INFIDELITY

Should I Stay or Should I Go? A Program for Couples After Suffering Emotional Abuse Trauma, Affair and Deceit in Marriage.

It Includes Divorcing and Healing from a Narcissist.

By
John T. Collins PsyD & Rachel Collins MD

Table of Contents

PART 1: Infidelity

PART 2: Divorcing and Healing from a Narcissist

PART 1

Infidelity

Introduction

To give meaning to "infidelity" using a single definition is quite challenging because its incidences vary from person to person. Usually, infidelity is also termed as "cheating" or "having an affair" with someone else. One is said to be practicing infidelity if he/she is not being completely faithful to his/her partner, but there are other ways to define infidelity:

Sexual attraction – This is one of the most common signs of infidelity. Sometimes, a person develops a sexual attraction towards another person even if he/she is committed to someone else whether they are married or simply dating. Infidelity occurs when a person develops a sexual desire towards another person and he/she acts on it instead of trying to overcome these wrong feelings.

Romantic emotional connection – A person is said to be cheating if he/she develops a romantic emotional connection with someone other than his/her current partner. This connection can manifest in different ways, whether through gestures or by feeling that the other person is someone he/she wants to be with.

Untruthfulness – Even without the sexual attraction and the romantic emotional connection with someone else, some people say that their partner is practicing infidelity if he/she is being dishonest with him/her. For example, they miss out on some important details when talking to their partner, but they reveal these removed details to another person. Another example could be seeing another person in secret or going out on dates without telling their partner about it. Simply lying to one's partner is a sign that something is wrong in their relationship; distrust is a sign of a dwindling relationship, most especially if you prefer to share your life experiences with other people than your partner.

The accusation of whether someone is cheating depends on the perspective of the partner. If the person is oversensitive, then even their partner's littlest connection with somebody else could scream infidelity. Nonetheless, infidelity is a huge mistake and it could cost you your relationship, and it causes a lot of pain and doubt for both you and your partner. Moreover, infidelity could cost you your partner's trust for life. If you are lucky, then you will be able to regain this trust back. If you are not, then you have lost a relationship forever. For these reasons, the purpose of this book is to provide tips on how to deal with infidelity, regain the trust of your partner, and save your crumbling relationship.

When a person finds out that his/her partner is cheating on him/her, he/she may ask the following questions: "Why? Is there something wrong with me?" "Am I not good enough?" "What did I do wrong?" There is no complete list of answers to these questions as well as the causes of infidelity, but here are the most common ones, separated into the physical and emotional aspect, that may help you address your questions:

Emotional Aspect

- Incompatibility – One of the main reasons why people cheat is because they are not getting along well with their current partner but they do not have the heart to break up because they think they can still "work things out". However, sometimes they don't work out and the person ends up looking for someone else to fulfill his emotional needs while forgetting that he/she is still committed to someone else.

- Romantic emotional connection – When a person meets someone else and they get along well, there is a possibility that they may develop a strong, romantic emotional connection without asking for it. In the process of getting to know each other, there is a possibility that one may feel like the other person is someone fun to be with and is someone who would make a good partner instead of the one he/she is currently with.

- Weariness and boredom – Another common reason why some people cheat is that they are already tired of the relationship in the sense that they are already getting bored. When someone feels like nothing exciting is happening anymore, he/she could go out and look for someone to provide him/her that lost "excitement".

Physical Aspect

- Sexual attraction – When it comes to the physical aspect of infidelity, one of the most common causes of infidelity and broken relationships is a sexual attraction towards another person other than the current partner. We all have our desires and fantasies, but sometimes some people cannot suppress these desires even if they know well that they are still committed, which is why they end up cheating on their partner because they try to fulfill these desires.

- Amount of time together – Partners may not always have the same careers. They meet different people every day and spend most of their hours with different sets of people. However, when someone spends a lot of time with another person, there is a

14

possibility that they will develop feelings for each other, most especially if their interests go along well and they do not allow themselves to be held back by prior commitments.

- Absence – Spending too much time away of your partner can also cause too much longing, and most of the time this "longing" is the cause of infidelity, for there is a tendency for them to look for someone who would fill the "gaps" that their partner had left.

- Long-distance – It is difficult for long-distance relationships to prosper especially if one is not always updated on the activities of the other. Same as absence, long-distance relationships barely survive because of either one of the two looks for some excitement and romance without thinking of their partners. Oftentimes, they do this because they think they can never be caught because of the distance separating the two of them.

Chapter 1. Defining Infidelity

Infidelity is perhaps the most challenging issue encountered by couples. The union of marriage is not held in highest regard by everyone; in some cases, it has become tainted with infidelity. By infidelity we mean physical or emotional affairs—either one can break up a marriage.

Cheating is a word commonly used with infidelity. Some of us have been there. The thought of your spouse being unfaithful can make you shiver in your skin. It may play into your insecurities. Once it is confirmed that you have been betrayed, you may experience the sensations of blood rushing out of your body, your legs weakening, your stomach dropping, or just plain nauseous. The feeling of betrayal—mistrust, deceit, being lied to—brings us to a physiological and psychological nightmare! This may be the reason that you're considering divorce.

Media and Technology

The media portrays extramarital affairs as common in our society, perhaps as a symptom of the twenty-first-century value system. It has even become "trendy" to have babies out of wedlock. Politicians, actors, musicians, professional athletes display their lovers and children in the public eye.

Just because celebrities do it, it doesn't mean that it is appropriate and acceptable for you.

In addition to the media blurring standards, our new and advanced technology—the Internet, texting, e-mail, Skype, and social networking—makes having affairs more accessible. Watching pornography, having cybersex, or engaging in sexual chat rooms can be considered forms of cheating. Therefore, even if people are not physically having sex with another person, the effects can be just as devastating. Believe it or not, some websites promote affairs; they make the connection for you and even provide an alibi for you. No wonder sex addiction is becoming so prevalent.

Temptation

In some instances, infidelity is motivated by temptation. We are well aware that there are temptations out there, some subtle, some blatant. You may find temptations in your workplace, in social gatherings with other couples, or even in your extended family. Remember the moral of the story of the forbidden fruit. What you think (or are told) that you cannot have, you want even more. Temptation can harm any relationship. Let's face it, there are some gorgeous men and beautiful women out there. However, this does not mean that you need to act on the temptation.

So why do people act on it?

It may be a character weakness. A person with a weak character cannot stand for something or have the strength to follow through with a commitment.

It may be a self-esteem issue. When people feel insecure about themselves, they constantly seek validation from others. This can be in the form of sexual, emotional, or intellectual attention.

It may be a lack of self-control. Some people have problems inhibiting their behavior. People who lack self-control do not think about the consequences of their behaviors until after they've already acted. They act on impulse instead of stopping to think about the impact of their behavior.

It may be influenced by unhappiness in the relationship. Some people think that engaging in an extramarital affair will take away their unhappiness.

It may be boredom with life. Some individuals do not pursue enough stimulation to feel fulfilled. They feel that their lack of excitement is the fault of their partner.

It may be pure selfishness. Some people are concerned only with satisfying their own needs without consideration of the impact it may have on the other person.

If you are the cheater, think about which of the former reasons you can relate to. Each individual has his or her own motives. By identifying the underlying factors of your action, you can do one of three things.

1.   You can work through it to resolve the underlying issues and attempt to reconcile with your spouse.

2.   You can work on resolving the underlying issues and not reconcile with your spouse.

3.   You can choose to go to a marital counselor.

If you choose to do nothing, you will likely repeat your behavior in other relationships.

Some people are tempted more than others. Some people put themselves in situations where self-control is more difficult. For example, after a business dinner you allow an attractive male co-worker to walk you to your car. Or you work on a project after hours with a beautiful and sexy single female co-worker.

To avoid falling into the trap of infidelity, be aware of high-risk situations. You may think that one time is "not a big deal." However, that one time may destroy your marriage.

Exercise for the Cheating Spouse

If your extramarital affair is a secret you have been keeping from your spouse, this exercise will help you confide in your spouse. Your spouse has the right to know the truth, and you will benefit from getting it off your chest. If you are the cheater, and your infidelity is the reason for you to contemplate divorce, work through the following exercise. Telling your spouse is the first step to coping with the situation and the beginning of the healing process for both of you. Although infidelity can be a traumatic event in a marriage, many marriages do survive after an affair.

Write down how you want to tell your spouse. Keep it brief, no more than two sentences. Be direct, clear, and empathic. Remember, it is bad news for your spouse. A more elaborate conversation may develop after you present the news. Be receptive to questions your spouse may have and be compassionate in your answers.

If you have already talked about your infidelity with your spouse, and betrayal and mistrust are causing conflict, this may be a reason to seek professional help. If your spouse continues to express feelings of anger and resentment, and you continue to feel regret and guilt, couples' therapy is necessary if you both feel the marriage is worth saving.

Exercise for the Betrayed Spouse

If you are the one who has been cheated on, now you have the opportunity to ventilate your feelings and thoughts on the lines below. This can be a difficult process. We encourage you to seek professional help if this is an obstacle preventing you from moving on in your life. Here is where you can use profanity if it makes you feel better.

The day you find out that your spouse has cheated is not just a bad day. Learning of adultery is a negative event that leaves you feeling confused, desperate and vulnerable. After you discover a spouse's betrayal, it is very difficult to cope. Your initial response may be shock and disbelief. Your trust is shattered. You may feel angry for being deceived and even beat yourself up for not knowing. Being deceived negatively affects your self-esteem. That is where depression may set in. You may feel that the floor has been pulled out from beneath you and you're falling without a safety net.

You may experience mood swings. One moment you may feel numb, then angry; you may burst out crying and screaming and then behave calmly once again. The effects of the marital infidelity—intrusive thoughts, lack of concentration, forgetting important tasks—may interfere with your daily functioning.

When you are the deceived party, you may think of getting revenge, think or act in self-destructive ways, use negative self-statements, or have thoughts of acting out destructively.

Not to do list:

- Question whether your spouse ever loved you

- Doubt yourself

- Harm yourself

- Lose self-confidence

- Lose trust in others

- Feel unworthy

- Feel ugly and unattractive

- Feel stupid that you did not know

- Feel ashamed

- Harm your self

- Binge drink

- Binges eat

- Take drugs

- Starve yourself

- Have unprotected sex with a stranger

- Quit your job

- Feel inadequate

- Obsess over the infidelity

Take time to heal by taking good care of yourself. The following is a list of coping strategies to help you heal.

- Eat healthy. People in distress tend to either stop eating or binge on unhealthy food. A first step to feeling better is to eat nutritious and healthy food such as salads, vegetables, fruits, nuts, and good proteins such as fish, chicken or lean meats. Believe it or not, these can be comfort foods if prepared your favorite way.

- Go for a walk. Walking is a good way to walk off the stress and leave your troubles behind with every step you take.

- Go to the gym. When you work out, your brain releases endorphins, which make you feel happier.

- Take an art class. Use each stroke to express your emotions through painting on the canvas.

- Take a dance class. Dancing helps to release and express your emotions through rhythmic movement.

Chapter 2. Types of Affairs

Object Focus

In this detrimental series of behaviors one partner focuses on something else to the extent it harms the relationship. A short, but not exhaustive, list is video games, work, the kids, friends, going out/partying, hobbies, travel, and anything you get caught up in and ignore your partner and relationship. Another way to think of it is you are giving your primary loyalty to something other than your spouse/partner. This keeps you from being there for them or your relationship.

Secrets

This one is simple to pinpoint; it is when a person does something, they hope their spouse/partner will never find out about. I'm not talking about planning a surprise birthday party or buying a gift and hoping they don't guess before the holiday; this form of infidelity is about having secrets from your spouse. Examples are giving money to someone and your spouse wouldn't approve, buying something and hiding the purchase, talking to someone your spouse would be unhappy about, saying you're doing one thing but you are doing something else. Secrets undermine trust, and trust is the foundation of a real and healthy relationship.

Inappropriate Behaviors

This is when one partner acts out in ways that hurt their partner. Examples can be: flirting, inappropriate touching, sharing a hotel room with someone who is of your sexual preference, putting your relationship down, insulting your partner, only being there when it's okay for you but not when your partner needs you, swearing or acting disrespectful of your partner or around your partner.

Emotional Affairs

One person interacts with intensity and emotional connection to a person other than their spouse/partner. In a purely emotional affair there is no kissing, touching, or sex, and they may not ever meet in person (emotional affairs are a huge pitfall of online interactions.) It is all about the emotional connection and often includes romantic sentiment, attraction, chemistry, and a sense of intimacy and love. One hallmark of an emotional affair is deep, intimate conversations often about the marriages or primary relationships. Another seemingly innocent example of emotional affairs is the "work husband/wife" who you can unload all your stress and angst to. That may sound good, but it's bad if you are talking to your work spouse and not your real one. Unfortunately, emotional affairs all too often become sexual over time, adding layer of hurt.

Purely Sexual Affairs

These are often referred to as opportunistic affairs. They are about sex and sex only. They are based on pure lust, risk taking and the surrender to a feeling in the now despite the love the person may have for their partner. People confuse attraction (which we all feel) with a need to consummate the feeling. Examples of purely sexual affairs are: "happy ending" massage parlors, hiring prostitutes, one-night stands, and random sex with known people. This type of affair is all about temporary pleasure, but it can lead to permanent regret.

Replacement Affairs

These are often a combination of emotional and sexual affairs. The infidelity replaces your primary relationship or marriage. It can fulfill all or some of the expectations one should have met within the primary relationship. Sometimes this happens when a person is looking for an excuse to leave a marriage; sometimes it is a way to stabilize someone miserable in a committed relationship. This is where the unfaithful partner believes they have "found the one" or are "truly in love" with their affair partner, and they may or may not be, but they are being dishonest in the rest of their life.

Addictive Affairs

Like Object Affairs, addictive affairs involve something outside taking the place of the intensity that belongs in the relationship. Examples are misuse of pornography, alcohol/drug addictions, gambling problems, workaholism, shopping addiction, and any dysfunctional behaviors that diminish your primary relationship. These addictions can be used for sexual gratification (porn or getting high and acting out sexually) or as a way to cope and stabilize unhappiness.

Chapter 3. Infidelity Statistics and Facts

Statistics on infidelity vary. The Kinsey studies and Hite report suggest that in up to 70 percent of all marriages a spouse will cheat. A major study by the University of Chicago in the 1990s was more optimistic, suggesting that infidelity occurs in no more than 25 percent of all marriages. When you add to the fact that the definition of infidelity varies (some studies require a sexual relationship, others include "emotional infidelity") then the real numbers are fuzzy. However, experts tend to agree that cheating will occur in 30 to 40 percent of all marriages. On the brighter side, some affairs occur after a marriage has all but died and weren't the cause of the marital problems.

It tends to be true (not always, of course) that men start affairs for sex—and it may or may not become emotional. Women are more likely to have affairs for emotional reasons. There are many types of affairs, and all can be devastating. Some people have cyber-sex with an online stranger. Some chat online with a "friend" and start developing feelings although there is no sex. Some people have purely sexual affairs. Some have emotional affairs that have not become sexual. Still, there are sexual fantasies, secret get-togethers, phone conversations, a passion to spend time with that person—all of which are usually hidden from a spouse. And finally, some people have affairs that are both sexual and emotional.

Regardless of the type of affair, any affair can seriously damage a marriage. That is because all affairs involve deceit and secrecy— both of which significantly undermine trust.

Cheating 101

Every spouse who is a victim of an affair wants to know "Why did it happen?" I have yet to hear an unfaithful spouse provide an answer that makes a partner respond, "That makes sense." In other words, no answer is usually acceptable. Any answer makes the unfaithful spouse sound like he or she is justifying the affair—which only makes the partner madder.

Still, an affair happens most often for the following reasons:

Sex addiction or character flaws. A philanderer may feel entitled to cheat. Someone addicted to sex may feel compelled to cheat while wishing to stop. In all cases, the wandering spouse made a conscious choice to cheat.

Unintentional involvements. Many people develop friendships that truly start innocent. Over time the friends look forward to time together, begin talking about personal problems or future dreams, and start to develop feelings. Many deny that an affair has started because no sex is involved. On closer examination, it becomes clear that each person made small, step-by-step decisions to spend more time together and to be secretive about the nature or frequency of those meetings or conversations. Or, a person may have an unexpected "one-night stand" especially if alcohol was consumed and a spouse is unaware of what might be going on.

A less-than-satisfying marriage. An "OK" marriage is vulnerable to an affair almost as much as an unhappy marriage. An unhappy spouse may get involved with another to feel listened to, cared about, have more passionate sex, or be better treated. Or the person may be wondering if in fact "the grass is greener" and is exploring "what's out there."

Tit-for-tat. Some people cheat to get back at an unfaithful spouse or to punish a spouse for some other disliked behavior (the spouse is too jealous, too controlling, is abusive, drinks too much, and so forth).

Overwhelmed by life circumstances. Some people cheat when a baby is on the way, or a parent dies, or when the kids leave home. In such cases, these life transitions hit a nerve for that individual and trigger a need to perhaps "feel young again" or to cope better with overwhelming feelings.

There are numerous possible other reasons. For example, people who marry at a young age are more likely to have an affair than people who are older when they get married. Someone afraid of deep intimacy might cheat on his wife as a way to regulate his level of emotional closeness.

The Immediate Consequences of an Affair

When an affair is discovered, the damage is not just in one area of the marriage. A partner doesn't think "We still have a great marriage and you are a good person except in this one area of infidelity." Affairs shatter the entire foundation of a marriage. Everything good is at risk for crumbling. Affairs splinter the image a spouse has of the now-unfaithful partner. "I thought I knew the kind of person you were," a distraught spouse claims, "but I don't know you at all!" It can be frightening for the betrayed spouse to realize that the partner once viewed as honest, upstanding, moral, and devoted to family life seems to be different.

After the affair, it's extremely hard for the victim to want to connect warmly. Usually there is hostility and perhaps loathing. At best there is silent contempt. The victim often obsesses about the affair, doesn't trust that the entire story has been told, expects more lies, and interrogates the spouse repeatedly. Positive memories of family vacations, holidays, Valentine's Day gifts, all become suspect. "When we were vacationing at the beach last summer, did you spend your time wishing you could be with her?" Petty annoyances that happen in any marriage—the spouse arrives home late, forgets a grocery item, doesn't have time to tidy up the house—all become reasons to lash out. For many couples, making love is now impossible. For others, making love becomes highly passionate—followed the next day by the betrayed spouse acting cold. All of that happens even when the unfaithful spouse is truly repentant and wanting to heal the marriage. Just as often, though, the unfaithful spouse still has feelings for the other person and may have doubts about the desire to stay married. That only adds to the couple's misery as they slog through their days trying to hold the marriage together.

Phases of Repair

Couples who are motivated to heal the marriage after an affair can succeed. If you are one of those couples who choose to stay in the marriage you can expect to have dozens of conversations about the affair and how to rebuild the marriage. It can be exhausting but is a necessary part of healing.

There are three broad phases a couple experiences after an affair and conversations will be different depending upon the phase. These phases tend to overlap and a person can be in two phases or even all three phases at one time. Usually, one phase tends to predominate.

1. The Roller-Coaster Phase. Here emotions are wild, conversations are heated, and optimism is almost absent. This phase is filled with conversations about what happened and why. Blaming and attacking is common. The victim usually finds it impossible to speak calmly and respectfully. Name-calling, put-downs, and

other forms of verbal attacks are typical. The unfaithful spouse is best advised to be understanding and accepting of such verbal lashings as much as possible. Calling them unfair or hurtful won't work. The victim will only respond, "But what you did to me was unfair and hurtful!"

2. The Depressed-Accepting Phase. Here the betrayed spouse has finally accepted the affair and has begun to learn to live with it—however painfully. That spouse is grieving the loss of faithfulness in the marriage, is probably coping with a damaged self-image, and is trying to rebuild trust slowly. Occasional mood swings may happen but for the most part things have started to settle down—although a bit grimly. Here the couple has a sluggish coexistence punctuated by occasional nice days or moments together.

3. The Rebirth Phase. Here trust is on the rise and the marriage is looked upon more favorably than unfavorably. The affair is regarded as a painful time but the unfaithful partner is viewed in a more positive light overall. The affair may not be forgotten but every day the betrayed spouse chooses to be forgiving.

Chapter 4. Causes of Infidelity

Transitional Anxiety

We believe that most extramarital involvement occurs from anxiety arising from individual or family transitions. Like individuals, families go through developmental stages. The anxiety that occurs in making the transition from one life stage to the next, whether it is an individual or a family one, is one reason people choose to be unfaithful.

Transitional life events include both losses, like death, separation, and divorce, and positive occurrences, like marriage, the birth of a baby, and job promotion. With every transition there is a loss. We lose a role or a view of ourselves, and with it the comfort of understanding what was formerly expected of us. Change brings not just a new role but the anxieties that come with new expectations and responsibilities.

It is during such transitions that infidelity is most apt to occur. The prospective bride or bridegroom, although not yet married, may have an affair—often looked at in the conventional wisdom as a "last fling." More likely, it is caused by anxiety over the approaching marriage.

Consider the case of Sharon, who came for counseling because of the stress she was feeling from what she termed her "home situation."

"Ten months ago," she began, "I discovered I had genital warts, and had to get painful medical treatments. I found out that my husband, Felix, was having an affair. He told me he was having an affair with a young woman named Trisha, a graduate student at the university where he works.

"I've really been a fool," she cried. "He told me he needed 'space' for a while. I can't believe I bought that, but I did. He said he would leave if he didn't get his 'space.'

"I agreed, but I couldn't eat, sleep, or concentrate. I asked him to go with me for therapy, but he refused. He said it was my problem. So, we are separating while he dates Trisha.

"You know, this probably sounds stupid to you, but Felix has never had an affair before. He's been a devoted family man and a well-respected faculty member of the university. This is not in keeping with his personality. We have a lot going for us—five terrific kids, money, a home, and lots of friends.

"Felix is sixty, and he is going to retire soon. I thought he was depressed. He always wanted to write a book. He talked of missed opportunities and disappointments. I thought there was still time for him to write the book. We had planned retirement together.

"Now I'm a fifty-five-year-old woman looking for work. They're calling me a 'displaced homemaker.' Do you know how horrible that sounds to me? But I am displaced. At fifty-five I have to find a new life, and I have a disease to deal with."

Sharon's husband was having an affair at a critical time in his life, as he was facing retirement. He probably began this affair as a way for him to fight off the demons he saw in aging. His wife was a reminder of his aging, and he labeled her "old and fat." The problems were not in their marriage but his concerns.

Transitions are anxious times for all of us. Successful transitions depend on our strengths, supports, and resources. It's a time of vulnerability when infidelity can become a way, albeit an ineffective one, of dealing with the anxiety.

Unfulfilled Expectations

When people marry, they do so with the expectation that they will be happy and have a satisfying emotional and sexual life, with many of their needs met by their partner.

Individual expectations can change in the course of a marriage, as people develop new interests and learn more about themselves. Generally, they can become incorporated into a marriage without any repercussions. When, however, the change is dramatically different from the way the couple has been conducting their lives all along, the equilibrium of the marriage can be greatly disturbed.

An example of such a case was Jacob and Rose. They came in for counseling about Jacob's flirtation and intense friendship with their neighbor, Lila. Although Jacob never had sex with Lila, he admitted that he desired her, and he knew this obsession with her threatened his marriage.

Jacob had developed a strong interest in becoming more Orthodox in his practice of Judaism. This is not an interest that one member could participate in alone because it is a way of life with strict religious practices and standards. It requires the work, support, and involvement of the wife. Rose would be obligated to keep a kosher home and carefully observe the rules of the Sabbath. There would be a prohibition against former activities, such as men and women dancing together. As a busy lawyer, Rose found it hard to accept, and there were many arguments about her "level of commitment and sabotaging" his needs. Jacob said that his religious scruples kept him from having sexual relations with Lila, but this attitude meant little to Rose. She viewed his relationship with Lila to be "an affair."

Jacob found he was getting more understanding from Lila than from Rose. However, in their counseling sessions, each of them learned to listen to the other's needs and problems.

Eventually, they became more understanding and supportive of each other.

Need for Attention

Although it may strike readers as dramatic or extreme, one partner in the relationship may sometimes become unfaithful as a way of getting the attention of the other. In these affairs the unfaithful spouse wants to change some unbearable aspect of the relationship rather than end the marriage. The purpose of the affair is to bring attention to the situation when prior attempts have failed.

The "need for attention" results from poor communication. Partners are not able to tell each other what they want or pay attention to the expressed desires of the other. This affair occurs out of frustration. It is a way of saying, "I can't communicate with you in any other way."

Such was the case of Claudette and Ralph, who have been married for fifteen years and have a thirteen-year-old son, Joshua. Joshua is developmentally disabled. They came for marriage therapy after Ralph realized that Claudette had been unfaithful.

Claudette began by talking her son. "Joshua is a very lovable little boy. We are very close." Ralph quickly interrupted. "I think that's part of the problem. She's overly involved. They're too close. That's how her damn affair started with that guy from the association, and she's always working on something with those people."

Claudette explained, "Ralph is talking about Harry, the ex-director of the state program. I've worked with him on many committees. He understands what I am going through."

"And I don't?" Ralph shouted. "I am the boy's father, for God's sake!"

In their counseling sessions, Claudette and Ralph began to talk honestly with each other. We then began to understand the dynamics of this triangle.

Now Claudette and Ralph were given the opportunity to cry together and comfort each other and also to release their anger. With this work accomplished, they were both free to love Joshua and to be sharing parents in his life. Ralph could resume his role of parent and free Claudette from assuming the whole burden. With Ralph's support, Claudette could develop herself and her other interests and still be the parent she wants to be to Joshua.

Although the problems she faced were quite serious, changes are possible. You can see from this case how an affair can develop in a marriage where two people care about each other but are unable to communicate their problems. The affair serves as a very dramatic way to get attention, to solve the problem, and to continue with their relationship.

Boredom

Affairs may also occur when partners become bored with each other. We often hear the phrase from our clients, "I've outgrown her." We know that adults continue to grow and develop throughout the life span. Our longer life span now ensures that couples will spend more years together than ever before.

Opportunities in education, travel, recreation, and entertainment are more available to this generation than to those in the past. The opportunity to grow can create boredom and stress in a relationship if one partner seizes these opportunities and the other does not. The results can be boredom in the marriage and anger at the partner for not keeping up. When such dissatisfaction exists, it leaves a marriage vulnerable to infidelity.

Jack and Mary, a couple who came for counseling, were good examples of this kind of marriage. They said that they had been having marital problems for years. They had separated three times and were on the verge of another separation when they came for marriage counseling.

Mary was very attractive and animated. Jack was handsome, quiet, and polite. Mary began. "We were high school sweethearts. We lived on the same block in a small town in Oklahoma. We started dating when we were fourteen years old and got married after high school. Jack joined the Army, and we both left home for the first time. Army life was great. I worked in a department store. The Army sent Jack to college to study engineering. Our families were very proud of us. They thought we had everything—Jack's college education, a family, a home—and when Jack left the Army, he got a good job as an engineer in Baltimore.

"Things were terrible. Jack picked on me all the time. He criticized and found fault with everything, from the food I served to the color I painted the kitchen. Almost every family outing ended in a fight."

Mary cried as she continued. "We began our separations about the time that our youngest child, Carole, started school. But Jack kept coming back. He said he missed the family."

"I grew bored," he revealed. "We had grown apart. About the only thing we talked about were the children and the routine business of running the house. I felt I no longer wanted to be married to her. If it weren't for the kids, I would have left."

This was a marriage characterized by boredom. Couples can grow apart as one of the pair expands his or her world and the other stands still. Jack and Mary continued to work out their feelings about the affair and then to understand what had happened to them over the years.

The Unavailable Spouse

Sometimes a spouse is emotionally and sexually unavailable to the partner, usually because of physical or mental illness, geographical distance, or military service. For some people these are not justifications to break a "till death do us part" commitment, but infidelity does occur under such circumstances.

The spouse who is not able to have sex because of physical or mental illness also deprives the other of marital companionship and support.

Chapter 5. Infidelity as Trauma

The Spin Cycle

The very nature of betrayal sparks reactivity—it's trauma. We are reacting to something we didn't know was going on. Our minds, emotions, and bodies spin like a top as our world is turned upside down. Our challenge comes in finding a path to stabilize what's happening inside of us while we're dealing with the sexual chaos that's happening around us. We have to find tools that help us rest and respond.

The more grounded we are, the more collected we feel on the inside. We're less reactive and more steadied and can make better choices. Finding a pause, the selah, during the chaos can help us move toward a more thoughtful, responsive place. The wisdom of the selah (see-la) is found seventy-one times in the book of Psalms. The Psalms are power packed with raw emotions like anger, longings, disappointment, grief, and joy. It's no wonder we relate to them and no surprise the writers added so many selahs. A selah is a musical interlude to help us pause, "think about" what was just said, or "watch for" a visual demonstration of what's around the bend.1

As women impacted by betrayal, we have to keep our wits about us and watch for visual demonstrations of recovery. Remember: trust his behavior, not his words. Adding a selah, a pause in the moment, helps us see things more clearly. Without a pause we can't find peace, and we jump from one crisis to another. A compassionate view of our reactivity requires us to look through the lens of trauma. When we are reacting to betrayal, we are often trying to:

- be seen

- be heard

- get safe

- find our choices in the matter

Finding a way out of our feelings of helplessness can turn our symptoms of stress around.

Let me start by saying it's not just one thing. If getting out of a trauma-induced spin cycle were as easy as taking laundry from the dryer, we'd do it. But it's not. The layers of impact to our bodies, brains, and emotions can be so fused that sometimes it's hard to see what's going on clearly. My motto is "Whatever it takes," because we are worth being seen and heard; we deserve a choice in the matter. Your willingness to try the options presented will help you find yourself again. Shame beliefs like "I'm not worth the time, effort, or money," or "I'm not important," or "I don't deserve it" rob us of what we need to heal.

Self-care is an act of personal fidelity as we take brave steps, we faithfully show up for ourselves.

SOS!—Stepping Out of the Spin Cycle of Shame

Whether you have underlying shame from your past or betrayal-induced shame beliefs from the present, your invisible wounds need to be treated. Shame produces unwanted self-sabotaging behaviors that cause us to relate in one of two ways:

1.   Shame moves us into a one-down position: a victim.

2.   Shame moves us into a one-up position: we attempt to have power or control over others.

With unhealed trauma and shame, wounded people wound people.

One resource created to help people break free from this spin cycle of shame is called the Karpman Drama Triangle. Dr. Karpman's design has been around for decades and addresses the unwanted behaviors caused by underlying shame and traumatic wounds.2 Inspired by Dr. Karpman and others,3 I've expanded the idea into what I call the Empowerment Wheel.

Every one of us has to wrestle with the influence of shame at one time or another. Trauma-induced shame beliefs can play havoc in our lives, especially when we're distressed. Shame is the culprit of conflict and chaos. Ultimately, it keeps us from peace. Let us look at the Hebrew word picture for peace (shalom): "to destroy the authority that establishes chaos."4 Much like a vessel nearly capsized at sea, when we're stuck in conflict or overwhelmed by our own shame, we get lost in the chaos and cry for help—SOS! We don't have to stay in a helpless spin cycle; we can send sound signals to others by changing what we do and the way we relate.

Let's take a look at four roles we take on when we're under the influence of shame: victim, rescuer, offender, and entitlement. Stepping Out of the Spin cycle means we listen to the cry for help inside and do something different. We respond in one of four ways: responsibility, collaboration, options, and humility. By identifying the roles and power struggles we get into with others, we can learn to follow the arrows and find our path out. As we learn how to move into more responsive stances, we feel less stuck and more empowered by what we can do.

- Problem: When we're stuck in the victim position, we feel trapped, react, and want a path out.

- Fact: We have no way of controlling what another person will do.

- Truth: When we decide what we need to do, we get out of the victim position.

- Good News: There is a way out.

The solution comes in changing the way we deal with conflict by learning how to move through it responsibly. Remember, these are roles we take on, not people; they are shame-influenced ways of being. See if any of these roles sound familiar to you. What can you do to find your way out?

"The Victim" Role

People in the one-down victim position often feel helpless, hopeless, fearful, and ashamed. While victims have been wounded by someone or something, their cluster of shame beliefs keep them reacting from a one-down position rather than finding a path out. They feel too overwhelmed to solve their problems, so they look for someone else to do it for them. When someone doesn't help them, they give up, blame, or expect help from others rather than choosing to take responsibility for themselves. This role can place unconscious demands on others, causing them to pull away. Trauma-induced shame beliefs include "I am helpless or weak," "I'm too needy," or "I'm not in control."

Stepping Out of the Spin cycle means we step out of the victim role, use our voices, and take responsibility for what we do or don't do.

- Determine what you need. What can you choose to do to get there?

- Use your voice to communicate what you need clearly.

- If no one is listening to you, pursue getting assistance for yourself.

- Don't let anxiety stop you. Anxiety is a normal feeling when you're facing your fears about doing something on your own.

- Reach out and ask for encouragement from safe and supportive others.

- Take thoughtful action steps toward resources and problem-solving ideas.

- Use the 180° Turnaround to move your nagging neggies into truths: "I am strong," "I have a voice," "I can learn to make choices," and "I can honor what I need."

I felt like I was jumping through a ring of fire when I confronted Chip with the porn I found on his computer. He was angry with me and denied it again. I knew I was right; I saw it. Finally, I showed him the proof. When I did, he owned it. He said he needed help and called a therapist.—Lilliana

Responsibility helps us learn to identify our needs, face our fears, take risks, discover our strengths, and grow from our mistakes.

"The Rescuer" Role

While people in this one-up enabling position may look calm and in control on the surface, inside they're often a ball of nerves. They feel worried, panicked, and out of control and try to manage another's problem. They feel helpless in knowing how to stop someone from hurting themselves or others. Their trauma-induced shame beliefs are often "I don't matter" or "I'm not in control," or they have guilt-inspired beliefs like "I should have done something." Many "rescuers" grew up in homes with insurmountable responsibility without a way out.

Stepping Out of the Spin cycle means we stop trying to fix or enable others. Collaboration involves two people each carrying their fair share of what's needed. Being over-responsible keeps others from learning how to own their part. Check the boxes below as you consider what self-care looks like for you:

- What is underneath your desire to help someone with their issue?

- What are your vulnerable feelings (hurt, fear, sadness, guilt) about their behaviors?

- You can't make choices for someone else, but you can advocate for what you need. You can begin to talk about how their choices (sexual betrayals) impact you.

- If someone is unwilling to work collaboratively, you can honor your need for truth, trust, and safety by establishing boundaries.

- Have you looked at how you might be avoiding setting boundaries or following through with consequences to avoid conflict, abandonment, or rejection?

- Use the 180° Turnaround to move your nagging neggies into truths: "I matter," "I can learn to make choices," and "I do the best that I can."

I was exhausted and kept worrying about Nathan's recovery. I knew I couldn't hold the marriage together for both of us. When I started some self-care, it felt really good to take care of me. Weird, but Nathan seemed more respectful. It's been a long, hard road. At dinner we talked about things other than what we're doing to recover. It felt good to just—be.—Roxanne

Collaboration is a necessary aspect of life that involves negotiation and active participation. As we learn how to take care of ourselves, initiate boundaries, and release others to take ownership of their own recovery, our load is lightened.

"The Offender" Role

While people in this one-up position may look powerful and together on the surface, on the inside they are often afraid, grieving, walled off by hurt, and fearful of vulnerability or losing control. Their childhood histories often include chaotic, neglectful, controlling, or abusive families. When someone is reacting in this one-up offending position, they use power, control, rage, blame, passive-aggressiveness, silence, gaslighting tactics, abuse, or they withhold affection or finances.

- Anger is a legitimate emotion, like sadness, fear, joy, or pain.

- Anger is a natural response to grief and loss.

- Anger as a "fight" reaction is an instinctive trauma response (fight, flight, freeze, fold).

- Righteous anger can be a motivator for addressing injustice when others are being oppressed or hurt.

- Anger is a legitimate emotion when you are reacting to betrayal, deception, or sexual violation. In his book Torn Asunder: Recovering from an Extramarital Affair, Dave Carder reminds us that people don't get better until they get mad.

Chapter 6. Symptoms of Post-Infidelity Stress Disorder

The effects of experience with emotional manipulation may leave the victim with trust issues and anxieties that last the rest of their lives.

Depression manifests in a prolonged emotional state of hopelessness or helplessness. Many sufferers hear voices in their heads that constantly tell them they are worthless or stupid or that they are not enough. This voice may manifest and may be persistent for days on end, especially at night when relaxation becomes impossible.

Anxiety is another possible aftereffect of emotional abuse and especially common in instances where there is a history of physical abuse as well. The anxiety will often stem from the creation of doubt and destruction of self-esteem. A once confident person may let down their guard just long enough for the abuser to poke their head in and plant an idea about how that failed relationship was their fault, or they are really too fat to be wearing that, or that supervisor at work probably doesn't think you're good enough, etc.

Towards the end of the abuse cycle, the victim may finally start to see the light and attempt to get as far away from the perpetrator as possible. This may or may not be successful.

This may initially feel tragic, as you've still got to deal with the emotional attachment that was cultivated. But soon, you will start to realize that you are a survivor of an abuser and you are lucky to be free.

One technique many abuse victims utilize after an experience like this is therapy, either in a group setting or a one-on-one setting. It can be very helpful to talk to others who have been through a similar situation and it is important to be able to ground yourself in the truth that you were not stupid or immoral or bad or not enough; you were manipulated, just like the others in your group. Talking to these individuals may go a long way in finding yourself again after a long and dreadful experience of narcissistic abuse.

There are several typical emotions and cycles of thought that victims experience immediately following the end of the relationship. The victim is usually quite tired and worn out, and this may last weeks or even months. Emotional exertion takes a toll just like muscle exertion. It will take time to recover and heal from this stress. You may feel disgusted with yourself for having fallen victim to something like this. As I've stressed before, it is very important that you try to talk to someone or wrap your mind around the reality that you are not at fault. You are not stupid. Someone who is an expert at emotional manipulation with zero sense of remorse has taken complete advantage of you and your pain.

It is common for the victim to go through feelings of guilt and shame. Let these feelings run their course, but again, it is important to put yourself in an environment which supports the truth that you have survived an ordeal, not committed a horrendous crime.

Panic attacks and anxiety may go hand-in-hand for a while after the abuse. Some people get out without experiencing symptoms like this, but others will need to address the issue through talk therapy and drug therapy.

You will feel a big blow to your self-esteem, and this may take some time to build back up again. Try to surround yourself with people who love you and who care for you. You will likely go through all kinds of emotional fallout, and it is good to let it out when you need to. You may feel like crying or screaming or releasing your emotions in some other way. Perhaps, you may find it helpful to join a gym and punch a punching bag for an hour. Whatever you need to do, try to express and release that emotion rather than bottling it up inside of you. This will only make the eventual release much worse and may even cause toxicity and additional emotional and psychological turmoil.

Chapter 7. How to Overcome Hurt and Rage

The worst form of destruction you can commit to your soul is to rest in your hurt. It is like resting on a dagger that stabbed your chest. You've got to step out and pull the dagger so that you can begin the process of healing.

7 Steps to Successfully Step Out of Your Hurt:

Step One: Make a Bold Decision

A bold decision is one where the various elements of its choice are fully optimized. Yes, it is optimized when the intent is the most supreme of them all (with the highest possible opportunity cost); the timeframe is of utmost priority and the effort is fully dedicated.

Our modern lifestyles have brought us the misconception that big is better. Thus, we focus on grandiose schemes of things to the detriment of small details that would actually add more value to our lifestyles and bring forth the grandest of our being.

It's the little decisions we make every day that will either bring us closer to our goals or further away from them. Be mindful of the choices you are making when going through a difficult time. For example: If your goal is to move through the pain of life and get out the other side with your head held high, then, your choices will come down to as simple things as going for a walk, taking up a new hobby, accepting friends requests to catch up, going to bed early and getting sleep, make the decision not to assign time to your trauma however pricking it is. This is the best way to snap out of it.

It all starts with a very minor decision such as making a call to a colleague; visiting a loved one; deciding to play with and entertain a neighbor's kid; taking a dog for a walk; deciding to teach some kids a music or art lesson; deciding to enroll with a charity, community mobilization, or relief organization, etc.

Opportunities are all over for you to start small and grow big. So, don't think there is such a big decision that you must make to get out of a hurting situation. Very small bold decisions can have a giant effect just like a persistent small ax felling a giant tree.

Step Two: Take Control of Your Situation

There are things within our control and there are things that we have no control over such as the weather. People with mental health issues will often spend much time and energy on things that they have no control over.

Be mindful of the amount of time you are spending thinking about things that you cannot change or are unhelpful to you. For example, if you are feeling angry or sad about things that have happened to you in the past this is not something that you can change. The past is in the past and you cannot change this. Energy spent dwelling on this past is wasted energy.

There are those things that you can change and there are those that cannot be changed. It is important to know the difference!

Many times, we spend a bigger part of our lives trying to move huge mountains when probably what we required was simply to acknowledge and admire their uniqueness. We only needed to take a step to climb them, see what is hidden beyond them and appreciate the panoramic view of that newness that we soon needed to discover.

The greatest determinant of what you can change and what you cannot change is your willpower. This willpower is fueled by a very powerful propellant – your ATTITUDE. Your attitude determines your willpower. Yet, your attitude and willpower are both products of your very own mindset!

What are the things that you cannot change?

You cannot change:

- Your past – your past happened and it cannot be changed. What matters are the lessons you learned. Don't attach yourself to the past occurrences but derive pure lessons for future applications.

- Your future – your future is not yet born. You are not certain that you will live it. Thus, it is good to plan for it, but, don't let it sweep away your joys of the moment. Don't let it take away more than a fair share of what it deserves.

- People's perception of you – for so long as you are not alone, there will always be people's perception of you. There is nothing you can do to change people's perceptions but there is everything you can do to change yourself.

What are the things that you can change?

- Your attitude – your attitude drives you. It is the ignition key to your willpower.

- Your willpower – your willpower is the kinetic energy that propels you to take appropriate action to change. Make sure that you are full of it.

- Your self-image – your self-image reflects who you think you are. Sometimes your self-image can be true or false. You need a true self-image in order to discover your true being, purpose, and aspirations.

Step Three: Take Charge of Your Emotions

Other than the physical hurt, emotional hurt is one of the most commonly talked about of life hurts. In fact, more people encounter emotional hurts than physical hurts. The most enduring elements of a hurting life are rarely physical but emotional.

To be able to take charge of your emotions, the most fundamental step is to understand what they are, what their purpose is, how they come about and how you can intelligently apply them to fit different situations.

Step Four: Be Focused

Focusing is a mental phenomenon. When you are mentally disturbed, such as when you are filled with worries, anxiety, stress and even depression, there are plenty of thoughts razing through your mind such that you cannot focus on a certain specific thought that is of importance to your present needs.

Thus, the best way to be focused is to de-clutter your mind from these razing thoughts. A mind that is free is a focused mind. Yet, for this mind to be free, it must not be tethered to the past nor catapulted to the future. It must be free to the present unwrapping in the moment of now.

Step Five: Engage the Right Association

To engage the right association is to experience life joys. To engage the wrong association is to experience life hurts. The choice is yours! Make yourself happy.

When you try to force a friendship that doesn't or ought not to exist, life will inevitably hurt. When you allow yourself to experience the spontaneity of friendship as it arises, you will experience a happy, joyful life.

You are the company that you keep. Friends are not just for interaction. Friends shape you and, in the process, you shape them. You become one in so many aspects. To become a better you, a joyful you, a happy you, keep the right company and surely life won't hurt.

Your relationships are a great investment - probably the richest investment that you could ever have. Like any other shrewd investor, you don't want to keep dead investments. Investments that consume more than they bring are not worth keeping. Keep assessing your relationships, and those like branches that no longer bear fruits, prune them off so that those that bear fruits can have healthier ones.

Negative people are like a very low ceiling that prevents you from standing up, leave alone jumping. They affect your self-esteem, self-confidence, self-worth, and self-actualization. They are a disaster for your wellbeing. The earlier you keep them off the better you are back on track to optimizing your potential to becoming all you've ever dreamt of becoming.

Life hurts when you are constrained. Frustrations are simply the energy of a potential that has not been allowed to actualize.

If you really want to change the way you have been, then, seek change-makers in your relationships. Yes, people who show you a different perspective of life; People who see opportunities in what you can only see as problems; people who are ready to take your hand and help you make a giant leap over an obstacle; people who are ready and willing to go an extra mile just to make sure that you don't give on your resolve. These are the change-makers that you need! Life will stop hurting when you embrace such people.

Step Six: Give Meaning to Your Life

The real meaning of life is not in the big things but in the small things that we so often take for granted. Life hurts when we take for granted small things like just sitting calm and taking a deep breath; playing around just to have fun; tending to a small garden – be it in your backyard or in your in-house pot; spending time to fetch clean, natural, organic ingredients for the meal that you are going to cook; playing with your lovely pet; having time to play with children; visiting and spending time with your parents/grandparents, etc. It is such small activities that absorb the shocks of the hurts of life leaving you to ride comfortably to your life's destiny.

Step Seven: Self Compassion

To practice self-compassion is to be in love with your being. It is to know without self-love actualized through action to relieve yourself of your very own challenges and suffering, you cannot achieve the same of others. You have to begin from inside. You have to tend to your own wound with tender love and understanding its sources and its eventual end. You have to heal your own wounds. Only then, can you be able to do the same to others. Having self-love accompanied by faith in your being is the true healing balm to your trauma when life hurts.

Self-pity, anger, remorse, bitterness are all life hurts that are symptomatic of pain for that which happened in the past. They are signs of a lack of happiness. It is not that you cannot be happy with pain. But pain must not degenerate into self-pity, anger, remorse, and bitterness. You must own your pain. To own it is to accept that what happened is irreversible and it had its own consequences which you are experiencing right now. You have to detach yourself from this sensitivity and experience pain for what it really is – a crying call for healing. Focus on healing.

Life is tough sometimes. Acceptance of pain without reacting to it brings emotional intelligence. Treat yourself for 10 minutes a day with a soft word, a hand on heart, and a level of understanding that what you are going through is painful. You are human, and as a human, you

Will experience pain and suffering and if you try to avoid this emotional experience through avoidance behaviors such as drugs or alcohol you suffer further.

Chapter 8. Overcoming the Resentment and the Danger of Trust

Attempting to Repair the Relationship

Yes, it's possible to repair a relationship after an affair. No, it doesn't always work, and no, things will never be exactly the same again (they'll definitely be different, they might be worse, but if you're walking this path then there's also hope that things might turn out better).

Attempting to repair a relationship after someone cheats really boils down to whether you want to stay in the relationship and whether the partner is genuinely sorry (both are necessary) though there are other factors as well, for example children and finances. Here's some things to start thinking about. The first one is mandatory:

Get Counseling

When cheating has occurred, it's a significant breach of trust. In order for the relationship to get back to where it was, it is essential that you both get external assistance. Talk to a couples' counselor who specializes in infidelity and get at least one counseling session.

Counseling requires a great deal of courage, bravery and commitment. If you decide you want to stay together it should be the first thing you ask of your partner. And when I say ask what I mean is ultimatum.

I can offer some general advice on these pages, but seeing a therapist offers advice specifically tailored to your situation, which is something I can't do. Importantly, they can also help get to the root of why this happened in the first place, and ensure it never happens again.

It's Okay to be Angry

Your partner has been an absolute a-hole and deserves you coming at them with all engines firing. Get it all out, it's healthy. But be careful not to get violent.

Observe how your partner reacts when you tell them off—are they sorry, or do they get angry back? Signs of your partner getting angry or pushing the blame back on you can be warning indicators that the other party is not truly sorry.

Don't Try to Get Revenge

Repairing the relationship is all about healing! Choosing to go down a reconciliation route means that even if you haven't forgiven someone (yet), you've decided to try and make things work. Trying to get payback in some form or another goes against that. If, for example, you go out and cheat yourself, you're doing something just as unhelpful as the thing that hurt you.

I get it. It's tempting. But don't do it. There're the moral reasons, but there are other equally important reasons as well. You'll lose all the emotional high ground, all negotiating opportunities, and if you ever do decide to leave, you're also shooting yourself in the foot for any legal benefits of being the innocent party.

Be Mindful of Social Media

Remember, once it's out there you can't take it back. Posting that your partner is a cheating dirtbag on Facebook might feel satisfying, but it will cause a veritable storm of additional stuff you're going to have to deal with. It will polarize your mutual friends and importantly, it will still be there 30 years later when you've moved on one way or another.

I'm not saying that you have to bottle it all up inside! That's equally as bad. Tell who you need to tell. Enlist a support network of close, trusted friends. Just... maybe, take a break from social media while you're trying to work it all out. I haven't once seen a circumstance where posting how much you hate somebody on Twitter has ever been a positive influence on the situation.

Request That Your Partner Cut Off All Communication with the Other Person

It's a no brainer but it's got to be said. If your partner is truly sorry and really wants to repair things, they're going to have to cut off their relationship with the other person and remove all temptation for relapse.

Do note that it's possible to have meaningful friendships with ex's from before you were together. We're very specifically talking about the person that your partner has had an affair with.

Deciding to Leave

Right, so either you don't think your relationship is repairable, or you don't want to repair it. Either way, this is your decision and nobody can make it but yourself. Once you've made your decision, here's a list of suggestions for you to consider, while making your own decision about what's right for you:

Don't Tell Your Partner 'til You Have a Plan of Action

First things first, once you have confirmation that your partner is cheating, and before they know you have that information, you're in a unique little pocket of power. There is a whole list of things you can do because your partner isn't watching you closely yet, that you won't be able to do afterward. Don't waste the opportunity if you can help it. Don't blurt anything out until you're ready.

Work out what you want to do, where you're going to go, or if you expect the partner to leave instead (and if so, how are you going to make that happen?). Consider your finances, and who controls the bank accounts, the car and the house. If you leave, can they cut your money off? Can they pull all the money out of your joint account?

Explore the steps you can take now to protect yourself in the future. If you have a joint account, start putting money in a private account for when or if you need it. If you don't have a joint account and they control the finances, try and find an excuse for this to change.

If you have children, have a think about how leaving will affect them. I'm not saying, 'don't leave.' I think that relationships where the parents stay together for the sake of the kids are miserable, and everyone would usually be happier apart. But you should know what you're going to say to them. If they're not staying with you, how will you ensure they aren't turned against you when you take off? Photographic evidence helps a lot here—the cheating partner can say terrible things about you all they want, but once that photo comes out it's a different story.

Basically: Get all your ducks in a row and see the family lawyer. Because as soon as you tell your partner that you know they cheated, they may start hiding assets.

Consider Physical Logistics

Again, before you tell your partner, consider where you're going to stay. If you expect your partner to move out and are in a mind to dump all their belongings out on the street, do you need to change the locks? If you'd rather move out, either because it's their house or you need your space, where are you going to stay?

Book a hotel or a couch at a friend's place. Be aware that there are men's and women's shelters in many large cities as well.

Stay Safe

If your partner is violent, make sure you confront them with your information in such a way that no danger is posed to yourself. Do it in a public place or even over the phone if you have to (you could hide incriminating photos in a drawer, then ask them to open it while you're on hold). Don't tell your partner where you are staying. You may even want to let the police know beforehand, if you feel at risk.

If your partner isn't violent, by all means have the conversation in the privacy of your own home. You'll be better able to judge their facial reactions and register the impact that this information will have.

You also don't have to tell them anything in person at all! A note will give them the message easily enough—your cheating partner has had the power for so long, but now you have it. Make it your decision where and how things go down.

Don't Involve the Kids

Your children are not pawning in your relationship. They are not tools that you can or should use against your partner. I'm sorry to say it, but your partner still needs access to their children as well. Just because they cheated on you doesn't make them less of a parent (only less of a partner). Be sensible, be calm and remember that what you do now, and how you both acts, has the potential to positively influence (or scar) your children for the rest of their life.

Get Help if You Need It

You don't have to do this alone. Draw on your support networks for advice, guidance and strength. Do this in person—i.e., with one on one conversations, rather than group chats or via social media blasts. There's a couple of reasons for this: firstly, it lets you stay classy and in control—you aren't airing your laundry for everyone to see and comment on, only selectively telling people that you know will be on your side.

Second, relationship troubles are a lot more common than you might think—no one is going to talk about their own experiences with everyone else listening, but they might just confide in you if you confide in them.

If you don't have a support network, or you don't want to tell your friends and family, remember that there are professional helplines available to you as well. There are free social work services in many countries for all genders, and there are depression hotlines if you're feeling down about the whole thing and just need an anonymous chat.

See a Lawyer

Okay, so this is a different kind of help but it's just as important. If you're leaving a long-term relationship with mixed finances, pets or children, you need clarity on what's going to happen next. Book an appointment with a family lawyer to see what options are available to you in your situation. In some states and countries if someone is caught cheating it gives you the right to ask for more in a settlement. Conversely, in many countries unfortunately it does not.

If you're worried about the money a lawyer will cost, think about this—the cheater has already spent hundreds and maybe thousands of dollars on their affair. You've got the right to spend money ensuring you're happy and safe as well.

Once you have legal advice, you'll be able to plan. Your partner will also know that you're taking what they've done very, very seriously—the look on their face when you tell them you've hired a lawyer can be kind of fun!

Move On

Remember—you're not the person who cheated here. It's heartbreaking, it's hard and it can take time, but you're not doing yourself any favors by staying miserable and refusing to move on. That just means the cheater has won. Surround yourself with friends. Remind yourself that you are loved, and important. Eat well, sleep, exercise (make yourself superhot, so your partner realizes what they're missing) and take care of yourself.

Chapter 9. Differing Responses of Men and Women

I will begin with a few statistics about men and women regarding infidelity and its consequences.

Men are usually considered to cheat more, but is that true? New research has revealed surprising facts about infidelity. Recent statistics show that more than one-half of men cheat on their partners, exactly 57 percent. But women are not far behind, 54 percent admit to infidelity.

Interestingly, they are more likely to seek a divorce than men. About 71 percent of divorces are initiated by women. Also, 53 percent of marriages end in divorce. Otherwise, 69 percent of women admitted they had chosen to be unfaithful because they no longer received any gifts from their partner, precisely of the kind of attention that make women feel valued and loved.

Healing from Infidelity

Cheating results in a loss of trust, and it is not a behavior that is unique to only one sex. Both

men and women cheat. At this time, we will focus on the woman's perspective, but that does not mean that men cannot learn something valuable by reading this. If I tell you this story from the perspective of both men and women, you will not understand this well. Instead, we will focus on one gender, so that you will understand this better.

There is a big difference in understanding cheating and the actual definition of infidelity, and it seems that different people come to different conclusions on the subject. For some, infidelity is the physical act of engaging in sexual relations with other people. Anything short of that does not count as cheating, at least not for them. Other people consider that infidelity is romantic physical contact, which should only be reserved for a partner, even if it does not include sexual intercourse.

Some believe that infidelity can exist even if there is no physical contact. If two people have shared something personal and intimate that would ordinarily be reserved only for a partner, that is also infidelity.

The fact is, if your partner is convinced that you have cheated, because of the time, attention, or attachment you have given to another person.

Your relationship should be the most important thing in the world to you and yes, friendships are wonderful, but if they impair intimacy and connection with your partner, then you are guilty of infidelity. That is a simple fact.

Relationships should be built on trust and mutual respect. When you are the "other woman" how can you trust a person who cheats on your partner with you? If he cheats with you, do you have enough ego and vanity to believe that he won't cheat on you too?

One thing psychologist know about cheating that the public ignores is that cheating never happens because of the quality of the relationship you are in. It is not because she was not good enough. Cheating happens because something is wrong with the person who is cheating.

There is no excuse that justifies infidelity. If the relationship is in trouble, then work on the problems. I have told you

If you find that the relationship cannot be rescued, then break it, with divorce if you are married, or by leaving your partner if it's a relationship. Do this before you go looking for someone else. Don't cheat! Cheating can never be justified and is never acceptable.

One thing as bad as cheating is being the enabler of the cheater. Of course, that doesn't hold true if the person doesn't know that their lover is in a relationship with someone. In such a case, the man should take full responsibility and consequences for his actions.

But if the other person is aware of the situation and chooses to continue the affair with the married man, then she is no better. It might be said that this other woman's infidelity is more unforgivable than his, because, as a woman, she should understand how much infidelity hurts and should never have entered into an affair.

As you look at the facts, bearing in mind that the problem of infidelity is not in the relationship, but in the one who committed the infidelity, then you will understand that the other woman can never be sure that she will not be deceived as well.

Once a cheater, always a cheater. If he is cheating, let him seek help. If it cheats again, you should just leave. But what do you do when you're with a cheater and you know he's cheated on other women before you? The truth is a man who has a past of cheating cannot be trusted in a relationship.

And if you are the "other woman" ask yourself this question: Knowing his unfaithful history, what do you think it will be like to become the cheated one, and learn that he has moved on to another?

Of course, you will think that things will be different with you. You will be everything he needs, but you are wrong.

There is nothing you can do, or give, or become, that will prevent a cheater from embarking on his "ventures". Cheating is cheating, both emotionally and physically, and if you allow it to continue, you are as guilty as he is. Don't worry, the time will come when, one day, he decides to move on to someone else, leaving you heartbroken just like the heart you helped him break when you participated in and encouraged his infidelity.

Not all men are cheats. Some are truly loving, willing to give anything for their partner, and be loyal to the end. This is the type of man you need to look for, instead of constantly trying to fix an irreparable cheat that will only break your heart and the hearts of other women.

If your man comes directly from the arms of another woman, you should flee, because it will soon be your turn. If you don't, well, you've earned you everything it will do to your heart and your soul. Cheaters never win. Be honest with your partner, and if you prefer to be with someone else, then end the relationship immediately.

If, you are the "other woman," you must also end the affair immediately. That is the right thing to do, or one day you will be in the place of this devil's wife, but, unlike his ex-partner, you will deserve every second of suffering.

Infidelity is a major social issue and I will not clarify or classify specific reasons. Do you wonder why? Because of that "golden rule". The truth is that there are no scruples in the cheater and they do things the wrong way. Both men and women are the same. And, there are no excuses.

Chapter 10. Understanding Your Unfaithful Partner

If you took the time to write down all of the ideas you cannot fully accept about your situation but that your husband (or others) want you to accept, you could end up with a long list. Every time you chip away at a belief it may seem as if you are not standing your ground. That will make you resist making an honest appraisal of the situation. Truth is often found in the gray areas. It's very rarely possible to pigeonhole people as all good or all bad. Good people can make bad choices and bad people can make good choices. When it comes to complicated situations, life is never open and shut. Consider the following five beliefs that, if you embrace them, can make your effort to get past the hurt and betrayal easier.

The Fact that He Betrayed You Doesn't Necessarily Mean He Doesn't Love You.

If he says he still loves you he may be telling the truth. Hurting people, you love is not a new phenomenon. If he loves you, his cheating says more about his inability to deal with his unhappiness, his impulses, or his emotional needs in a constructive way. As long as you claim "If you loved me you wouldn't have cheated" you have no other conclusion to draw other than he doesn't love you. But is that really true? Look deep in your heart at the totality of who he is. Do you really believe he has no love for you? If you cannot believe he loves you when he insists, he still does, you have reason to doubt him. After all, he's lied before. But for now, it's best to accept both sides of the issue. I accept that I believe he must not love me if he cheated, and I accept that it's possible he still loves me. You don't need to make a final decision on the truth of his love. If he wants to make the marriage work and you wish that it could work, you must go with the flow (a right-brain response) until more accurate information comes your way in time.

He May Have Lied but That Doesn't Necessarily Make Him a Liar

Infidelity and lying go hand in hand. They're a package deal. At first it is a lie of omission—not telling you what he's been doing. Then if your suspicions are aroused, he will lie to prevent getting caught. Lies soon build upon one another as he must continue to lie in order not to reveal that his former statements also were lies. And once the truth of the affair is out in the open, he may still lie because he fears making the situation worse by telling you more details of the truth. Or he will lie when he denies he was in contact with "her" after he strongly claimed he'd never speak to her again. (To be honest, everybody lies. Researchers claim that in an average ten-minute conversation with friends a person will lie up to three times. Usually the lies are done to enhance self-esteem or to avoid hurting someone's feelings.) If your husband was a fairly honest guy before his affair, and he wants to be trusted by you again, you're better off viewing him as someone capable of lying under certain conditions but not completely label him as a liar. If you are unsure about that, ask yourself: Have I ever lied after having done something I was ashamed of or didn't want others to know about? If so, does that make me a liar or a person who has lied and who has also spoken the truth?

He May Regret He Hurt You, but Not Regret the Affair

Unless he had an affair to exit the marriage purposely or to be vengeful, most affairs are not committed for the purpose of hurting a spouse or the children. If he had feelings for the other woman— even a little bit—he may still regard some aspects of the affair positively, even though he feels badly that you were hurt. If he does have some positive feelings about his affair, you will probably feel threatened by that. You may worry he will want to return to her. Keep in mind that no one continues an affair unless there is something worthwhile about it. But even when aspects of the affair are worthwhile, people can end affairs and remain faithful to their spouses afterward.

Similarly, he may have fond memories of the affair after it has ended. If you keep asking him about that and he admits it, you can choose to view that as a threat to your marriage or as an understandable (but somewhat unpleasant for you) consequence of many affairs. Again, if you are honest with yourself, you may fondly recall many parts of your earlier life (before you met your husband) and even fantasize about those things—and that doesn't necessarily mean you wish you weren't married. If your husband sincerely regrets how he hurt you and has taken clear and persistent steps to prove to you his devotion and commitment to the marriage, it is best to accept that any positive memories he has of his affair are memories only, and not a threat to you.

You May Never Know the Whole Truth

Getting to the heart of the matter seems like a sensible thing. Why did he do it? And has he told you everything? The trouble is when you ask him certain questions he will likely respond, "I don't remember" or "I don't know." It will look like he's being evasive. And that may or may not be the case. If he is being evasive to hide the fact that he is still carrying on with the other woman, you will eventually find that out. Some men are evasive because revealing additional details will only inflame the situation and they hope to focus on rebuilding things instead. For example, some men will refuse to describe their sexual activities with the other woman in any graphic detail. One husband told me in private that he had taken his mistress to a vacation spot that was one of his wife's favorites because he was familiar with the area. He also never told his mistress that he and his wife vacationed there many times. When his wife pressed him for details about his weekend trips with "her," he lied about where he'd gone knowing it would devastate his wife if she knew the truth.

If he isn't consciously hiding aspects of the truth, he still may not be that insightful. "I don't know" may be an honest answer. He never thought out why he was having an affair and never thought through the implications should he get caught.

Sometimes, more parts of the truth come out in bits and pieces over time. That's because as the marriage improves and trust is being restored, his anxiety and defenses will be reduced and he may suddenly have more insights or believe it is safer to reveal more.

Finally, you may know the truth about why he cheated but refuse to accept it. It will still seem as if a piece of the puzzle is missing. In reality, you're just having a difficult time accepting the fact that he did indeed cheat. Cheating is inexcusable, you believe, so no reason for it could ever be good enough.

He May Feel Ashamed (Deep Down) for a Long Time

As I've stated, there are many good men (and women) who have affairs. When I speak to these men, they struggle trying to accept themselves. They may have reasons for why they cheated but those reasons were not good enough in their hearts, either. You may think that it's appropriate he feels ashamed and you may even be thinking he deserves to suffer in any way possible. But my point is that in the years after an affair when a marriage has been restored, the infidelity can be an ugly part of his own past. It can always make him think less of himself. He has to somehow come to grips with what seems like a contradiction: "I'm a decent, honest man—who cheated on my wife and hurt my kids in the process." If his children were teenagers when the affair happened, they may have had strong negative opinions of their father. He may believe he lost his "hero" status with them. It is easy to focus completely on your own pain and victimization—and that is appropriate. But at some point, it can be helpful to understand the price he may have paid, as well.

Ideas to Erase

Any idea that paralyzes you or makes you feel defeated before you've really begun must be tossed aside. The trouble is that your mind (your left brain) will insist that you think of every possible negative outcome and worst-case scenario to help you better prepare for that possibility. But unless you or your husband are seeking a divorce and have no intention whatsoever of salvaging the marriage, it's too soon to tell what will happen. Be realistic. If you both desire to reconcile you can succeed, although the process is difficult. For now, accept that you may be thinking very pessimistic thoughts and also accept that there are other ways to think.

You'll Never Be Able to Trust Him Again

Actually, trust can be restored. And if you wish to have any peace of mind it is important to trust. Always being skeptical and on edge cannot result in happiness. Day by day you will discover that he seems to be trustworthy and keeping his word. An unwillingness to trust is really your way of saying "I will not be made a fool of again." But you sacrifice happiness instead. Trust involves taking a risk. Anyone who reconciles with someone who has betrayed them must be willing to risk being betrayed again. Only you can decide if it is a risk worth taking. He will prove himself over time to be trustworthy or not.

You Should Have Seen the Signs

You may be driving yourself crazy by thinking back about all the signs you may have missed before your husband's affair was brought into the open. But if you are upset that you should have seen the signs and did not, you are focusing on the wrong issue. His affair is the issue, not how easily you put two and two together.

She Must Be Better than You

Making comparisons is normal and understandable. But if you make this a competition you take a lot of the anxiety away from your spouse—he should be worried about losing you more than you are worried about coming in second place to some other woman. If in the process of working things out you realize that you have made mistakes in the marriage, by all means aim to correct them. But that doesn't mean she is better than you. In fact, when a person leaves a marriage to be with an affair partner, that relationship succeeds only 10 percent of the time.

Chapter 11. It is Crucial to Understand Why Your Partner Betrayed You

Once you have quite an idea on whether you should stay or go, the next thing to ask yourself is if a cheater will always be a cheater. Will your spouse still commit the same mistake even after he has promised you that the first time, he cheated would be the last one as well? Is the temptation too much that he has succumbed to it?

Why Is Your Spouse Cheating on You?

There are tons of reasons why your other half can be lying to you. It could be that he is just tired of living with someone else and want to be left out on his or her own. Maybe he fell out of love with you; it could be as simple as that or as complicated as him having a problem with you that you do not know about. What should you be able to do? It is going to be so hard during the first time but you are going to get through this. What are the common reasons why he is cheating on you?

Cheating has been going on for a very long time in the society. It is something that is very hard to stop as trust is lost during the process. What do you do to prevent the one you have made your vows with from deceiving you and finding someone else to love? The answer is simple: you need to consider the reasons why people are deceiving their partners and try to fulfill them.

1. Not satisfied with partner in a sexual manner

Men love to experiment especially with sexuality. They want to explore and look for their limits. Women, on the other hand, tend to be more laid back on that topic. People have a different hunger for sexual desires and if you do not want your partner to cheat on you, what you need to do is figure out if they are sexually satisfied with your relationship. If you can fulfill that, you might be able to prevent him from lying to you. Sex is a very vital part in most relationships so you need to keep this in consideration.

2. Wishes to engage with others sexually

Sometimes, one partner is not enough for a person and after years of settling down, suddenly the person gets an urge to engage sexually with another person. The person wants to get another feeling or is searching for something different than his wife. This sort of reason as to why he is having an affair with someone else cannot be easily resolved. Can you willingly let your husband have sex with someone else as long as he is not romantically involved with that person? If you are then, this should be easily resolved; the problem arises if you are not willing to go through that.

3. Not satisfied with emotional support from partner

Your husband/wife is your main source of emotional support, he is the one who you expect to give you advice, comfort you whenever you feel sad, be there for you when it seems that the whole world is against you and love you unconditionally. Sadly, there are times that your partner seems to lack the emotional support you are searching for and you feel that you need to seek it from someone else. He might feel the same way and try to look for that support from another person. If you want to stop him from going in another direction, then be more supportive and understanding of him and let him know that you are enough.

4. Wants to be appreciated with another person

Sometimes, your other half feels that your appreciation of the thing he does is not enough. As if you do not express it enough or he does not feel it at all. You need to be more expressive; you need to show your spouse that every simple thing he does, you appreciate more than ever. If you do appreciate it and it seems that he seems to be looking for more, then it is not a problem with you anymore, just that he thinks that your appreciation for the things he has done is not enough and he wants more.

5.   Fell out of love

As the marriage progress, people tend to lose the interest they once had in their partner. Love is such a big word and you have both promised to love each other for the rest of your lives but a person is always capable of loving another person. At some point, maybe the lowest point of your marriage, your husband might find another person to love and, in the process, fall out of love with you. Of course, the love he has for you will always be there but it can certainly be overshadowed by another. When he falls out of love with you, the only way to solve it is to make him fall in love with you all over again.

6.   Wants to get revenge on partner

If you have ever cheated on your partner before and he knows about it, there is a high chance that he is doing the same to you only because he wants to seek revenge on you. Your husband wants you to know how he felt when you were the one doing it and wants to make you suffer for it. After all, the best way to get revenge on someone is to ask for an eye for an eye that was lost. Since trust is gone between the two of you, he finds it easier to cheat on you.

7.   Wants to have new experiences

There are also times when your partner is simply tired of how the two of you are living, he may be bored and want to have new experiences with another person. Because marriage becomes stagnant after so many years, it is certainly possible that you want for adventure might decrease while your partner is still searching for a thrill, danger and something like that. When this happens, he might want to seek it from someone else if it seems that you cannot give it.

8. Lack of intimacy and attention

Do you not have the same way of showing your affection as you did before? Has time changed the way you intimately talk with each other or touch each other? Do you not have the time to spare for your husband anymore and you do not even give him enough attention? If so, then you really cannot blame him if he cheats on you. After all, intimacy and attention are some of a human's basic needs and he seeks that from you, the wife. If the relationship lacks these two, then you must really expect it not to work out.

9. Lack of self-esteem

If your partner is not confident, you will want to find someone who is more confident about himself or herself, someone who is able to stand up for the things that he wants. If you lack self-esteem, keeping your husband might be hard because you will always think that you are not good enough for him and eventually he will get tired of proving to you that you are worth it because he loves you. If you want to keep him and you have a lack of self-esteem, make the love he has for you into something that will help you have more confidence in yourself.

10. Financial problems

Money is one of the worst problems out there and it has ruined a lot of marriages in the past. When the husband or the wife cannot provide enough money for the family and the couple has kids, then things are set out for the worst. You cannot live without enough money to feed your family and it certainly is very hard to keep on loving each other when you are trying to find how you are going to feed yourselves or pay for the bill or prevent your family from getting kicked out of the apartment you are renting in.

Chapter 12. Manage Negative Emotions

Negative thoughts come from our core beliefs and as such they will never go away. There are people who always seem positive, and it is true they might be more positive than others, but that is due to their own system of core beliefs. There is no such person who doesn't have negative thoughts. We all are victims of our insecurities. They are either better in managing their responses to negative thoughts or their core beliefs are completely different. They might be the lucky ones who grew up in a safe, loving environment but if you ask them, they, too, have insecurities and negative thoughts to some degree.

Negative thoughts are cognitive barriers that your relationships are dealing with. When you make progress and turn from insecurities-driven negative behaviors to those driven by your values, you will still find yourself dealing with negative thoughts. If you want to learn how to manage them in a way that won't hurt your relationship, you will have to understand what they are and how they work.

Negative Thoughts May Come as:

1.   Predictions you make based on your core beliefs and past experiences. These may include rejection, abuse, failure, or abandonment. Predictions are not to be seen as premonitions; they are more expectations. We are so convinced that they are

going to happen no matter what and our behavior is leading us into more situations that can cause these expectations actually to happen. This is why we call them predictions.

2.   Memories of past situations, losses, and failures. We are prone to remember situations that hurt us much more than the ones that are happy. This is due to our defense mechanisms being at work. We have to remember hurtful situations and experiences to avoid them in future.

3.   Negative judgments, that we have about us or the others. Negative judgment comes from insecurities, and it also reflects on others. In them, we see our own insecurities and we easily pass the judgment as a coping mechanism.

As you accepted your core beliefs as something that is constant, and you have no influence over, so should you do with negative thoughts. They come from core beliefs, and we cannot stop them. They will constantly pop up in our minds whether we try to stop them or we don't. The fight you would put in trying to think only positive is futile, there is no amount of strength that will help you achieve this. You may succeed in pushing away negative thoughts temporarily, but they will always come back. You need to accept that negative thoughts happen to everyone and are not controllable. Again, what is controllable is your reaction to them.

At all costs avoid coping behaviors such as drug use, alcohol, gambling, risky sex... These behaviors will numb you so you don't feel emotions that accompany negative thoughts, but you will never get rid of them. This behavior will only create more negative thoughts about yourself and it will spin you in enchanted circle of bad coping mechanisms.

There is a tactic how to manage your negative thoughts properly and it consists of observing, labeling, and letting them go.

Observe Your Thoughts

The key to successful observation of your thoughts is objectiveness. It is not easy to be objective when it comes to something as personal as our own thoughts, but it can be learned. Put yourself in a third-person position and use ration and logic to engage your thoughts actively. See how they come to understand them. There is no need to act on them. The next time a negative thought comes to your mind, don't pass the judgment. Instead, take time to ask yourself why did you just think of this? What situation caused your negative thoughts? Where did it come from? Then think if there is a better way to have more positive view on the given situation. Don't be afraid to ask yourself "what if" questions but do it only from objective and rational third-person view.

Label Your Thoughts

When you acknowledge your thoughts and when you are able to accept them without judgment, you will take away their power. Putting yourself in the third person will give you the necessary objectivity to observe thoughts, but you will also be able to label them for what they are. Give them names and think of them as what they are: "My abandonment thought" or "Mistrust and abuse thought." Choose a label that works for you and categorize your thoughts. It can even be a thought associated with someone who reminds you of a said thought. For example: when you think "What did I do to deserve my partner?" it might remind you of your experience with your mother. During your schooling she may have been less supportive and frequently asked "What did you do to deserve that grade?" or "What did you do to deserve the main role in the school play?" You can simply label these as "Mom thoughts" if it will make it easier for you to categorize them.

You do not need to write them down, simply practice this in your mind with active thinking. If you do feel the need to write down your thoughts and label them, please feel free to do so. Creating your own ways of dealing with problems is amazing motivation and the path to success.

Let Go of Your Thoughts

Remember the meditation exercise we did for letting go of your emotions? We can do the same exercise for thoughts. Instead of emotions, visualize your thoughts passing by, see them as objects you are willing to give up on. Now that you labeled your thoughts, it is easier to visualize them and make them pass by without interacting and reacting to them. Imagine you are driving a car and your thoughts are signs next to the road. Use the labels you gave to your thoughts. Imagine a sign saying, "Mom thoughts" or "Abandonment thoughts." Observe them, acknowledge them and drive past them, letting them go.

Practice observing, labeling, and letting go of your thoughts daily. Practice putting yourself in objective position of a third person to make it easier. Do so with positive thoughts, too, for the sake of practice. In certain situations, it may come as a helpful thing to do with positive thoughts. For example, if you need to hide the excitement so you don't give up on a surprise you are planning for your partner.

When our insecurities are triggered, what we feel is emotional pain. This emotional pain is responsible for our actions. We react to it, and it makes us behave in unhelpful ways that will only add up to already existing emotional pain. No matter how hard you try, you can't get rid of your negative emotions and thoughts. They always keep reemerging. Just like with behavior and thoughts, you need to learn how to manage your emotions properly. You need to learn how to accept them for what they are even though they are the main reason why you feel the pain.

When your emotions manifest due to your insecurities, you feel pain and you start remembering the situation that caused the insecurity. You start reliving the past, either through your memories or just by feeling the same as you did back then. This will make you blind to the fact that you are in the present and in a different situation. Your behavior will reflect your insecurities, and they will be unhelpful and harm you even more.

Learn to Tolerate Your Emotions

What you need to do when your emotions appear is choose the reaction that will not keep hurting you; it won't make you or your partner feel bad, and it won't damage your current relationship. Let's observe what happens with emotions when our insecurity is triggered: once the situation presents itself and you feel at your worst, your emotions are very painful, overwhelming, and you can't bear to feel that way. It is quite normal to want to get rid of them as soon as possible so why should you endure the pain? You start behaving in unnatural ways, ways that are against your own core values. This is why you feel even worse after you let your emotions cause unhelpful behavior. Sometimes these behaviors will make you feel better in the short term, but in the long term, emotions will be back and will strike you even harder.

Emotions are unavoidable, and there is nothing you can do not to feel. What you can control in this situation is a response to your negative emotions. Don't allow them to control your behavior. You are the only one who should have the full control. Accept the responsibility of the way you feel, and don't give in.

Distract Yourself from Negative Emotions

If you are afraid that negative emotions are going to overwhelm you and you won't be able to tolerate them, or take control of your behaviors, there is an option of distracting yourself. Be sure to use only healthy distraction activities; this means engage yourself in any helpful and healthy activity that will divert you from the negative emotions you are feeling.

Exercising: We do not need to mention the health benefits of exercising. It influences your whole body in a positive way. It will help you to lose weight, it will improve oxygen flow and help with elevated blood pressure. Be sure that you choose an exercise that is to your liking. We are not all capable of doing extreme sports no matter how much we want. Start with some light exercises. Even dancing can be a good exercise that will distract you from your emotions.

Hobbies: Another activity that will distract you is engaging in hobbies. It can be anything you want and find interesting. Identify activities you find interesting to and don't wait. Start doing it now. We are often lazy about our hobbies, thinking there is never enough time and there are always more important things to do. Stop thinking like that; hobbies are great way to entertain yourself and stay distracted when needed. It can be anything you find interesting: photography, learning how to play an instrument, cooking, knitting. The possibilities are endless.

Volunteering: volunteering is about having a purpose or a task that goes beyond you and your own needs. Helping others puts focus on a good cause that will distract you from what you feel. It also feels rewarding to help someone else. If you want, you can join big organizations that will help you decide how best to spend your time volunteering with the programs they offer or you could do simple stuff such as helping your elderly neighbor shop or walk his dog on a daily basis. It doesn't have to be anything grand. The main thing is to move the focus from yourself to someone else. It will make you feel good about yourself in the most unselfish way.

Chapter 13. The Blame Can be on Either Partner: Working on Self-Awareness

Being self-aware implies that you become conscious of your own character and feelings.

1. Spend some time alone and meditate

In the stillness and quietness of your mind, you will become conscious of the thoughts and feelings that you have. You will have the opportunity to think about things that influence your attitudes or behaviors.

Once you figure out your thoughts and feelings, you will begin to make sense of your actions. As a result, you will have a better understanding of your emotions and the way the feelings relate to specific experiences.

2. Start journaling about your self-awareness journey

Keep a record of the reflections you have during meditation and identify any patterns you will discover about your thought process. Journaling will help you to see and evaluate the gaps between your thoughts and your actions, and you will make out the pattern involved in your decision-making.

Think about what you write and improve on anything that needs a change in behavior or thought. Most importantly, write out your thoughts, feelings, and actions every day in a way that you can understand.

3.   Ask yourself reflective questions

When you ask yourself questions, you discover things that help you to understand yourself better.

Ask questions like, "What am I feeling right now?" "What do other people think of my behavior?" "Why do I feel this way?"

When you find the answers to your self-reflection questions, you will become aware of your strengths, weaknesses, and the driving factors that explain your response to situations.

Reflective questions are therefore important because they help you to look inward for solutions, instead of looking outward for affirmation.

4.   Forget about your worries and be present in the moment

Focus on what is happening to you now and analyze your feelings concerning the event at that particular time.

Are you reading a novel? What are your thoughts about the page you are currently reading? How do you think the story will end? Why do you think so?

Are you going out for a walk? Where do you plan to go? Why do you want to go there? What do you expect to find there?

Are you having a conversation with your friend? How can you show that you are interested in having that conversation? Do you enjoy spending that time with your friends? How can you contribute effectively to the talk?

Whatever activity it is that you are doing, focus your attention on it, and live that moment.

The benefits of becoming self-aware include knowing who you are and what you want, welcoming setbacks as stepping stones to triumph, replacing reactivity with pro-activity, and finally, appreciating who you are.

Exercise and Eating Healthy

Nutrition and fitness are important aspects of loving yourself. A healthy lifestyle and a balanced diet can give you the energy you need to fuel your daily activities.

How can you capitalize on your health and fitness?

1.   Start with eating a healthy meal in the morning

Incorporate whole-grain cereals, low-fat milk, bananas, and fresh juice in your breakfast. Remember to take carbohydrates to boost your energy for the day.

2.   Watch the amount of food you take

When you plan to have a bounty meal, eat at least three hours before your workout session begins. For small meals, you can expect to exercise one hour after you finish having your lunch

3.   Carry a healthy snack with you

A fruit smoothie, an energy bar, fresh fruit, yogurt, or sports drinks are some of the healthy options of meals you can carry.

The best time to eat them would depend on how you are feeling. Follow what works best for you, but make sure not to overdo snacks.

4.   Eat healthy carbohydrates after working out

Eating foods like whole-grain bread, vegetables, white meat, or fruit, and yogurt can help you to recover your muscle energy.

Treat yourself to a meal that has both protein and carbohydrate within an hour or two of your work out session, if possible.

5.   Take in as many fluids as necessary

Your body will need enough fluids before and after workouts, to help avoid dryness and dehydration.

Stay well hydrated by taking 2 to 3 cups of water two hours before you work out and the same amount of water after the workout.

Water is commonly the best fluid to drink, but sports drinks can work as well when you have extended hours of workout sessions. Sports drinks contain carbohydrates that help to preserve the electrolyte balance in your body.

Exercise and healthy eating are vital in promoting healthy lifestyle habits, shedding off excess weight, boosting the physical appearance, making life more diverse and exciting, and lastly, stimulating brain chemicals that produce feelings of happiness, relaxation, and contentment.

Keep Your Eyes Up

Be on the lookout for anything that may cause trouble, or that may not be good for your well-being.

You can keep your eyes up by:

1. Learning to express yourself honestly and openly

Transparency helps you not to hide behind a fake smile and a phony head nod when you are not saying what you think.

Get in the habit of speaking out openly without being too much obliging or defensive, and you will realize that people are willing to hear you out and incorporate your ideas.

2.   Being assertive

Be polite, but do not let bullies run all over your emotions. Stay calm in a conflict situation and express yourself confidently when it is time to do so. Do not react with low blows to people who like to make a sport of others. Instead, be the more mature person and take the high road but stand your ground.

3.   Identifying what could be unsettling you

Whether it is a person's behavior toward you or an uncomfortable situation, uncover the issue, and have the courage to stand up to it.

When you fail to identify and talk about what is bothering you, no one will know, and therefore, a real talk cannot begin to take place.

4.   Defending your time

Realize that time is precious and that every minute counts. Therefore, do not feel overstretched to give your time when you have the ability to say no. Appreciate that 'no' is a complete sentence and that you do not have to explain your reasons.

Engage with people and in activities that fit into your schedule, but do not be afraid to push back when you need to.

5. Appreciating that your view may differ from another person's perspective

Own your beliefs, thoughts, emotions, and actions and acknowledge that other people may think differently. However, no one else can control how you think or feel and thereby invalidation your sentiments.

Consequently, do not be around people who seek to invalidate your thoughts and ideas and, likewise, do not override other people's opinions.

The benefits of keeping your eyes up include becoming confident, feeling more comfortable around your peers, improving your self-esteem, freeing up your mind and time, building self-respect, and finally, respecting others.

Affirm Yourself

Affirming yourself means that you put down in writing your inner self-talk about yourself and about the things you value. That exercise makes you own the aspects of yourself and your life that you could be overlooking.

You can affirm yourself by:

1. Stretch your limits

Develop a new habit or start doing an activity that you usually would not do before. When feeling low, instead of playing all the sad songs in your playlist, go out for a jog or take a walk.

Find something better to do with your time and develop your knowledge and skills.

2. Create time to volunteer

Volunteering allows you to help other people and thereby feel good about your ability to make someone else happy.

Happiness is contagious. When you inspire someone else's life, that person's joy becomes your joy when you see him or her feeling more positive about himself or herself. Similarly, when you encourage those who struggle with self-esteem, you will learn to improve yours too.

Find something helpful to do, or something kind to say to a person who may need a kind word.

3. Set out to accomplish your goals

Make a list of what you wish to accomplish, and that will be a step closer to getting to where you desire to be.

When you begin to accomplish your goal one-by-one, you will experience a sense of direction in handling your time and a sense of fulfillment whenever you finish a task.

4. Avoid being around negative people

It is difficult for a person to develop positive attitudes when negative-minded people surround the person. Negative people will cause you to walk with your head down because you feel that there is nothing in your existence to be happy about.

Avoid being around negative influences that drain you emotionally and leave you feeling dreadful about yourself.

If you cannot avoid being around such people, interact with them on your own standings. Do not allow negative mentality to infiltrate your mind and to control your life.

5.   Talk yourself out of negative thoughts

Do you imagine that other people believe the unwanted thoughts you may have of yourself? When you fill your mind with negative thoughts about whether your group leader dislikes your ideas, or whether your contribution to the group project ruined the chances of that project becoming successful, you judge yourself without anyone else having to do it.

Negative thoughts reflect a person's insecurities about whether he or she is worthy of approval from other people. When you feel bad about a situation, think about the emotions that are contributing to that feeling and filter your emotions through objective reality. Fine-tune yourself until your inner satisfaction becomes better and more objective.

Affirming yourself helps you to become aware of your thoughts and words, and as a result, you prevent negativity from getting in. Similarly, asserting yourself helps to keep you bounded by the things you desire in your life and to keep the small details in perspective. Additionally, self-affirmation keeps you focused by helping those around you and being in a constant state of gratitude.

In conclusion, loving yourself may come across as selfish in a world that teaches people to put others first. However, you must acknowledge that self-love is the basis for who you are. Everything else falls on that reality, and life begins to move forward with ease when you learn to love yourself. Subsequently, connect with your deepest needs, enjoy the freedom of being you, and honor your authentic self.

Chapter 14. Controlling Emotions

Forgiveness

Forgiveness, whether it is forgiveness for yourself or for others, is very important to keep your emotions in check. How? Well, it is simple; when you forgive yourself and others, you get rid of the emotional baggage that you have been carrying in the form of guilt, anger, regret and hurt. Hence, forgiveness becomes the ultimate step to overcoming your emotional habits and saying goodbye to them for good.

Let me explain this with an example. Imagine you are mad at yourself because you lost a tennis match at your school's sports festival. Until you forgive yourself for the loss, you will carry the pain of that defeat in the form of guilt and anger. However, if you forgive yourself and let go of the defeat, you will feel a sudden relief and the guilt will disappear. Moreover, if you have been hurt by your loved one and haven't been able to forgive them, you will carry the hurt, pain and grief with you until you forgive them. Therefore, forgiving yourself and those who hurt you is important to keep your emotional habits in control.

Self-forgiveness and forgiveness for others can be practiced in the following ways:

1. Empathy: Empathy is the ability to understand the feelings of others. Moreover, being empathetic helps when you want to forgive someone or yourself. For instance, if you want to forgive your friend for hurting you but it seems hard, ask yourself how you would feel if you had hurt your friend and they wouldn't forgive you. If you are having trouble forgiving yourself for something, practice the same empathy and lend yourself the same courtesy you would lend another person.

2. Let it go: The best way to forgive yourself or someone else is to let go of the grudge. In order to let go of a grudge, stop ruminating over it and tell yourself that the only way to feel at peace is if you let go of it. Letting go of negative thoughts and that experience will help you forgive yourself or someone else more easily. To do that, write the negative thoughts about yourself or others that bother you on your journal and then tear off that page and throw it in the trash can. For instance, if you are mad at yourself for being rude with your mother and this upsets you now, write it down on paper and then discard it. When you forgive yourself for your flaws, you feel better and get the courage to improve yourself

Assertiveness

Your journey to control your negative emotions doesn't end yet. You need assertiveness to master them completely. Let us find out what that is and how it helps you take charge of your emotions.

Importance of Assertiveness

Assertiveness means being able to stand up for your rights or the rights of others in an appropriate, direct and honest manner. Assertiveness and emotional intelligence go hand in hand; you cannot achieve one without the other.

For instance, if you think that your boss is violating your rights, it is important that you stand up for yourself, but it is also essential that you take a stand in an appropriate manner. For example, throwing a temper tantrum in front of your boss is not the right way to be assertive. Instead, to be assertive, you must take legal action or state facts that make your boss realize that he violated your rights.

Similarly, if you want to be emotionally intelligent and overcome your negative emotions, you must be assertive in your ways and take charge of your life. For instance, if you want to get rid of grief and depression, you must be assertive in order to make a change. If the reason for your grief and depression is other people, use assertiveness to express your feelings. Follow the strategies given below and learn to be more assertive:

#1 – Respect Yourself

To be assertive, you must respect yourself. This includes respecting your feelings, emotions, thoughts and opinions. If you don't respect yourself, you will never become assertive because you will not value yourself enough to take a stand if your rights are infringed upon. On the other hand, if you respect yourself, it becomes easier for you to be assertive because you consider yourself worthy and believe that your rights deserve protection. In order to respect you, always be positive, don't indulge in negative self-talk and practice self-love.

Self-love is the act of loving yourself despite your flaws and imperfections. If you want to respect yourself, it is imperative that you love yourself first. To do that, always be kind with yourself and comfort yourself when you err instead of being harsh on yourself.

#2 – Be Clear About What You Want

If your siblings constantly tease you about your weight and that has caused you to be anxious, depressed and self-conscious all the time, express yourself clearly in the following manner: 'I don't like the way you people treat me and it is best that you refrain from making fun of me in the future'. When you are clear with people about what you want from them, they see you as assertive and think twice before insulting you next time.

Moreover, if you want something from yourself, be clear about that as well. Let us take the above example; if your siblings tease you about your weight and you don't want yourself to react to their insult by drowning in depression, tell yourself 'It doesn't matter what my siblings think; even if I am overweight, I am still a good person and the next time they insult me, I will stay calm'. Try this technique to be assertive and you will feel its usefulness for yourself.

Once you have learnt to be more assertive, you will be on your way to becoming an emotionally intelligent person. The only thing left to do now is learn patience and the art of forgiveness.

Patience

Patience is the ability to accept trouble, delay and suffering without letting your emotions take control of you. It is one of the key elements required to overcome your undesirable emotional habits. For instance, it has been a year since you invested in a business venture and it has not given you the return you had hoped. Instead of getting depressed and hopeless, be patient and hope for the best and soon your dark cloud will show a silver lining.

Moreover, if you want to master your emotions but it is taken longer than you expected, patience will come in handy and it will keep you going. Learn to be more patient and take charge of your life in the following ways:

#1 – Know the Consequences of Impatience

First, ask yourself what happens when you are impatient. If you recently became impatient because you couldn't find a file at work and went to report it to your boss but later found it on your own cluttered desk, ask yourself how impatience made you look in front of your boss. The purpose of this activity is to get you familiar with the negative impacts of impatience. Once you are aware of the consequences of impatience, you will not rush yourself the next time you are in a similar situation; you will be more patient.

#2 – Slow Down

If you have the habit of rushing around and trying to do things in a hurry, slow down. For example, if you are stuck in traffic and it is getting you all worked up, ask yourself if your anger will make traffic move any faster. Try to observe patience and distract yourself by listening to music.

As you practice being more patient, your negative emotional habits will start to vanish and you'll find it easier to stay confident, assertive and in control of yourself all the time.

In addition to having patience, you also need to learn the art of forgiving yourself and others to be in control of your emotions. Let us find out how forgiveness frees you from your emotional demons and how to practice it.

Chapter 15.   Rebuilding Trust

All throughout this we have talked about jealousy, anxiety, and insecurity and how the three of these things often lead to trust issues. As you are already aware trust is a big part of any kind of relationship, if you don't have trust you won't have a relationship for very long. As we have talked sometimes the trust issues are not the fault of your partner, they are based on your relationships. However, sometimes it is the fault of your partner; they do or say something that shatters the trust you have given them.

Once your trust in your partner has been shattered your relationship often starts to go downhill. You are literally second guessing everything that your partner says and does, and the reason for that is the lack of trust. Once the trust goes, so does the sense of security and safety you had in your relationship. Once trust is broken the feelings of love, respect, and friendship are often replaced by anger and fear.

Trust issues can stem from all sorts of scenarios, whether its lies or infidelity, the reason doesn't matter, just the end results do. Once that trust has been broken, it might seem like all hope is lost. I mean after all; how can you reasonably expect to trust that person again when you have never felt so violated in your life? Now even if your life currently right now is filled with nothing but arguments and everything seems hopeless, there are some things that can be done to help rebuild the trust that you two once had.

Step One: Come Clean

The first step that you will need to take when trying to rebuild the trust in your relationship is to come clean with what you have done. Nobody can move beyond the hurt and the anger, if you continually deny that it happened. You have to step up and take responsibility for what you did, which includes admitting what you have done. Taking responsibility doesn't necessarily mean including all of those minute details, sometimes sharing the details only causes more pain and anger, so be honest but don't over share.

Step Two: Be Aware of How you Act

You need to pay close attention to how you are acting. Being on the defensive or even acting casually about the problem at hand can have disastrous results. If you act like what you did doesn't really matter, your partner is not going to be very willing to work things out. You need to put forth a very sincere effort to show your partner that you do feel bad for what happened. This comes down to the way that you communicate. There is verbal communication of course, where your apologies for the mistake that has been made and try to make up for it. Then there is also your nonverbal communication which reveals much more than the words that you say. With your non-verbal communication, you can express your remorse over having broken trust, or you could reveal an attitude that shows you do not really care. It just needs you to be sensitive to what you are doing.

Step Three: Talk About It

After you have come clean about what you have done, you will want to find the time to talk to your partner about what made you do it. I don't recommend doing it right away, wait a few days for things to calm down a little bit. Talking about why you did it, how you might need help, as well as how you plan to fix things so it doesn't happen again is a great way to show your partner that you are serious about working things out, and just might convince them that you can be trusted again.

Before you decide to do this, take the time to carry out an intense self-analysis, so that you can determine what happened that you broke trust. Unless there is something wrong with your personality, such that you have a personality disorder, it is unlikely that you purposely went out to break the trust of someone. There will be something that is lacking for you, a gap that you needed to fill, or something deep down inside that drove you to do the wrong thing.

When you sit down to talk with your partner about everything that has happened it is important to do it correctly. When talking you want to sit so that you are facing each other, and as we learned from trust building exercises, as close as possible, to help reestablish that trust. Proceed to tell your partner the entire truth, do not go into hurtful details, but be honest about exactly how you feel. If you make things seem better than they are, you are not doing yourself or your relationship any favors. Honesty really is the key to rebuilding trust.

Step Four: Be Gentle

Communicating is vital to rebuilding trust, as long as it is done correctly. While you want to be perfectly honest and open with your partner, you don't want to be harsh. Coming right out and confessing might make you feel better, but it isn't how your partner deserves to be treated. Talking openly and honestly doesn't mean you have to forget about tact, you can still get your point across about how you are feeling while being tactful. And, no matter what happens or who confesses what, the worst thing either one of you can do is attack the other.

Also ensure that you do not put your partner in the wrong, or in any way blame them for the mistakes that you have made in the relationship to break trust. This will be the easiest way to ensure that they clamp up. It is so important to take responsibility for the role that you have in breaking the trust, and that is why this is a point that is raised over and over again.

Step Five: Let Your Partner Talk

Part of communicating freely involves letting your partner speak. This can be especially hard if your partner has recently hurt your feelings, but you won't be able to resolve anything if you don't listen to what they have to say. By listening to what they have to say, even if it's not something you necessarily want to hear, it is something that they need to do. It can also help you decide if it's worth trying to rebuild the trust, just don't make that harsh decision while you are still feeling angry.

There is a difference between hearing what they have to say and listening to what they have to say. Hearing what they have to say is easy, as this means that you do not really take it in and consider the implications of what is being said. When you are listening to what your partner has to say, it is more the words that you are taking in. You are also absorbing the emotions that surround these words, the anger and sadness that they may be feeling, the defiance that may come through and everything else. It may not be what you want to experience, but your relationship will be much better off if you choose to put yourself in the shoes of your partner by truly listening.

When letting your partner talk that means they are going also to have questions. The worst thing you can do is avoid answering your partner's questions. No matter what question they have you need to respond to the questions, avoiding them makes you seem guilty of something. And, remember, when answering their questions, you need to remain honest, yet tactful. Belittling them or attacking them is only going to work against you.

The way that you ask these questions is also important, as is the way that you respond. At the back of your mind, you need to remember that you should be coming from a place of love all the time.

Step Six: Be Transparent

In order to prove that you are doing everything that you can to be trusted again you are going to need to make yourself entirely transparent to your partner. Making yourself transparent to your partner includes giving them access to everything, emails, voicemail, etc. While this might sound easy, it really is not because you are simply giving up your privacy and that can make a person edgy. Being edgy often means you end up getting defensive with your partner, which can cause even more problems. Just remind yourself it's either your privacy or your relationship, only you can decide what one is more important.

In addition to being transparent with your partner, you also need to share information willingly. If you feel like you have to withhold information from your partner, you are setting yourself up for trust problems on down the road. If it is something that you have to hide, either you shouldn't be doing it, or you shouldn't be in the relationship. Being open and honest with your partner means they have less reason to doubt you when you tell them something.

Step Seven: Renewing the Vows

Most people think that in order to renew their vows they have to be married, but that is far from the truth. If you are simply in a relationship you and your partner need to sit down and talk about what you first felt when you entered into the relationship. Talk about the values that both of you considered sacred. You need to have a serious talk as to what you want and how you want things to be in the future. Each partner can write up their own vows and you can even perform a ceremony in front of your friends to help make it even more official.

The one thing that you need to remember when it comes to rebuilding the trust in your relationship is that it is not something that is going to happen overnight. Even though the trust was lost overnight, the actions that lead up to the loss of trust probably took place over an extended period of time. If you really want to rebuild your trust in your partner or you want to start believing in your partner again, you are going to need to put forth the effort required. You can't give up just because it's not easy.

Chapter 16. Cultural Differences and Scientific Considerations about Monogamy, Open Couple, and Polyamory

Many cultures have sanctioned monogamy and upheld it as the center of civilization. However, there are some aspects of civilization that have not been understood completely. Everyone is aware, either completely or vaguely, that monogamy produces a social contract that is peaceful to a large extent supporting a framework for economic advancement and cultural harmony. Still, this realization has not been studied extensively. There lacks a comprehensive report on why we settle for monogamy while there are other options.

And like every other hard-won battle, monogamy is not a perfect choice for everyone. Whence examined closely, we can realize there are a good number of private dissatisfactions in monogamy. These imperfections form a nagging undercurrent of discomfort in any culture. Under ordinary circumstances, these dissatisfactions are seen as a form of deviance and are generally disapproved and suppressed by the vast majority. However, they are impossible to eradicate from society. The only time that culture may experience some relief is if people begin to appreciate the weaknesses of monogamy and look at other possibilities.

The silent question in our society today is how much of anti-monogamy practices can we accommodate in the community before we lose our culture. A good number of people already appreciate the idea of open relationship; others are choosing to bear children out of wedlock, while others are taking divorce as a norm. There are some practices in the society that hold the ideology of monogamy since ancient time but have examined them as times are changing.

Polygamy persisted since time immemorial for both human beings and animals. However, as human beings became civilized, they reinvented monogamy. This reinvention did not do away with polygamy entirely because of the basic nature of mammals except a few animals such as orangutans, gibbons, and beavers. Over the centuries, the debate of monogamy versus polygamy has brought different results and opinions in people. However, monogamy has held the forefront.

What Makes Monogamy So Successful and Appreciated Across Cultures?

Firstly, it reduces sexual competition among the male species and creates a social contract. Looking at the animals, males do not have a fair chance to mate, rather, it is about strength and getting as many females as possible. With monogamy, however, there is the rationale that every male will get a chance to mate. Consequently, the do or die mating competition among men reduces. If one male can collect many females, then the competition becomes deadly intense. However, monogamy promises a democratic outcome, and the bachelor herd disappears.

Secondly, monogamy reassures everyone in the society that they have a chance to reproduce; therefore, another social contract develops. There is no risk of a certain group out-casting or pulling in people from other groups through reproduction. The society can function as a whole. Monogamy ensures that people can pair off for reproduction purposes, but they have to keep other social and familial relationships. Consequently, the community can cooperate. Monogamy also ensures that men and women can easily work together in non-sexual settings even though there is role tension as the world gets more complex.

Monogamy also ensures that we develop a complex personality allowing us to maintain sexual relationship privacy and at the same time maintain a multilayered network of friends, relatives, associates, acquaintances, strangers, and even coworkers who we interact with without sexual intentions unlike other mammals living in collective doubt.

We can, therefore, say that although monogamy has its discontents, distinct advantages are making it most viable for human beings. These advantages have a price.

In a monogamous setting, everyone has the chance to get a partner regardless of their status. A high-status woman does not have to worry about sharing her mate with a low-status woman, and a low-status man has a chance of getting a mate. In this case, status is defined as the quality of beauty, characteristic, strength, brightness, speed intelligence, and any other admirable character. With human males, there is a crucial character that women look for: the willingness to provide for the offspring.

Keeping all these factors in mind, let us account for the major areas of dissatisfaction with monogamy. First, the one-mate-per-person idea limits the mating urges of males. Naturally, male species have the underlying desire to mate with as many females as possible. The Coolidge effect explains that a barnyard male animal will get a resurge of sexual desire as soon as a new female is introduced into the barn even if it had just exhausted its energies.

Monogamy has resulted in serial monogamy, whereby a male or female changes partner as he/she moves up the ladder. Because a low-status person would probably be forced to mate with a person of the same level even if he/she is unsatisfied, one of the results is divorce, and marrying someone better as the standards rise. This effect is more visible in men who marry women who are way younger than them after leaving their wives and children. On the side of the woman agreeing to marry an older man, it is a case of choosing a man who can provide rather than a man who looks good yet cannot offer support for the offspring.

People who are unsatisfied with monogamy settle for other options such as single motherhood, divorces and remarrying, not marrying but having several partners in different locations, open relationships, et cetera. Male dissatisfaction with monogamy is normally very open, unlike female dissatisfaction.

Should we then accept a more practical alternative such as polygamy? That is, should we allow people to choose the side they want to settle in openly? This kind of freedom might open the world to acceptance, but it might also bring confusion. People will no longer be sure of whether their spouses will be monogamous for life or they will get to a point where they change their agenda.

To sum up, the above analysis shows clearly why monogamy is best suited for our society. Polygamy might bring in confusion and aggression as every mate tries to identify the best option. Monogamy is essential for humankind to keep the current family values. Most of the family values followed today is based on a husband, wife, and children setup which makes the human society progressive and peaceful. Practices challenging the monogamy contract such as divorce, legalized prostitution, pornography, single parenthood by choice, and homosexuality should be addressed because they pose a threat to the norm. If we accept anti-monogamy practices without real analysis and understanding, we might end up confused and non-progressive.

Polygamy might seem appealing for people unsatisfied by monogamy and may choose to support their cause, but they should take note: looking beyond the personal dissatisfaction, which we all might feel at one point or the other, we all have a responsibility of retaining a permanent stake at ensuring that the society remains peaceful and orderly. We should ensure that in the world, everybody has a reasonable and fair chance of achieving happiness. And although monogamy makes tough demands on us, it also offers complex and unique rewards to society.

Chapter 17. Changing Expectations – Case Studies

"Wants" Versus Core Values

All of us live with values that can be negotiated and some that cannot. Dr. Murray Bowen defined a person's core self as made up of both types. The non-negotiable values are our solid self and cannot be changed, and no number of lectures, persuasion, or coercion will alter those beliefs. The preceding example of the husband who does not want to change his religion may illustrate one such value. The values that can be changed are part of the pseudo-self.

How to Solve the Problem

Unfulfilled expectations do not necessarily spell the end of a relationship, but they must be addressed and accepted. These are the expectations that Sager has indicated are beyond our awareness. Therefore, to find out what these expectations mean to an individual, the couple must have an honest talk. For example, the woman who must have a lavish lifestyle may have a background of poverty and deprivation that is unimaginable to her husband, one so terrible that she has kept it hidden. That may be a problem that can be worked through when effective communication is used.

Some core issues or values, such as wanting to have children, may be unfixable. These expectations are non-negotiable for some, so their expectations cannot change. In these cases, unfulfilled expectations may mean that the two partners are no longer compatible in some vital way.

Case Study: Beth and Joshua

Beth and Joshua met on a college expedition to an archeological dig in Israel, where they both had a wonderful time. As a couple, they traveled the country and toured as many neighboring countries as they could. During the year after that, they saw each other often before graduation. Then Joshua went to graduate school in New England, and Beth in New York. Both made frequent trips to visit each other. After graduation, Joshua got a job on a research team, and Beth worked for a television news network as an assistant producer. They felt fortunate that they both were hired by firms in the same city, Atlanta. They made a commitment to each other that they would always be together and agreed to make decisions that would honor that commitment. That was the extent of what they said about their expectations for their future together.

They were like many of today's young generation who are excited about their careers. Beth was moving up at the network and was given increasingly more responsibility. She put in long hours and traveled to many places to work on stories. Joshua was left alone, and more and more he began to realize that this wasn't the life he wanted.

One day, when Beth came home from a trip to Dubai, Joshua surprised her with tickets for a long weekend at Hilton Head, where they could relax and enjoy themselves in the water and at the beach. She was delighted. It was just the kind of vacation she loved. On the second day of their holiday, Joshua said he wanted to talk to her about something.

Joshua: I know our careers are going well, but what about children? We can't wait too long.

Beth: We never talked about kids.

Joshua: I thought we had. You love my nieces and nephews. We have all these great get-togethers.

Beth: I do love them. But I'm on such a roll with my career. I don't know what to say.

Joshua: Beth, if you get pregnant, they can't fire you. There are laws against that.

Beth: Yes, but I won't get any of the good assignments anymore.

Joshua: Don't you want children?

Beth: I don't know. I don't not want them, but I'm not excited about them. I want the kind of life we had in college. Not being torn between work and children.

So, they decided to put off the talk for six months. No definite conclusion was reached. As the decision continued to be put off, Joshua became more and more depressed. He started telling his problems to his coworker, Leah. They would have dinner together on the nights when Beth worked late. As their relationship developed, Joshua felt very close to her, and they began sleeping together.

Joshua and Beth came in for therapy after he told her that he was attracted to Leah and was sleeping with her. Beth was very upset.

Beth: So, it's my job or a baby?

Joshua: Why can't it be both? Your job and a baby.

Beth: I don't want a baby.

Joshua: Why didn't you tell me that sooner?

Beth: I never knew it was so important.

Joshua: You saw my family—all the kids. I thought you would understand.

Beth: You saw my family—I'm the oldest of eight children. I had to work, work, and work. I don't want that again. I thought you were a career guy and wanted the same for me.

Joshua and Beth had not verbalized their desires for the life they wanted together, so they had expectations that went unfulfilled. Joshua cheated on Beth by having an affair with

Leah, rather than really talking about their problem further. We spent time helping Beth with her feelings about the affair.

Conclusion

The shock of the affair caused Joshua and Beth to talk about their different expectations for their future together. After hours of talking, they could not come to a compromise. Neither one could give up on their expectations. They were intelligent people who loved each other, but both found the expectations of the other unacceptable. Their therapy goal changed to helping them separate. They did not separate in anger; they said appreciative things to each other and they assessed every way they could possibly make it work. At their last session together, they gave each other a gift that had special meaning for them and each wrote a letter to the other. Writing the letters was therapeutic and provided something they could keep and read when needed. Their breakup was sad, but it was a separation that had meaning, not bitterness.

Retaliation

Couples who have been disagreeing with each other for some time are often angry. One of the least effective and most destructive ways to cope with anger is by having an affair in retaliation for some hurt. Yet this is somewhat common. Retaliation affairs are an expression of rage at the partner. They can be a result of knowing the partner had an affair or multiple affairs. Other reasons relate to years of mistreatment that ate away at the person's core values. The person who retaliates is for some reason feeling too angry from living with an emotionally abusive spouse or feels powerless in his marriage to act in a more assertive way, so he resorts to a very destructive way: an affair. Such an affair could be a way of getting back for other hurts, but in any case, it makes a statement—a statement about anger, pain, and powerlessness. Retaliation affairs can complicate life and create many more problems than were there to begin with.

How to Avoid Retaliation

Some couples face infidelity based on retaliation because they do not have good communication skills. Because they aren't able to speak with each other personally and intimately, they can't find out what the problem is, how the other is feeling, or what they want from one another. Their marriage could be richer and grow in intimacy if they could effectively speak with one another. If they keep their problems to themselves and do not even approach one another because they know an argument would ensue, they are only increasing the distance between them. Effective communication skills help a couple to problem-solve without the negativity that may have hampered any prior attempts. Most people react positively to being spoken to with respect and being shown empathy, which is the aim of good communication. Reacting with retaliation shows an out-of-control person. His anger must be understood, but you must tread carefully and with help because you do not know what behavior such a person is capable of. If this is your problem with your partner, first see a therapist alone so that he can give you an idea of the degree of anger and guide you and your husband through this process.

Case Study: Sophie and Ted

Sophie and Ted, who had been married thirty years, came into my office because Ted had an affair with a woman, they both knew. It was not long before a more complete, but complicated, story came out: They had both had affairs.

Sophie had an affair first, and then Ted had one to retaliate for Sophie's affair (which was with her dentist, Dr. Harris). At that time, Sophie had been very worried about her marriage to Ted, thinking he was overinvolved with work, and that they spent very little time together. At one of her dental appointments, Dr. Harris asked how she was, and as she talked, she started to cry so badly that he was concerned for her and started to talk with her. He was very comforting and supportive, and he provided the attention that she needed. He continued his support through talks with her outside of the office. Then they started meeting for lunch, after work, and on weekends. Soon, they were in bed together. Ted found out about their relationship because of some confusion in the dentist's bill and he "hit the ceiling," as he put it. He threatened to report the dentist to the licensing bureau. Ted's anger seemed to know no bounds. Dr. Harris had a change of heart and refused to see Sophie privately and also suddenly had no dental appointments available for her.

Ted's anger increased until he felt he had to get even, which he did by having a brief affair, and then telling Sophie about it as soon as he could. Sophie was devastated, and eventually she and Ted made an appointment with me to sort things out.

Both affairs hurt and caused pain. Ted wanted Sophie to know how much her affair hurt him, so he saw to it that she experienced the pain the other partner feels. This did not solve their problem, but instead worsened it to the point that the marriage was on shaky ground.

Conclusion

In our work together, we started from the beginning and found that Ted and Sophie were a couple who had lost sight of one another and ignored the situation until they were in a crisis. Their life had become routine to the point that they hardly spoke to each other. Both affairs were flings, not romantic love affairs, and they were easy for them to end. Ted loved Sophie and wanted the two of them to breathe new life into their marriage. The most significant problem was that both felt their marriage was in trouble, but neither spoke to the other about it or did anything constructive that would have started them on the way to finding out what was wrong and what could be done. Fortunately, marital problems like these are not as difficult as others to resolve.

Chapter 18. Can this Marriage Be Saved?

Some marriages do survive infidelity. But can your marriage survive it? That vital question is one that only you can answer, because your recovery from your infidelity lies squarely in the hands of you and your partner.

But either way, it's going to take some blood, sweat and tears. Your trust has been severely violated, and nobody bounces back from that as if nothing has happened. You loved, and for that love received deception, betrayal, lies. You were treated like a troublesome inconvenience rather than the loving partner you believed yourself to be.

How will it be possible for you ever to trust again; to feel comfortable in any relationship, much less one with your betrayer of a spouse; to relax into the happy, comfortable feeling that love is supposed to engender?

How will you ever again get back what you lost? How will you ever know if you had, in the first place, the love that you thought you did?

Was it all an illusion? Was it all a mistake? Did he ever really care for you? Was there ever a time when you weren't being made a dupe by your own inability (or unwillingness?) to see the lie behind the "love"?

Will you ever be able to trust love again?

Statistics show that almost two-thirds of marriages in which one (or both) partners have an affair don't survive that affair; the majority of such couples officially divorce one to two years afterward. This means that there is a fairly long period of time during which the couple looks for possible solutions and ways out of the troubles in which they find themselves—where, in other words, they give their relationship a chance to heal. But nearly two-thirds of the time, that chance fails.

Reasons for Getting Over Affair Fail

Here are six primary reasons why:

1. They don't get the proper help. They try to fix themselves, when what they need is a trained counselor who has experience helping couples to get through that critical first year or two following a discovered affair. There are some things that couples can do on their own. Surviving infidelity is rarely one of them.

2. They stay in survival mode. Instead of moving forward, the couple stays in what amounts to a state of shock, hoping or assuming that their relationship will somehow magically heal itself. They talk about the infidelity from time to time—a conversation usually

started by the betrayed partner—but rarely come up with any ideas, plans, or agreement about how to go productively forward.

3. They stay the course. Often couples stay together in spite of infidelity not because they love one another, but because they'd basically rather pretend that the affair never happened than they would disturb their status quo. They stay together for the children, for their property, for their careers—for a whole host of reasons having nothing to do with the emotional core of their relationship. But such unhappy, post-affair unions rarely hold together. People want and need a genuine loving relationship too much to typically be able to sustain the illusion that they can contentedly carry on without it.

4. They can't stop fighting. The affair launches a war which, lacking anything resembling constructive and ongoing peace talks, relentlessly continues, skirmish after skirmish, battle after battle, until finally there is nothing left of what once was that either side cares to claim.

5. Suspicion reigns supreme. The aggrieved spouse is constantly tracking, inspecting, suspecting, testing, and trying to trap the husband who did her wrong. As far as she is concerned, he can now do no right. And

since healing is right, hers isn't exactly a helpful position to maintain.

6. The revenge binges. The betrayed partner gets her revenge by also cheating, believing that this will restore balance, and so ultimately peace, to her damaged relationship with her husband. It never does.

Note: It is quite amazing how often betrayed and hurt women, when they are in a state of panic about losing their partner and marriage, think that getting pregnant will bind their estranged partner to them—when, in fact, pregnancy and a new baby are very stressful for both partners, and stress is a well-known risk factor for infidelity. A baby should arrive at a time when the relationship of his or her parents is defined by happiness and mutual attachment, not by stress and uncertainty. In my twenty years of practice as a psychologist, I have never seen getting pregnant work as a means of saving a failing marriage. So, if you are thinking about taking this course, DO NOT. Countless women before you have tried it, and it has never helped.

It is critical that as a couple you understand that what the two of you do together in response to the infidelity is significantly more important than the actual infidelity itself. It's not the bad times, in and of themselves, which matter: it's how you respond to them. If you and your husband respond poorly to his affair, the chances of your marriage surviving diminish accordingly. If you respond well—if you take control of the situation, if you use it to help you grow, if you don't allow your despair and feelings of anger and fear win over your desire to use the affair as fertilizer to grow a marriage even stronger than the one you thought you had before you discovered how wrong you were about that—then your marriage stands an excellent chance of not just surviving, but thriving. There's nothing like fire to harden steel.

Chapter 19.   Practical Program to Heal Infidelity and Love Again

Here are a few examples of situations that people have faced in their lives and what they can do to heal or react after finding out.

"He cheated on me and was unable to take responsibility for his actions or even admit it for that matter until I kept questioning him. I found out he cheated with two other women and he made the same excuses and now he is trying to get back together with me and is claiming he is a different person."

It is mostly construed that the betrayed is the only one in pain and needs to be healed. However, the offender may also shut down due to the guilt of cheating, and to cope with this they may end up blaming the other person. The narcissistic behavior may be caused due to certain events in their past or just their nature of fearing commitment. This has nothing to do with the betrayed. In addition, the betrayed must try to be aware of their emotions and feelings. The rage and the grief of losing someone they cared so much about should be patiently understood and dealt with. If this person returns after causing all the trauma, check if they are remorseful and don't rush into anything. Take it slow and maintain a continuous stream of conversations and explain or point out any oddities you face in each other's behavior.

"I've been cheated on, lied to and abused by my ex-fiancé. I was 7 months pregnant with our daughter. One month after I gave birth I learned about his affair. He kept on denying it until he admitted the affair when he went back to his work on a cruise ship. It really hurts because we've been in a committed relationship for eleven years. He blamed everything on me. And he even dared to deny that he is the father. I told him no one had ever touched me except him and I'm willing to have my daughter undergo a DNA test to prove to him that he's the father. He kept accusing me of

cheating on him when in fact he's the one who cheated."

This is extremely excruciating. Having a child while facing this situation makes it extremely hard to cope with. The first thing that needs to be done is to get help or get in touch with your family or some trusted person. The recent abandonment and indifference of the partner can be too much to handle. An expecting woman is already at a sensitive time in her life. So, the priority must be to lose correspondence with this cheating partner and find a safe environment where you are nurtured and loved. Having a child assures companionship between you and your child for life. This is precious. Even if the other person has the thought of shrugging off all responsibilities, you are enough. Visit a psychiatrist and have good and long therapeutic sessions to release inner emotions. Finances can be a big factor especially when an infant is involved. Sort your life out with the help of your loved ones and try to put your focus away from anything that reminds you of the unfaithful partner.

"When the mask slipped on my covert ex-wife and she left me and the children, I had no clue as to why. She was drinking and staying away from home and I thought that alcohol was the issue. As a consequence of my divorce, I discovered that my mother was covertly narcissistic and my ex-wife was one as well. My ex-wife never gave me any concrete reason why she left other than I "didn't change." What was I supposed to change into? A butterfly? It made no sense."

Women want emotional support, fairness, friendship and sensitivity in their relationship. Even though this seems a lot, but when you are entering into a relationship with a person, it is necessary to know and understand the person. A woman wants a man to have a good heart and work hard in the relationship. It may even be about having money or being attractive. She wants someone who loves her unconditionally who she can love back. However, it is necessary to look for signs if a person is dissatisfied with you. Any relationship, no matter how compatible, will suffer issues if couples don't talk about their feelings and emotions openly to each other. Ignoring one another while in the relationship only increases the distance between the partners. It is hard but the key is actually to understand what the other person expects of you, and to decide based on the possibility of fulfilling their expectations. Otherwise, it is a waste of time for both people.

"My boyfriend of three years told me he had been cheating on me for the last few months with some girl both physically and emotionally. He said he wasn't happy with me and that's why he did it. I did everything in the world to make this man happy. I was there for him through so much, including the passing of his mother. Most of our arguments centered on him always going out with friends, clubbing, drinking, and not spending enough time with me and making me feel special. He pointed out how "annoying and needy" I was when I asked for more in the relationship, which in turn caused him to be unhappy and seek out this other woman. I had this gut feeling all along and he told me I was crazy and couldn't be more wrong, and he repeatedly denied there was anything going on with them. Now I can't help but wonder how he gave everything we shared away to some other girl so easily."

Finding the person who you cared about so much and whose life you invested in turn away from you is unbearable. It can crush the nervous system of any person, and it's very common to feel belittled and dumb. The gush of emotions engulfing you can get the best of you. For the victim who is hurt, it is necessary to think about the moments in the relationship when the other person reciprocated their emotions. More likely than not, if the victim reflects, they may find out that the other person never showed the same level of affection and care as they did. The imbalance can make a person take you for granted and may construe you to be something of a pushover. This usually surfaces only after the shock of betrayal. The person who has gone out of the relationship starts to fear commitment because their partner is too present for them. This is completely the offender's fault, who is not clearly viewing the person in the same light as they are. Their real fault is that they could have ended the relationship by being transparent rather than cheating and then summoning the audacity to reveal their affair and blame the other person. The victim should have looked for signs of cheating earlier, and if nothing seemed suspicious, then such person is an obsessive cheater; no matter how attached they are, they are most likely to cheat repeatedly. The victim needs to accept the fact they should finally move on and refrain from letting self-doubt to clog their minds.

"Years ago, I was deeply in love with a guy and I thought that we would get married. When he left me, I honestly thought that I would die. I even considered suicide. It took me three years to get over him. I am now married to a wonderful man and I am happy. I rarely think about my ex these days, and I know that I have forgiven him because I don't hate him anymore. I hope that he has found as much happiness as I have. It's a cliché, but it is so true that time is a healer."

Time truly heals. It's about attaining maturity and controlling your emotions from getting the best of you in the situation. Once your partner cheats, the adrenaline rush that flows through the body makes you either shut down or become violently aggressive. You can get drawn into these emotions and may get as down as wishing to end your life. But what is important is at those moments you just hold on to something positive in you. It shouldn't be external; it has to be internal. A strong mind and a drive to live a better life independently must motivate you to reach a better phase in your life. Take this as an experience where you learn something and not let it paralyze or scar you for good. This is not the only relationship that you will have in your life. You need to work towards getting your confidence back and know your worth. No one should be so important that they claim a right over your life. Everyone is sufficient for themselves. The feeling of ending up alone is an irrational fear that the mind creates, and the other person becomes irreplaceable. However, they can be replaced by someone capable of loving you even more than them and you can have the life you deserve with them.

Marriage is not easy. Even if it is a happy one, there is no manual on how to navigate through all the challenges that will come your way. Couples have to learn each other's needs and basic nature, and most importantly, communicate well. Communicating may sometimes be too hard to do, but the better the communication, the lesser is the build-up and the less fights. It is a personal choice to take back a person who cheated on you. It must be a well-rounded decision and must be done for all the right reasons. To stay together amidst societal pressures is not a good idea. This can hamper everyone who surrounds them - their family members, friends or children. If a couple is still emotionally dependent, they should be willing and ready to work on their differences. Transparency is promised and kept, and communication about any issues faced by either are welcomed and explained properly.

Chapter 20. Types of Men Likely to Cheat

Studies show that as many as 60% of women and 75% of men cheat on their partners.

There are certain traits and characteristics that make a man more likely to cheat on you. That said, even if a man has every single trait on the list, it does not mean he's already cheated or is doomed to cheat on you -- it only means that he has a higher likelihood of cheating than the general population.

How many of these common traits of cheaters does your man have?

He falls asleep immediately after sex

Some men like to snuggle and engage in a little pillow talk after sex, some men just roll over and pass out. A recent study from the University of Michigan found that men who snooze immediately after sex are more likely to suffer from insecure attachment and are more likely to be unfaithful.

He's pathologically afraid of getting close.

Insecure attachment, characterized by difficulty connecting to others and problems with managing their own emotions, makes men more likely to stray than men without. Men with insecure attachment tend to have low self-worth, a fear of getting close, inability to trust, and a need to be in control.

He's had a brain injury, multiple concussions, or has a history of high contact sports

Was your guy a linebacker on the football team in high school? Men who have had multiple concussions are more likely to cheat than other men. Why? Multiple smacks to the head damage the front lobe of the brain, the part that controls our inappropriate impulses.

He has a specific variation of DRD4, a dopamine receptor gene.

A Binghamton University study linked a specific genetic variation with infidelity. While everyone has the gene, the longer (7 repeat allele) version of the DRD4 reported 50% more likelihood of cheating. Scientists report that one in four people are born with the thrill-seeking, in-the-moment "cheating gene." The gene affects the reward centers in the brain, flooding it with dopamine, which makes us feel pleasured and excited. Men with the "cheating gene" need more stimuli to feel excited than other men, and they take bigger risks. How do you know if your man has the cheating gene? A DNA test (usually under $100) can tell you for sure, but the five traits below are a tip-off.

He's had a lot of one-night stands.

People with the longer DRD4 gene are more likely to have lots of one-night stands. If your guy has a long history of sleeping with strangers before you were together, he may have the cheater gene.

He loves horror movies

Men with the cheating gene are more likely to enjoy watching horror movies than other men. Men with the longer DRD4 are much more likely to be attracted to slasher movies than men with the shorter DRD4. Why? He needs more stimuli than regular men, so the usual car chases and romantic comedies just don't do it for him.

He drinks a lot or is an alcoholic

Alcohol addiction and cheating go hand in hand. First, alcoholics are accustomed to hiding their behavior from friends, coworkers, and family, so cheating is practically second nature. Second, alcoholics have problems with impulse control. (They say, "just one" and two hours later they're face down in the gutter.) Men with the longer DRD4 gene are more likely to be compulsive drinkers.

He's a gambler

Here we go again with the impulse control issues. Thrill-seeking guys who have the longer DRD4 gene are also more likely to have gambling addictions. Yes, the same guy who ran up $7,000 on your credit card last month in Vegas probably slept with a showgirl or a hooker in the same weekend.

He's an adrenaline junkie

Thrill-seeking men, the kind who jump out of airplanes or drive too fast or are always looking for a big rush need more stimulation to feel alive than other men and are more likely to engage in cheating.

He's tall

A study reported in Psychology Today reported that tall men are more likely to cheat. Experts aren't sure if its related to testosterone, (which may influence not only height but also infidelity) or something else, but it certainly puts a damper on tall, dark and handsome.

He's wealthy

The more money he has, the more affairs he's likely to have. Not only do wealthy men feel more entitled to cheat, they have the means to afford to cover it up.

One of his parents cheated

When one of his parents betrays the other, it affects him in a profound way: namely, his ability to trust is severed at the most basic level. Fast forward twenty or thirty or forty years, and he's highly likely to repeat the pattern, even if he despises his parent who cheated.

He believes that he's not getting enough sex

This is a tough one, because what man hasn't complained about not getting enough sex? That said, men are more likely to feel justified when they cheat if they are not getting as much sex at home as they'd like.

Your relationship is on the rocks

Many men actually feel justified in cheating if they are unhappy in their current relationships. While it makes sense that a relationship on the rocks would be more susceptible to one of the partners having an affair, it is a surprise to many women that their partners feel they deserve to have an affair if they are unhappy at home. (Even when they have neglected to mention this to you.)

He's easily sexually excited

Men who are more easily sexually excited, easily turned on, are more likely to cheat according to a study conducted by the Kinsey Institute at Indiana University.

He worries that he won't orgasm or stay sexually aroused

Paradoxically, people who have a high level of worry or concern about their ability to either have an orgasm or just stay aroused cheat more often. (Women who worry about orgasm/arousal are 8% more likely to cheat; men with the same worry are 6% more likely.) You would think that those kinds of worries would keep a person from flashing their genitals in public, but you'd be wrong.

He's not really concerned about the consequences of sex

If he doesn't really worry about pregnancy, STDs or sending naked pictures of himself to complete strangers, he's more likely to cheat.

He's narcissistic

Yes, narcissists are more likely to cheat on their partners. It's always all about him, right?

He's an extrovert

Extroverts are more likely to be optimistic, talkative, thrill seeking, risk taking, and socially assertive. Extroverts are highly sexualized who are not only more likely to experiment sexually than their more introverted counterparts, they're also more likely to have affairs.

He has impulse control issues

Does he call at all hours or hang up on you when he's mad? Fly off the handle before he has all the facts? All are signs of a lack of impulse control, a classic characteristic of cheaters.

He proposed to you in February

Cheater matchmaking site Ashley Madison reported that that a whopping 57% of their male members proposed in February. And although December is traditionally the most popular month for engagements, men who proposed in February may have done so due to pressure from family, society, or the bride to be herself, rather than waiting until they're actually ready. Or, it may be that old impulse control issue again -- maybe he had no intention of proposing but got swept up in the romance of Valentine's Day, even though he was nowhere near ready to get married.

He's a high school dropout

A study by the National Marriage Project found that high-school dropouts were more likely to cheat

than high school graduates.

You make all the money.

Guys who are completely dependent on their wife or girlfriend's income are five times more likely to cheat than men who earned as much as their partner. Men are least likely to cheat when their female partner earns approximately 75% of what they do. Sucky, but true.

He makes all the money.

Men who make significantly more money than their wives or girlfriends are more prone to cheating as well.

He's employed

Who knew employment could be a drawback? Men who have jobs are more likely to cheat than men who don't. Money plus a valid reason to leave the house every day equals higher levels of infidelity. That said, men who are unemployed are only slightly less likely to cheat.

Speaking of employment and cheating

Studies show that 70% of affairs begin in at work. Ashley Madison, an Internet dating site for people actively looking to cheat on their spouses, studied their 1.9 million users and found the most common professions held by cheaters:

Men Who Cheated Were Most Likely to Be:

1. Physicians

2. Police Officers

3. Lawyers

4. Real Estate Agents

5. Engineers

1. Women Who Cheated Were Most Likely to Be:

1. Teachers

2. Stay-at-home Moms

3. Nurses

4. Administrative Assistants

5. Real Estate Agents

Other professions that are ripe for affairs?

Entertainers, politicians, speakers, consultants and sales reps (Any job that provides a high salary, long work hours, and lots of travel plus an expense account means plenty of opportunities to cheat.) And this won't come as a shocker, but 80-90% of male athletes cheated on their spouses, according to CNN. (No surprise here, they're men, they're wealthy, and they probably hit their heads a lot more than an accountant would.)

Is He Genetically Programmed To Cheat?

Is it just hard-wired into a guy to screw around? Sometimes the answer is yes. Does this excuse their behavior? Absolutely not. But it's important to know that some guys have to work a lot harder than others to stay faithful. Some men have a genetic code makes them more prone to cheating. The only way to know for sure is a DNA test, but many of the "cheater" genes are linked to other behaviors as well.

He has a short vasopressin receptor gene

Men with a longer vasopressin receptor gene are more likely to be faithful and happily married. Men with the shorter version of the gene are more likely to be bachelors.

He has a low number of oxytocin receptors

Oxytocin is a bonding chemical (scientists call it "the cuddle hormone") which helps you bond with others, form relationships, feel love, and causes you to trust people. Men who have fewer Oxytocin receptors form weaker relationships and are more prone to cheating.

He has high self-esteem

Men who are confident and have high self-esteem cheat more often than men with lower self-esteem. Why? They feel entitled to cheat. If he's self-assured and wealthy, it magnifies the cheating effect.

He's creative

Creative types are more likely to cheat. Why? The same trait that allows him to come up with new ideas and consider alternate possibilities is the same key in helping him justify his dishonest behavior.

Chapter 21. How to Become a Human Lie Detector

Get a Baseline

You need to be aware of what she does when she's acting normally, and how she generally behaves when she's telling the truth. This is her baseline, her normal. You'll need to know her baseline so that you can recognize when she behaves unusually or responds to a question differently than her usual. Does she make eye contact when you're talking to her? How about when she's answering a non-threatening question (For example, at a restaurant, "How's your steak?" or "How is your sister liking her new job?") Whether she makes eye contact or doesn't make eye contact, whether she smiles when she talks or doesn't, whether she speaks fast or slow, whether she pauses before she speaks or starts speaking immediately, whether she crosses her arms or she doesn't cross her arms does not particularly matter. What matters is that you figure out her pattern of behavior when she has no reason at all to lie. The way she consistently behaves when she's telling the truth is your baseline. Every time you ask her a generic, non-threatening question, write down her response in your journal. Pay very close attention. Write down what she says, how she says it, and any body language clues that you notice.

Once you've established her baseline behavior after a few days or weeks, you can begin to ask her questions about things that matter. When you ask her where she was after work, for instance, you may notice that she speaks more quickly, or adds much less detail than in her baseline. You may notice she snaps at you in a way that is different than her baseline. Perhaps her body language is different, or her eye contact is different, or the sound of her voice is different. If you have done your homework, and studied her baseline, you should usually be able to tell the difference between when she is lying, and when she is telling you the truth. The key to spotting a lie is that she will behave differently when she is lying to you than she behaves in her baseline. When you ask her a hot-button question such as "Bethany mentioned that she saw you downtown yesterday afternoon, what were you doing way down there?" and she responds by breaking eye contact, or offering fewer details than usual, or shuffling her feet, write that down in your journal as well -- note her behavior and body language when you believe her to be lying. Does she blink, swallow, or scratch when she didn't before? She may have a "tell."

It is important to note that most people believe that someone who is lying to them will avoid looking them in their eyes, or will shift uncomfortably in their seat, or wave their hands around nervously. This is simply not true. In fact, some studies have found that a person is more likely to look you directly in the eye if they are lying to you, because they've heard the same thing and want to be perceived as telling the truth. The only behavior that tells you that a person is lying is a different behavior. A deviation from their baseline.

Lie Detection When Confronting

When you confront her about cheating does, she says something like, "I know you can't believe I'm telling you the truth!" Or does she say, "I don't believe you think I'm lying to you!" It is highly likely she's being truthful with the first sentence (her statement literally contains the words "I'm telling the truth.") With the second sentence, it's far more likely that she's lying to you. (Her statement is focused around the phrase, "I'm lying to you.") The truth seeps out.

Next, pay special attention if she laughs unexpectedly when you ask her if she's been cheating on you. It's a serious subject, isn't it? Why is she laughing? Nerves? Is she buying time to concoct a response?

When detecting a person's lies, it is critical to pay attention to the words she uses. What signals does your partner use when she's lying? From a logical standpoint, people realize that the more information they give away when they lie, the more likely they are to trip themselves up and get caught. As a result, liars say a whole lot less (and provide fewer details) than truth-tellers do. We use about half the number of words in a lie as we do when telling the truth.

We also have been taught from a very early age that lying is wrong so that most people will distance themselves psychologically from their own lies -- they tend to use many fewer references to themselves ("I") in a lie than they do when telling the truth. If you're having trouble discerning when your partner is lying when you're speaking with her, try recording the conversation instead. In a study, participants were correct more than 70% of the time when they simply listened to someone to discern whether they were lying or telling the truth.

Listen for words that express emotion. A person is far less likely to use emotional words when she is lying, such as "hurt" or "scared" or "angry." They are also less likely to use cognitive (thinking) words, such as "understand" or "comprehend" or "realize."

The word "BUT" should set off your alarm bells as well. She might say, "This is going to sound crazy BUT we just work together"

Lie Detection: Non-verbal Cues

When we're in love, our bodies line up with each other's. Your heart will face her heart, your head faces her head, your toes pointing at her toes. When you confront her about her cheating, or where she was on Thursday night, or what happened to all the overtime she was supposed to be earning, watch her body language carefully. Not only are you looking for a deviation from her baseline behavior, but you'll also be looking for defensive behaviors as well. First, she'll break the heart to heart, belly to belly line, and turn her body away from yours, or lean away from you. Shrugging her shoulder is an indicator that she is uncertain or not telling the full truth. If she crosses her arms in front of herself, or covers her genitals with her hands, she's defensive.

If You Still Cannot Tell

If you're having a rough time figuring out whether she's telling the truth or not, focus on two things -- her words and her baseline. If you're still having trouble discerning lies from the truth, just work with what you know for sure. I know that it's practically impossible to look at this situation from a purely analytical, rational perspective. It is your life we're talking about, after all. Don't be too rough on yourself if you're having a hard time here, just move on. It's far better to confront her with three rock-solid facts than seventeen strong hunches. You don't need to know everything that happened right now. You just need to know enough to elicit her confession.

Put it All Together

Now is the time when you take out your journal and put together all the evidence you've collected so far: Any physical evidence you might have found, call logs, any research on the other man, notes on where she said she was versus where she actually was, situations in which you believe strongly that she was lying, vehicle tracking evidence, and put the whole thing together on the kitchen table like a puzzle. Try to piece together a timeline the best you can. If you find holes in your research, go back and scour the records and your journal again for any other bits of information on that particular day/trip/event.

Your partner will attempt to lie or downplay your accusations by telling you it was nothing, or that she was just flirting or messing around, or that it was all just some great big misunderstanding. This is why you need to anticipate every excuse you can think of that your partner might concoct and gather as much evidence as you can to counter her lies and excuses before you actually confront her.

Now that you have concrete evidence of what she's been doing, you're ready to get the answers you need.

Take a Deep Breath.

It's all going to get better soon. Nothing is worse than what you've been living. You are strong and powerful and smart and you deserve to be treated with respect.

Chapter 22. Rebuild Intimacy

For every good relationship to occur, both parties must have integrity for their individual personalities.

You must act and say things you mean, according to how you feel and the empathy built must be within you and your spouse and not from a perceived external feeling or opinion.

You must keep your promises and request your partner to do the same.

Integrity must be completed between two partners in order to get its full effect on the strength of your intimacy.

Integrity is the Root and the Pillar for Trust.

The importance of trust in a relationship is almost untold, which can only be achieved when both sides have a decent amount of integrity.

Integrity involves doing things according to your individual abilities even though you don't want to do them; even when you are not actually comfortable, just to make each other happy.

It also entails talking to people about the less flattering sides of their personalities instead of talking about them with other people.

This means, integrity is keeping your marriage business within the confinement of your home.

It also involves treating people with respect even when you are not getting paid.

It is like helping the helpless without bragging about it.

Also, the man or woman of integrity does not allow situations or circumstances to change or compromise their moral standards. Instead, they push even further to become better people by handling situations and accepting people as they are.

- "Integrity also means being the same person in the public and in private. You don't intentionally hurt your significant other and you believe that the theft for one dollar is still a theft, so you keep the standards of doing the little things right". – Shannon Terrace

Both Partners Are Open to Each Other

Only when partners become really open to each other will they overcome the obstacle of misunderstanding.

The basic relationship problems begin when one person misunderstood the other person's intentions and then reacts in a way to get back to that person out of resentment or jealousy.

Both sides must be frank and should not hide anything from each other.

They should be able to speak about the less flattering sides of their endeavors without feeling challenged or offended.

They should employ communication as the first step in taking care of misunderstandings instead of taking other negative actions.

They should find a respectful way to be more open, not to offend each other. This will become a stronghold where the better relationship is built, providing you and your spouse an atmosphere to become better people for the sake of your intimacy.

The Equal Support Principle

The effort of active listening is not enough for a strong and long-lasting intimacy; support is also needed from your significant other in order to find a better validation for your efforts.

In an effort to find a solution, you don't just listen to your partner, you should respond positively to their problems.

In order to be mindful of the benefit of helping each other, partners should adhere to the law of reciprocity.

When you show support to your partner in their time of need, support shall be shown to you in your time of need.

Be aware of the seed you sow in the process of helping your partner, for you shall sow the exact variety of plant.

Law of reciprocity: "When we do good to others, they will also do good to us".

Supporting each other means to back each other to get what you need.

Keep in mind that when your partner is doing well, you are the first person to get the credit.

This will boost your social presence, in return aids in the cultivation of affection toward each other, which also automatically affects your intimacy.

Understanding Your Partner

Focus on understanding the efforts your partner is making and also the effort you are expected to make.

You have to decide to be reliable and honest, to act in advance, to prepare or even avoid the rainy day.

Build a consistent way of handling situations; make yourself reliable at all times, so that your partner will be able to trust your actions and judgments.

Beware that a single betrayal can destroy the trust you've built for long. So, the journey demands actual consistency, and withdrawal means withdrawing forever.

Never approach love from the perception of fear. Do not love just because you want to avoid a fire.

Love because you want to love. Love because this marriage is about love, the only thing that cannot be bought or traded.

In all these, do not settle for less. Do not seek for completion from your partner, instead build yourself to the best and allow your partner to see and pursue the best they could recognize about you.

Do not settle for a one-sided relationship either; do not accept bad behavior for the sake of staying in the marriage or because you don't want to be alone.

Design a standard and demand for your spouse to follow through with consistency and discipline.

Admit Mistakes

A good marriage provides an atmosphere for both to admit of a wrong doing or mistakes.

Fear will be replaced by confidence and the desire, to be honest for the sake of the relationship.

Defensiveness is replaced with strong honesty and the desire to do better. Excuses will be replaced by love and the desire to trust and be trusted.

Instead of making the other person feel hurt or even less than a semi-vegetable, both partners will make effort to correct their mistakes and to create a strategy to avoid such mistakes in the future.

This endeavor demands strength from both partners.

Patience and resilience for a considerable amount of time are required of partners to fully understand each other, create the right support system and strive to win against their differences.

Humility and the desire to be humble are also important in order to admit your mistakes and be honest about it.

The love for self and the urge to feed one's ego must be eliminated for a marriage relationship to thrive.

The Willingness to Change

Regardless how good your behavior, choices or principles, there is always a chance to become even better; to have a better perception of things around you; have a better sense of judgment; learn effective communication skills; employ good behavior, more pleasant than the one you have now; and also make a good impression in influencing other people to be better, which include your spouse.

Couples must be willing to change for each other.

They must admit to the fact that no one among them is perfect and the best of their personal self is yet to be explored.

They must together aim for improvement. They must align their thoughts toward positive change, and to see every mistake and wrong doing as a signal to work on a particular aspect of that relationship.

Look deep into an annoying situation to see if there is something you can both change for good.

Do not push all the blame to one person just to avoid pressure.

Work as a team; if the other person is willing to change something, you should also compromise on something to encourage them.

The aim is to make your relationship stronger and to keep growing day after day. This way you will both enjoy the company of each other and as you conquer one challenge to another, your intimacy becomes better and better.

Chapter 23. Coping

The news of infidelity hits most people like a speeding freight train. Instead of killing you, you end up plastered to the front of the train, terrified and unsure how to slow it down. You may think you want things to work out, but you can't begin to heal your relationship until you've learned to cope with your emotions.

The good news is most people can learn to cope once they've been taught how. Coping allows you to confront and deal with your emotions instead of keeping them bottled up inside and letting them fester. Coping allows you to move past the pain and eventually start getting better.

Some people can cope on their own. Others need help. If you're having troubling coping and moving past the pain, don't be afraid to seek counseling. It can work wonders.

For those of you who are suffering the initial stages of the effects of infidelity, I can't place enough stress on the importance of not acting on your initial emotions. The natural healing process takes time and you need to give yourself time to cope with what you're feeling. What you feel the day after you find out is going to be different than what you feel a week from now. What you feel a week from now may be different than what you feel a month or two from now.

Don't act on your initial emotions or you risk taking action that isn't in line with what you're ultimately going to end up feeling. If you immediately agree to try to work things out, you may find you regret that decision in a week or two. On the other hand, if you tell the other person you want to break up and there's no hope of reconciliation, you may end up driving them into the arms of the other person only to find out you want things to work after it's too late. Your best bet is to take some time off to reflect on the good and the bad in your marriage so you can make a rational decision as to what you want to do.

A short separation can help jump-start the coping process. Seeing your partner during the first few days after infidelity can be too much to handle. Taking a short vacation to a spa, visiting family for a few days or staying at a close friend's house for a short time can make the initial pain more bearable. It's going to be tough but try to relax and think things through during your time away.

Don't beat yourself up about the way you're feeling. Give yourself permission to grieve. Intense anger bordering on rage, intense sadness bordering on depression and unfounded fear and paranoia are all common emotions you may find yourself feeling as you progress through the grieving process. Learn to accept these emotions and ride them out without endangering yourself or others. It's OK to cry, scream out loud and yell—as long as you aren't doing it at 3AM in a condo with paper thin walls. You might get the cops called on you then.

Don't try to internalize your emotions. When you push everything inside and box it up, you're creating an inner demon that will slowly but surely eat you up from the inside. The victim needs to be able to express his or her rage and anger at what happened. Yelling allows the victim to push some of the inner turmoil out instead of leaving it all bottled up.

While it's OK to feel emotions, you need to make an extra effort to continue taking care of yourself. You still need to eat and drink. No, alcohol doesn't count. You also need to make sure you're getting enough sleep and are performing at an acceptable level at work and at school. You don't want to add dropping out of school and losing your job to your list of worries at this point.

Take note of any physical symptoms you have that are associated with the way you feel. You may find that in addition to the emotional rollercoaster you're on, your body may start showing signs of distress. Diarrhea, headaches, shaking and even vomiting and passing out are all side effects that can occur because of your fragile mental state. If the physical effects of stress are severe or they don't subside in a day or two, consult a medical professional.

Give yourself a day or two, a week tops, to mope around and feel sorry for yourself. This will allow you to go through the initial burst of emotions without trying to suppress them, which can be difficult at first. Don't try to fight back tears. Let them flow and let yourself grieve. Holding back the tears does more harm than it does good.

At some point, you're going to want to know why. Be aware that the cheater may not know why things happened the way they did. The best thing a person who engaged in infidelity can do to help their partner cope is to be completely open and honest. Lay it all on the line and let the person who's been cheated on make an informed decision as to what they want to do. Nothing will kill a marriage faster than going through the grieving and healing process under false pretenses, then having something else come out later on down the road.

A relationship built on lies won't work. There's no good reason to try to rebuild a relationship on the same shaky ground. Demand honesty and institute a zero-tolerance policy on lies. The cheater needs to own up to what has been done.

After this initial grieving period, it's time to get on with your life. Go about your daily duties, eat, drink and sleep normally and spend time with your friends. Try doing fun things with your friends to help get your mind off of what happened. The more you laugh, even if it feels forced at first, the better off you'll be.

You may think you're tough and can figure things out on your own, but counseling really can help. Depending on the situation, it might benefit you to seek independent counseling to help you deal with the emotions you're feeling and marriage counseling to help you work through the infidelity. Watch for signs you may be suffering post-traumatic stress syndrome (PTSD). This is the same thing many soldiers suffer when they come back from fighting in wars. It isn't uncommon for people who are grieving to show signs of PTSD as they come out the other end. If you're nervous and jumpy, are paranoid all the time or your physical maladies worsen or don't go away, seek immediate help. Let your doctor know what you think is going on and why.

Putting time between you and the act of infidelity is the best way to cope with what happened. The amount of time it takes is highly individual. One person may be able to shrug it off and begin healing in a day or two, while it may take another person a month or two before they're ready to move on. Give yourself time to heal. At times, it's going to feel like you're taking two steps back for every step you take forward. Push through the initial sadness and anger and eventually you'll start feeling better.

The person who has been cheated on has to decide as to whether or not they want to continue in the relationship.

Sometimes this decision is made for you when the cheater decides they'd prefer to be with the other person. When this happens, the best thing you can do is to go through the healing process on your own, learn to cope with the pain and eventually move on. It hurts, but it doesn't hurt as much as harboring false hope of eventually reconciling your shattered marriage while your partner is out enjoying life in the arms of someone else.

Chapter 24. Dealing with the Blame

Wanting to blame is common in any horrific situation because most people want someone to take responsibility for the unbearable situation. Infidelity impacts you in a major way; therefore, you are looking for someone to hold accountable. Blame serves as a buffer against owning the responsibility for the hurt and pain.

Blame happens because the relationship has reached a place where the actions cannot be reversed. It is natural to want to point fingers at a betrayer for a relationship having gone bad. You want someone to take the blame for the losses incurred. Someone needs to take responsibility for the failed relationship. Sometimes blame is used as a license to remain bitter or unaccountable.

There are no good reasons for anyone to cheat in a committed relationship. The simple fact is the cheater decided to commit adultery. Adultery is a sin in most cultures across the globe. Any reasons that are provided as explanations for cheating are mere justifications and excuses for their selfish act.

With or without the betrayer's help, you can

- admit to yourself and recognize that infidelity occurred. This is the most difficult step.

- experience the loss of your relationship. There is sadness and grief at the thought of the end of a significant relationship.

- reach out to an unfaithful partner to get answers to the unanswered questions so you can decide.

- start taking steps to get past the blame game. The betrayer blames you and you blame him or her.

Be careful, because the unfaithful partner may use blame to excuse his or her own bad behavior. Excuses serve as a buffer against owning the responsibility for the hurt and pain he or she has caused you. Some people believe that if they deny their wrongdoings, then it absolves them of their responsibility for or contribution to your hurt.

To ease their conscience, cheaters will pass on blame to their faithful partner to ease their guilt. Blame is used to pass the responsibility. If the betrayer does not blame you, then, in a sense, he or she is taking the responsibility for his or her horrible actions. Blame is the scapegoat used to justifying the unjustifiable.

In reality, the blame game had started in the cheater's mind long before the affair was discovered. Blame was the way cheater became emotionally prepared to carry out his or her actions. The cheater blamed you for not being available to him or her, not being attentive, gaining some weight, or other garden variety excuses. Without finding faults and without the scapegoating techniques, most people are unable to carry on affairs for too long. Most people have a conscience and know the difference between right and wrong. Blame is the tool used to make them feel better or justify their selfish act. Somehow, they validate this wrongful act by placing blame outside of themselves and onto something or someone else. This makes it easier for them to tolerate and continue to do the wrong deeds. Eventually, you will move to a place in your healing where blame doesn't matter so much, as it becomes irrelevant after some time.

Be careful. Because the unfaithful partner may use blame to excuse his own bad behavior. He or she knows that he or she is in the wrong but doesn't want to place himself or herself in a position of weakness. Excuses serve as a buffer against owning the responsibility for the hurt and pain he or she has caused. How do you deal with it if an unfaithful partner is blaming you?

• Do not accept the blame.

• Only take responsibility for what you have control of.

• Hold the cheater accountable.

• Know that the decision to cheat was 100 percent the cheaters.

- The relationship is irreparably damaged, so taking on blame does not reverse the clock.

The fact is, if there were relationship problems or issues, they should have been addressed before taking any action. If the betrayer's needs were not being met, then he or she should have tackled and communicated this openly with you.

First and foremost, you are not responsible for your partner's cheating. These actions are his or hers and not yours. It is OK to do an autopsy of the relationship to identify where things went wrong. You may have contributed to things going wrong in your relationship, but by no means are you responsible for your partner's cheating actions. In a nutshell, a virtuous person in a relationship will communicate or try to work out his or her issues with their respective partner rather than straying or cheating. Therefore, this is in no way your fault.

What you are responsible for is paying attention, being aware, and addressing what is going on in the relationship. You might have put off things or not addressed them because you were overwhelmed, busy, irritated, annoyed, or just did not want to. You are really not to blame if you were a loving, caring, and supportive partner; then, it is not right to take ownership of this horrible act.

You need to realize that you did not do anything to throw your partner into someone else's arms. You do not need to accept the blame, because no matter what the cause was, an honest and open talk can resolve most relationship discords; you can also partake in marital counseling or make a clean break. It is easy to take the blame for things having gone wrong. However, there are more rational ways to deal with the situation.

You cannot hold yourself liable for anyone's selfish, short-term, self-gratifying behaviors. It is OK to feel that the cheating spouse did not care or have any respect or any positive regard toward you. You cannot take the blame for someone's bad behavior. You cannot buffer or protect your partner by taking responsibility for his or her bad behavior.

Self-Blame

Another important thing to remember is that, sure, your ego is bruised. Some women tend to get caught up in self-blame, turning it internally into "it's all my fault." Sometimes your heart may cry for your partner but know that this will pass. And please, above all, remember this is not the reason to accept his blame. The best thing to do is to realize that the betrayer made a mistake out of his or her greed, weakness, and ego. Please remember that you are worth a healthy, happy, and faithful relationship—you absolutely deserve that.

In general, cheating is reckless and escapist behavior, and those engaging in it just aren't thinking! It is very easy for a betrayed person to blame himself or herself because he or she is feeling unworthy of their partner's love and feels confused in the aftermath.

Blaming the Betrayer

It is normal to feel the unfaithful partner should be held responsible for his or her sordid acts and the end result. Your mind will search relentlessly for a root cause and the source of your agony. In my early days after the betrayal, it was easy to view the world in a very self-righteous way by passing the blame on to him.

You'll need to be honest with yourself during this part of the healing process. It is easy to get caught up in blaming the unfaithful spouse. However, recovery and healing are about you and not about your partner. There comes a time when you will need to come to grips with this unfortunate life experience and take responsibility for yourself. Focusing on your future and being responsible for your own healing is the way to go, rather than pointing fingers.

Another reason why you may want to blame your partner is to punish him or her. It is normal to have fantasies about holding your spouse accountable for inflicting all the pain and hurt. He or she actively participated in the creation and escalation of this horrible situation. You want him or her to pay for what he or she has done. You want him or her to fix things that went bad in the relationship. This is one of the hardest things to get past, because in all actuality the infidelity is an act that can never be reversed. It is like crying over spilled milk.

- What is it that you want and makes you happy?

- What are some of the lessons learnt from this event?

- Since it takes two to make the relationship work, what was your contribution?

- This now is an opportunity to design your future.

- How can you identify distress signals or warning signs of relationship discord?

Blaming your partner or dwelling on the event does not change the course of the event. The unfaithful partner is responsible for this and making peace with that is the best option for your healing. Pointing fingers does not serve any purpose. In my experience, looking back, blame was a

Guarding Yourself Against Feelings of Jealousy

Jealousy after the discovery of infidelity is normal and expected. In the early days, I held bitterness in my heart toward the other woman. If you are currently struggling with jealousy, I recommend you search your heart. Most likely, something is behind the feeling of your jealousy. For me, it was fear. I wanted to be needed; I wanted to be loved and desired. I felt jealous because of my fear that the other woman was taking the source of my love, desire, and need away from me. I was fearful of losing my partner. Somehow, the irrational feeling of jealousy was equivalent to the feeling that my survival was being threatened!

There is frequently sadness and grief at the thought of the end of a significant relationship. There can be fear at the prospect of being single again and possibly for a long time.

It is not unusual to feel jealous, because you are losing your partner's attention and love. Jealousy is caused by the fact that you have lost the number-one spot in your partner's heart. So, it seems for now. It is caused by the emotional fear that you are being replaced. Your emotional brain translates this into the belief that you are no longer wanted, desired, or loved.

When you catch your partner cheating and having an affair, it diminishes your self-esteem a bit, leaving you feeling worthless and ugly. However, please understand that leaving or choosing another woman or man has nothing to do with you. Those are the betrayer's choices and preferences and by no means a reflection of you or your worth. It may be difficult, but you know in your heart of hearts that if your partner were really such a catch, then he or she would not lie, cheat, or deceive. It is easy to think he or she is a prized possession, but in reality, he or she is not.

Getting over jealousy can be tough for many, but it quickly destroys your heart and spirit. You cannot successfully live in the present and plan for the future if your head and heart are still living stuck in the past.

Just know that your cheating spouse has lost something greater, and that's you. You have to be confident and know that you are still a good person with many strengths and talents.

Chapter 25. Exploiting Spousal Prerogatives

Gathering Your Allies

Nothing is new under the sun. From the beginning of time, otherwise sensible, reasonable, honorable humans have left their homes, abandoning mates and children, all because they've "fallen" in love or found passion with someone new. Unlike times before, however, today's science informs us that infatuation, with all its physical manifestations, is temporary by biochemical design and rarely worth the cost of leaving the life and lover that you already have. Sometimes hearing these facts from someone other than a spouse (such as a sibling, friend, parent, or uncle) is enough to make a husband stop and think about what he's about to do—especially if there's a business or reputation at stake and a public divorce would cause all sorts of legal woes for everyone involved.

We've already tackled how as social animals people depend upon their fellow humans for survival. (Recall, no man is an island.) Living among a network of loved ones and kin provides a person with a sense of belonging and peace, as well as mutual allegiance and support. (We are a tribal species, after all.) The family will protect its general interests as it promotes the individual well-being of its affiliates. When your marriage is threatened, your network can help you, depending upon your relationship with its members and the dynamics of the families within the group. Some family members will respond to a call for help by offering to run interference. In-laws, for instance, might take their kin (your husband) aside and try to find out what's happening and set the matter right in a way that accommodates all affected. Not everyone will take an active role, however. Some family members will refuse to get involved; others won't see a problem, especially if infidelity was the norm in their household. (If they put up with it, you can too.) But for the most part, families do not encourage infidelity and will be there for you as a form of unified support, particularly if you have children.

Naturally, before family members can come to your aid, they must know of the imminent danger. Though many people find it difficult to talk about marital trouble—especially if a third party is involved—it is a necessary antecedent for rounding the troops to your defense. Consider confiding in one trusted family member so he or she can offer you emotional (and maybe financial) support. This confidant could perhaps use his or her personal influence over your husband, and others in his circle as well, to explain the damage that could be irreparably wreaked upon your family if he leaves you for a stranger or continues fooling around, risking your permanent departure.

As a generally competent person, think about how you can best use your social support network in a time of need. Your wifely status not only gives you the benefit of a loyal family— definitely yours, and often his—it also offers the advantage of having the entire community (religious leaders, mutual friends, neighbors, and colleagues who support you and your marriage) show open and notorious support for your position. There's no question concerning the villain's identity in your drama. From a community point of view, the woman having an affair with your husband is an evil doer and homewrecker and should be brusquely dismissed. (She is a threat to everyone's marriage as she flouts decorum and disrespects boundaries and legal and moral obligations.)

But to set the wheels in motion you must disclose your need for help. Bear in mind, humans who remain isolated do not generally fair as well as those who can rely upon others to help them. If you can't work your problems out with your spouse or your therapist, show yourself to be one of Darwin's adapters and seek support, if you need it. Even if you ultimately decide that staying together is not feasible, giving yourself the benefit of social support at a critical time of need can provide you with comfort and the moral high ground no matter what comes to pass as a consequence of others' ignoble actions.

Homewreckers Not Welcome

Widespread community and family backing for you and your marriage are found on one end of the relationship support scale; universal opprobrium for a secret affair with a married partner is found on the other. Unless your husband is brazening or itching for a marital exit, if he's engaging in an extramarital affair, chances are very good that he's tried to keep it a secret. Even if you've recently learned about the transgression, it's likely that the interloper has not shared information about her affair with friends and family. Think about it. Who in their right mind would brag about being involved with a man whose primary and legal relationship is to another woman and her kin?

How Her Hiding Helps You

Initially, having an illicit affair can seem more exciting than an open relationship, as lovers are preoccupied with their clandestine meetings and their need for secrecy. But as time goes on, the burden of keeping the liaison hidden outweighs the excitement (or, in more scientific terms, the physiological arousal) one feels when doing something dangerous or forbidden. Instead of fostering the allure between the partners, the burden of having to conceal the affair from one's support system becomes a drag on it, eventually reducing relationship satisfaction for the person with the least to hide and the least to lose (typically the unmarried one).

Pillow Talking It Out

No matter what's happened before and how you found out about it (or, even if you're not completely certain but you feel that something isn't right), there is no one in a better position than you are to talk with your husband. Whether you are still sleeping together in the same bed or are living in separate rooms or separate states, you remain the one who has the most to say and the most to learn from a dialogue with your spouse. Besides, apart from his attorney or therapist (if he's got either or both), you still have the best access to him (assuming no restraining orders!).

Formerly, we explored your support-seeking skills, this part will examine the conversation practices that promote frank exchanges and a chance to learn and grow closer after hearing each other's experiences, thoughts, feelings, worries, and perhaps explanations for past behaviors. Plus, as you will see next, the ability to communicate is a predicate to handling conflict in a positive, constructive way (a necessary skill for every successful, healthy relationship involving more than one human).

Emotional Expressiveness

We assessed how having a rant is generally not productive and if revenge is the motive, you're better off to wait till you cool off, using Houston dentist, Clara Harris, as an example of what not to do.

Here, you're not in the midst of a marital emergency as much as you're beginning the marital repair phase. This is the time when you have the opportunity to begin a dialogue with your husband that can lead you on the road to recovery or, if that's not possible, a better understanding of where you are, how you got there, and where you are headed. Even when it's difficult for you (as you are probably still hurt and angry) to reach out to your husband, if you want to re-establish a rapport with your mate—or take him back—this is the time to bite the bullet. Ask the right questions (How did we get to this point? What did/do you feel you get from her? How do you feel now that I know?) and listen to your husband to help him resolve the situation he created with the affair. Other items high on the must-tackled priority list are how to remove the mate-poacher from his life and how can you both save your marriage.

Mars and Venus Revisited

Research tells us that men and women communicate differently. No surprise there. Men tend to be competitive and domineering, while women tend to be cooperative (seeking understanding and consensus) and subordinate. Men and women also differ in the use of questions (and quality of responses to questions) and attitudes towards advice giving and problem-solving. Men's language is generally rule-oriented (dealing with achievement, rules, laws, facts, and abstractions), whereas women's is relationally oriented (dealing with seeking or maintaining interconnectedness). Knowing these general differences will help when you encounter a response that you could otherwise interpret as defensive or hostile. It might just be masculine, without a value judgment attached. No matter your gender role, when you speak with your husband, remember that you are not agreeing with him or forgiving him by giving him your attention and lending your ears.

Chapter 26. Communication

Why Is She Talking So Much?

The stronger sex is convinced that women are too talkative. In general, there is a considerable share of truth in this. But how to communicate, if not talk?! Men can be silent even with a close friend, sometimes understanding each other without words. Women associate communication with a conversation. Such are the differences in the psychology of men and women. And both sexes must take this into account.

Ideally, it would be desirable for women to moderate their speech activity, and men - to be more condescending to this weakness of the weaker sex, but In life, it does not always happen, and sometimes mutual irritation arises on this basis.

"When my wife starts talking, you can't stop her," complained 37-year-old Eugene. - In everything else, she is a sweet woman, smart, and I respect her very much. But if she chatted less! The main thing is that she is talking about various trifles. Many topics of the eaten egg are not worth it, but she can talk about them for hours. Well, she would say monologues - I have already learned to disconnect and almost not hear her. I nod, grunt, assent, and she does not even notice that I think of something else. But the whole trouble is that my wife very often demands my participation in the conversation, asks my opinion. And I didn't even hear what she was telling me. Sometimes she manages to evade, saying that she will understand everything better than me.

If she spoke less, I would probably respect and love her even more. Sometimes, if the wife starts talking again, I catch myself thinking that I want to shout: "Yes, shut up you!" and I can hardly restrain myself. I come up with some excuse and leave for my room. But if the wife did not speak out to the end, then I could not escape from her. She follows me and speaks, speaks, speaks...

The fact is that Eunice, the wife of Eugene, is a biochemist. At work, she deals mainly with flasks, test tubes, and laboratory rats. She has no one to talk to. With whom else could she talk, if not with her beloved husband?! But Eugene, on the contrary, work is associated with communication - he is the head of the marketing department, but he does not have a separate office, and the three of them sit in the same room. Around all the time, people - sometimes to one, then to another employee constantly someone comes. And although he is a "boss," sometimes he undertakes to go to another organization himself, at least on the road to take a break from the constant hum of voices. When driving, he manages to relax a little, although Denver roads are congested, but the street noise is not as annoying as talking. In the end, he developed neurasthenia (or asthenic neurosis, sometimes also called chronic fatigue syndrome), and he turned to me.

The stronger and weaker sexes have different ideas about what is of interest and what is not. For my part, my husband and I have no disagreements, because there are many common interests. But I must admit that they are more unilaterally - I tried to get interested in everything that is interesting to my husband. By the way, I did not lose anything from this; on the contrary, I only gained. I speak freely with him (and not only with him) about politics, football, hockey, boxing and athletics, rock music and philosophy, and other "high matters." And with any other man, I will always find a topic for conversation that will be of interest to him. But the husband patiently listens, if I want to share my opinion or burning problems with him and is equally patient with respect to my duty to admire when I get in front of him in a new dress or a new hat. But he still gets tired of my chatter. True, he was lucky that I simply did not have time for this.

The principle: "You will give in to me, and I will give in to you," helps a lot in family life. If men learn to be condescending to women's weaknesses, understand women's psychology, and will not pull a blanket over themselves, I assure you, family scandals will immediately decrease.

Why Is He So Secretive?

Wives often accuse husbands of unwillingness to explain their affairs and regard this as secrecy. However, this is a typical trait characteristic of men. It has been said more than once about the difference in psychology between the strong and the weaker sex. Men are used to behaving differently. And in general, men are more secretive than women.

Since childhood, boys and girls are brought up differently. Boys are taught to be restrained, not to show their feelings. "Be a man!" The father strictly says to his son if he came running home in tears when his peers offended him. "A real man should not show weakness to anyone!" - This is how boys are taught. The same stereotype of behavior in teenage companies. If one of the teenagers "hesitates" will complain and whine to everyone, everyone will despise him and consider him a "wimp." Frankness is not encouraged. Guys, even close friends, never open their hearts - they are used to this from childhood, and this stereotype is maintained throughout life. They prefer to carry their feelings in the shower. Every normal man wants to be considered a strong, real man. And if he will demonstrate his doubts, vacillations, indecision, - then he will no longer be considered a strong nature.

Girls are raised differently. At any age, both in girlhood and in adulthood, a woman can demonstrate her feelings, be open and frank. The mother teaches her to tell her everything, and she is interested in who she is friends with, how she spends time, what kind of relationship she has with peers, and boys (if this is a good mother, of course). A woman is accustomed not to conceal her feelings. If she is upset with something, upset, if she has trouble, she trusts her feelings to a loved one. Emotional instability is a typical feature of the female psyche. Men who understand female psychology do not condemn their girlfriends for this - why condemn what is inherent in the weaker sex?!

If men and women were the same in their psychological manifestations, they would quickly get bored with each other. Opposites attract, right? But such a relationship develops only in those married couples where both spouses understand each other's psychology differences and treat them adequately. Disagreements arise only in those families where men value women from their bell tower and husbands' wives from their own.

"What are you thinking now," is a frequent question that an inexperienced wife asks her husband. And you hope that the spouse will immediately "turn the soul inside out" and tell everything after your persistent inquiries if he himself does not want this? Maybe he has trouble at work, but he does not want to upset you. Perhaps he was wrongly wronged, or he did something that he doesn't want to talk about because he doesn't want to lose your respect. Or maybe the spouse is just dreaming or fantasizing. It is possible that on erotic themes, and there is nothing wrong with that—sexual fantasies are common to all men (and many women, by the way, too).

Perhaps the husband does not share his problems, believing that his wife's advice will not be useful. But this will add even more confusion to his doubts, and he wants to carefully think everything over and independently come to an optimal solution.

Or maybe your husband is just resting and not thinking about anything —and this is the most likely explanation for his unwillingness to talk. Why should a person constantly think about something? The brain must also rest. Therefore, the answer: "About nothing" is quite legitimate. Your spouse just relaxed and disconnected from external stimuli, and do not bother him and blame him for stealth. You will only cause his irritation with your persistent inquiries. There is nothing wrong with the fact that at the moment, the spouse is not inclined to frankness or does not want to talk. Reluctance to share their experiences can be regarded as a purely masculine trait. And this quality in men you must respect.

Imagine that he will burden you with all his doubts, hesitations, and thoughts before making an important decision. Well, if you have a trusting relationship with your husband, and you are a reasonable woman, listen to him with understanding and give smart advice. However, there are women who are not able to appreciate the confidence of men.

In any case, many men do not like to be frank with women because they believe that they can regard frankness as a weakness. And the strong sex does not want to show their weakness or insecurity. A man wants to look strong, decisive, and confident in the eyes of a woman.

Want to Play? – Talking to Your Spouse

A man or woman, loving and beloved, accepted by a single person, can act and more successfully reveal himself in communication. He can be himself without defending himself. He's less concerned about protecting his own self.

The periods of evening activity in men and women do not coincide. The man, after being alone for some time, rested, gained strength, usually not averse to chatting with his wife. Women are "dismantled" immediately, as soon as they cross the threshold of their apartment.

As already mentioned, communication for the weaker sex is not at all difficult. As a rule, a normal woman does not get tired of it. Therefore, overflowing with impressions after work, she wants to immediately layout to the faithful all the latest news. If the husband does not want to listen to her at this time and wants to be alone, she is offended.

On this basis, many couples have conflicts. "He does not listen to me at all! - the wives are indignant. "He is not interested in what happened to me, and in general, he does not care about me and my problems!" This is not so, ladies. It's just that your husband doesn't have a desire (and forces, by the way, too) to communicate at this very moment. Later, when he rests, he will already be able to listen to you.

If you do not constantly communicate with each other or do it in fits and starts, then sooner or later you will move away from each other. Everyone will live their own autonomous life, believing that the husband (wife) is not interested in her (his) problems. If you are already at this point, communicating with your spouse with these in mind will lead you on a path to re-building.

Chapter 27. Long-Term Benefits of Rebuilding Lost Trust

The work that you put into your relationship does not only help at the moment but in the future as well. All of the efforts that you put into your marriage right now will carry over into your future interactions. This means that you aren't only solving problems and dealing with current issues together, but you're also learning how to practice longevity. All couples strive for longevity in their marriages. Because you want to be with your partner for the rest of your life, you need to understand that everything that you do right now is going to make a difference in your relationship. Be cautious about what you say and do in times of anger or stress. These things that might seem insignificant right now can become magnified over time, leading to fractures within the bond you share.

As you work through this guide together, you are both making a commitment to the overall health of your marriage. You are stating that you believe in the relationship and that you see it working out in the long run. Those who have to question their significant others about whether they still want to be together will likely not be going through these exercises together. Know that if your spouse is willing to make changes and improvements, they are likely to believe that the love is going to make it and that the relationship will last. You need to have faith in one another as you explore this together. Rebuild your trust and enjoy the newfound connection that you discover.

What You Will Learn

- Instead of coming up with ways to pick apart flaws and point out weaknesses, you will learn how to accept these things about your spouse.

- Holding on to resentment/bitterness is only going to end up hurting you after a while. You will learn how to let go of it and to move on from it.

- The focus will shift to the qualities that you can appreciate most about each other instead of the qualities that could use some improvement. Being able to acknowledge these things will allow you to pay your spouse better compliments.

- Talking about hardship or difficulty doesn't always have to result in a fight.

- The longer that you work toward overcoming your differences, the shorter your fights will last. Once you get into a method that works well for both of you, this process is going to become easier.

- Instead of keeping your distance when things get hard, you will learn to come together and begin working on your issues immediately. There is nothing worse than allowing separation to overtake your relationship, causing emotional distancing.

- On a daily basis, you should be able to do things for one another that show you truly care. These things should be unprompted and done because of the love that you share.

- When healing is necessary, you will both be able to rely on constructive methods of getting to this point instead of continually resorting to behavior that ends up hurting you or the relationship.

- Reframing your approach can be beneficial when you're trying to solve problems. Instead of jumping straight into possible solutions, you will learn how to see things from new perspectives to see if it helps make things easier.

- Issues in the past can stay in the past if you move on from them properly. There shouldn't be anything residual that you're holding on to that is hindering your marriage today.

- When you see negativity, you will start with the attitude that you do not wish to carry it with you. After having this in your mind, you will be a lot more likely to find a solution for it rather than starting fights over it.

• You will learn how to enjoy what feels like a new life with your significant other. It can be a very refreshing feeling to realize that you do not have to be controlled by your trust issues and your problems.

• Couples should also be friends. When you can have a genuine friendship with your spouse, this is going to make your bond even stronger and show you different sides of each other.

• The two of you should be able to come to an agreement of what your "dream relationship" looks like. This kind of vision should come from how you wish your relationship could be in an ideal world. Together, you can strive to make this a reality.

This is only the beginning of what you will learn as you work through this guide. All of these examples can serve as motivation for you to use moving forward. A part of changing your behavior is changing your mindset. When you have the above examples to think about, you should be able to let go of any negativity that you might still be holding on to. Think deeply about why you might still feel the need to hold on to it, then let go of it in the best way that you know how. Understand that you don't need to remain in a state of worry or anxiety if you can personally clear your head enough to focus on the positive things about your marriage. If any issues come up, trust that your spouse will make them known and then you can work on solving them together.

Long-Term vs. Short-Term

When thinking about their problems, couples usually make the mistake of only considering what is going on in the present moment. Think back on the things that frustrated you the most last year. Do these things matter as much to you this year? Do you even remember what they are? Your mood has a lot to do with your reactionary impulses and you cannot necessarily help that. If something bothers you, then you're going to react to it — it's that simple. What you can do, however, is to learn how to think about the bigger picture. Understand that what might be bothering you right now might prove to be insignificant in the future.

When defining "the future," know that this can be anywhere from years later to weeks later. You need to consider if any issue is important enough to hold on to and if it will impact you in the future. If the issue is very temporary, meaning that it is likely to be resolved quickly, this is something that you shouldn't need to hold on to and take with you into the future. It is only going to take up negative space in your brain and hold you back from being the best partner that you can be.

For more serious and ongoing issues, you might need to carry them for a little while. This still does not warrant carrying them in a way that places weight onto your relationship. Know that the only reason problems need to go unresolved is if they need additional time to fix. For example, it might take time to rebuild trust once it has been broken. For anything that has a clear solution, do your best to consider it as handled. This way, you won't feel the need to bring it up again unnecessarily or use it against your partner in the future. You will feel a lot better when your conscience is free of these things that simply take up space.

Consider this example:

You and your spouse have been fighting a lot over the amount of time that is spent going out with friends rather than the amount of time that is spent with each other. It has been causing fights that come to the same conclusion — you want your partner to stop going out. This has then caused a negative chain reaction and your spouse has become emotionally distant, avoiding you and avoiding having this conversation again. They continue to go out with friends and it continues to make you upset. There is no resolution.

Short-term solution: You don't talk to your partner until they stop going out as much. This causes a lot of tension in the relationship and the issue often gets brought up in fights, even when they have nothing to do with this subject. Your partner develops a defensive type of aggression that tends to come out when you nit-pick at them for going out. The cycle repeats itself until you both feel exhausted. You both keep doing it because it seems easier than addressing the issue and working on finding a solution that you feel would benefit you both.

Long-term solution: You both sit down and talk about the issue, expressing both sides of the story. Your partner wants to feel that they have their own individual life, but you don't want them gone late into the night. You come to a compromise, showing one another that you both value your marriage. Instead of going out all the time, your partner has their friends come over. This no longer makes you mad because your boundaries are respected. With this solution, you both feel that the issue has been taken care of, therefore, you don't continue to bring it up again in the future.

As you can see, each solution would result in very different outcomes. When you think that you are "handling" a problem, you might realize that you're only coming up with a temporary and short-term solution. Recognize these instances and see how you can change them for the better. Adjust what you're doing so that you can make them long-term, instead. The latter is going to leave you feeling a lot better about the solution and it will encourage you both to speak up about what you feel should be done.

Passive-aggressive techniques should not be used, as they are solely meant to make the other person feel bad. Remember, you need always to make sure that you are acting out of love. No matter what the situation is, that love for your partner should not simply disappear. Allow it to guide you and provide you with a new way of thinking. Understand that you aren't always going to get exactly what you want, but there are ways to come up with a compromise that will leave you feeling just as satisfied. It's all about being willing to work with one another. Long-term solutions leave you with long-term results. You know how frustrating it can be to repeat the same cycles, so do everything that you can to avoid this from the beginning.

Chapter 28. Do's and Don'ts After Discovering Infidelity

Mistakes you need to avoid at all cost

Mistake #1: Do Not Recklessly Talk About Your Partner's Infidelity with Friends and Family.

What?! Don't talk about it? You may be wondering why I would offer you this kind of advice, right off the bat, because many of us are taught that talking about our problems will help us. While that may be true in most cases, I must caution you against spilling your guts about your partner's infidelity while you are still reeling in shock, anger, and pain.

Mistake #2: Do Not Rush to Make Significant, Life-Changing Decisions Right Away

I do realize this advice may not be ideal for all couples, depending on the level of commitment to recovery and the specifics of the situation. However, for many couples, postponing your major life-changing decisions for at least 12 months provides you with some time to gain clarity about the situation, even if you do end up leaving the relationship down the road.

Mistake #3: Demanding Explicit Details

Do not demand explicit details about the betrayals.

If you recently discovered your partner's sex addiction, it can be almost impossible to avoid asking for some of the dirty details because you need to know the depths of your partner's sickness and betrayal. But there is also a fine line between the features you need to know and the circumstances that cause you additional pain unnecessarily. Remember, once those details are in your head, it is almost impossible to forget them. For many spouses and partners of sex addicts, this is one of the most challenging mistakes to avoid when dealing with the trauma of betrayal.

Mistake #4: Failing to Set Boundaries

Do not fail to set reasonable boundaries.

Boundaries are rules for the relationship. Crossing the other's boundaries means you have broken the rules that were set in place. There are mixed opinions on the setting of limits with sex addicts. I know that some spouses and partners in recovery feel that boundary-setting is a disguised attempt to control the addict. In some cases, this is true. If you find yourself setting boundaries that require the addict to report their every move to you or else they must deal with the consequences you've set, you may need to rethink your underlying reasons for setting these boundaries. Of course, you are trying to protect yourself, and that is entirely normal and understandable. But are your limits an attempt to control the addict by keeping constant tabs on him? Healthy boundaries are an effort to keep the lines of honest communication open between the two of you. For instance, setting a limit that requires you both to practice honesty with each other at all times is usually healthier than setting a limitation that requires the addict to explain his whereabouts every time he leaves the house.

Mistake #5: Pain Mining

You should not torture yourself by continuing to look for pain.

The term "pain mining" does not describe the first remembrance of something unpleasant because sometimes those initial thoughts would unexpectedly pop into your head without a warning. Pain mining begins once you have that first painful thought or memory. After the unpleasant feeling comes to your mind, you always indulged in pain mining because you are forced to drop everything else in your life to search for other things that would cause you additional emotional pain. You can go from one hurtful thought to the next, replaying stuff your partner told you over and over in your head. Then those memories lead you to create awful scenarios in your mind, imagining your husband engaging in one or more of his betrayals. Once you are entirely devastated by the thoughts in your mind, you will often start to look for evidence of more deceptions on their computer or written in their private journals. You end up wasting hours upon hours of your life indulging in pain mining.

Be prepared for the pain – 10 things that will help to turn the page

1.   Relational Trauma

At this point, you may feel as if the person who betrayed you has taken everything away from you. Your sense of self has probably been shattered. You could be feeling a wide variety of emotions as your heart has been broken. You might feel rage toward the person/people they were with for stealing your companion and lover away from you. You might feel deeply hurt and not be able to put words to what you are feeling.

You might feel scared. You could be scared about the future or even feel afraid about the present. What will happen to the kids? Will I have to start dating again and go through that all over again? What if I can't trust anybody anymore? Why did this happen? Simply not knowing what to do or what will come next can be terrifying.

It is essential at this time to recognize precisely how traumatic this experience is for you. Emotionally, this is very similar to post-traumatic stress disorder (PTSD), except it could be happening right now, and it also continues to happen instead of just being an experience in the past.

Psychologists and health care professionals suggest that getting the help you need as soon as possible is vital to prevent developing long-term post-traumatic stress disorder or so that the symptoms do not get worse. These symptoms can take hold of your life and thoroughly shake it. But with time, professional help, and taking care of yourself, complete healing and peace are possible.

2.   Talk to Someone

On your path to healing, you will need to talk to someone. At first, it may be difficult finding someone you feel you can trust that won't judge you or the situation. There may be those around you that are unhealthy to talk to. These are the people that leave you feeling drained and discouraged after the conversation. They will continuously tell you their opinion rather than listening and having healthy lectures. You will know these people by how you feel during and after the conversations. They may not, and probably be not, intentionally trying to make you feel this way, but some people are not good at conversing and listening. It is a skill that needs to be developed because very few are "born with it."

Your goal is to find the people who have uplifting words for you and who listen to what you say. These are the people that help you answer your questions by giving you their ear and allowing you to follow a train of thought-leading you to your solution. The conversations you have with these people will leave you feeling empowered and energized, and you will feel yourself letting go a little bit at a time. This will take time, but it is crucial to have someone to talk to. Do not try to go through this all by yourself.

3. Journaling

Journaling is a powerful tool on the path to healing. A study was conducted in which three groups of individuals were being treated for varying degrees of depression. They were each given a different kind of therapy. Of the three different types were talk therapy, psychotropic medication, and journaling therapy.

The journaling group was given the task of writing for ten minutes every day. It didn't matter what they wrote, they were just told to write. They were told to write as if no one would ever read what they wrote. It could be thrown in the trash or burned after they had written it.

After six months, the talk therapy group had shown improvement; the psychotropic medication group was right where they started six months earlier. The journaling group was the one who healed and got over their depression the fastest. The healing power that writing can unleash is unmatched in many cases.

If at any point you find yourself holding back your writing and you are not allowing yourself to write what you want to, ask yourself why. If it is because you are afraid someone will see what you have written? If that is the case, then burn or throw away your paper when you are done. Or keep it under lock and key. All that matters is that you don't hold back for whatever reason.

4.   Enjoy Nature

Using nature for healing is sometimes called green therapy, ecopsychology, or ecotherapy. This type of treatment is used for many different emotional and traumatic situations and is found to be very helpful for most people. Many researchers worldwide agree that having a connection to nature can better a person's emotional well-being and interpersonal relationships. The whole idea is to be removed from your office or the walls of your home that you are in every day and be in the outdoors. This is done to develop an emotional bond with yourself and with nature.

Psychologists say that when a person finds this connection with nature, they experience feelings of stability, harmony, timelessness, and balance. Many sudden feel a sense of something bigger than themselves and outside of themselves when they find this connection because they know they had nothing to do with the creation of these things. It requires them to recognize a higher power, which is necessary for the healing process and will also be talked about more later on.

Nature is the strand that binds everyone together. We all live on this good Earth. Often, we forget about life and the natural beauty that is there. A stroll in the park or a drive in the country can be very healing. The grandeur of the earth can help us put our lives in perspective. Our lives can seem quite small when taking in the vast beauty that is nature. The sting of our pains can be swallowed up when we allow ourselves to enjoy something as broad as nature. I remember talking to a wilderness survival expert once, and he said, "In a wilderness survival situation, you find out that no matter who you are or how much money you make, nature does things her own way, she doesn't respect anyone." It is true how insignificant we are.

Nature allows us to see that the world goes on. Usually, after a betrayal or traumatic event, we would like the world to stop so we can take a time out. Unfortunately, it doesn't stop, but WE tend to stay. It is a lot like standing in a river, the water (or the world) keeps moving around us. Mostly if we are not moving forward, then everything else is moving around us. There are many lessons and things we can learn from nature. I'll leave those for you to discover on your journey.

5.   Find Something to Laugh at

Laughter is the best medicine. Scientifically it has been shown to reduce anxiety and stress. It is incredibly beneficial in helping cancer patients cope with the constant pain of some cancer treatments, as well. The bottom line here is that it has many applications in the medical field, and grief is a pain. Our job is to make that pain go away in a real and meaningful way.

Chapter 29. Prevent Infidelity

Don't Ignore the Importance of Sex

Sex is an important part of marriage and most committed relationships. We know that at one end of the spectrum you might find a couple who are both perfectly happy with having sex once every few months. Or who are fine with regular missionary sex once a week at a set time and day. However, even most marriage counselors would tell you that for the majority of couples, mixing it up once in a while by adding some "spice" should happen in any long-term sexual relationship, to keep the sex exciting and fun.

While both the men and women who contributed stories will tell you that exciting, novel, and occasional "naughty" sex are important components that cheated-on spouses frequently leave out, the men especially comment about their wives on this topic, and frequently use that as an excuse to begin an affair.

The most common complaint from men is that their wife won't give them a blow job. The second most common is that their wife isn't "into" sex, meaning that she sees it more as an obligation (or at least that's the way he perceives it). From women the complaint most of us have is that men don't spend enough time on the "play" part of sex—whether that's foreplay (especially oral sex), romantic play, varieties of positions, or even a little bit of role play. And frankly, there are a lot of husbands out there who still don't know how to bring their wife to orgasm, many times because the wife herself isn't willing to tell him and he hasn't done any research to find out.

When both genders complain about sex in their marriage, the common denominator is that the sex within their marriage needs to include more frequency and more variety. This doesn't mean you have to change your sexual self each time. It means that every once in a while, your "regular" sex routine should be prioritized and changed. It's like always having frozen vanilla yogurt after dinner, but then every once in a while, going for a full-on banana split.

This isn't a sex handbook so I won't go into great detail here, but there are plenty of books and even internet articles that will provide suggestions on how to improve your sex life and bring more variety to it even if you are a little more on the conservative side. Role playing, including a sex toy now and then, getting a wig, changing positions, playing a sex "game", surprising your spouse in the shower: these are all things you can do every once in a while, to change things up.

Don't Forget to Flirt

After you've been in a long-term relationship, it's easy to get complacent about verbal banter. After all, how many times over the course of your marriage do you need to tell your wife she looks beautiful? Answer: however, many times you can.

It's the same with husbands. They want to be told they are handsome, sexy, hot, and desirable. Most men and women love flirting and especially men love it when a woman foreshadows sex so that he knows he's going to get laid that night. In an affair, there is a lot of complimenting and flirting. When you have a relationship with someone you don't see all of the time, there are only so many things you can write in a text message. So, compliments and flirtatious comments are typically common during communication in an affair.

As a spouse, you need to flirt with your partner like you did when you were first married. Of course, you still need to talk about the more mundane items of life like laundry, dinner, and the yard. But within that don't forget to add compliments to make sure your husband knows how handsome he is, or that your wife knows how fabulous that new dress looks on her. And put it in writing, too. There is something about seeing compliments and flirting in writing that adds more power to their impact.

Another reason to flirt and give compliments is what Dr. John Gottman refers to as the "Rule of Seven". This means that for every negative interaction you have with your spouse you have to "make up for it" by having seven positive ones. Some marriage experts refer to this as putting marbles in the jar.

You need to pack the jar with lots of those positive-feeling interaction "marbles" so that the normal fighting and arguments which might occur in any long-term marriage don't deplete the jar.

In other words, if you fill your jar with plenty of positive interactions, the negative interactions won't have as large of an impact on either spouse's emotional well-being in the marriage.

Don't Have Too Many Separate Interests

While it's important to have interests apart from each other, it's also important to share common experiences and fun. There was a research study which found that when two people shared a "new" experience together, the endorphins created were similar to those created when falling in love. Thus, the researchers concluded that couples should create new activities to do together as one way to maintain that feeling of being in love.

Similar to staying out of a steadfast sexual "routine", you also want to break up the potential monotony of a long-term relationship by finding different activities to try as a couple, even if they don't become a part of your regular routine. They don't have to be expensive, either.

For some, it might be a hike in a new location. For others, it might be renting a movie they wouldn't normally see.

Vacations and hotel rooms and dinners out to new restaurants are great, but they will break the budget for most people if that's the only way you share interests.

Sharing interests also includes asking questions about your spouse's day and spending time with him/her at some point just talking about what's going on in general. This is another reason why prioritizing sex and alone time is important. It seems that after those times is when spouses feel more relaxed and ready to explain whatever annoying or exciting or even mundane events are going on in each other's lives.

Even watching TV together, touching each other, can create "connectivity" moments. In an affair, those moments are naturally created because you make time to have them; you actually schedule time to be alone together, usually to have sex. When spouses aren't prioritizing that time, it makes it easier for the cheater to place a higher value on the time with his/her lover.

Don't Ignore the Signs and Don't Avoid "A Talk"

Sometimes spouses have a false sense of security or even think they know their partner so well that he/she would "never" cheat. All of us in the gang have had experiences with individuals who even we thought would "never" cheat. And yet, the temptation or attraction just became too great. But if you want to have the information, and you start noticing some signs that your spouse may be having an affair, then it's time to do some snooping.

The signs of an affair can be anything, and any one item certainly isn't cause for concern, but several together could be. Changes in the normal routine are a big red flag. For example, let's say your husband has a regular nine to five job not normally required to work late. Then all of a sudden, he begins working late a few times a week, puts a lock on his cell phone, and begins receiving "work" texts and emails at home. It may be a change in his work, but it may be an affair.

Do some snooping without him knowing about it by looking for his car at work and calling to see how he's doing if it's not there. See if you can catch him in a lie or two. He may have a plausible explanation for working late, but if he lies outright about being in the office, and he's not, then that is a strong sign he is hiding an affair.

Ironically, another sign of an affair could be that your spouse becomes nicer and stops complaining about various aspects of your relationship. Maybe she doesn't ride you anymore for not putting your laundry in the basket and just does it herself. Maybe he says he's "accepted" that you're not interested as much in sex anymore.

It's been our experience that men and women differ slightly in this area. Men having affairs tend to be nicer to their wives, go out of their way to be sure they get gifts for them and do nice things for them. Women in affairs tend to simply quit complaining about whatever it is they complained about before, and seem to need less "couple" time, withdrawing more within themselves and becoming more independent to their spouse.

If you do snoop and catch your spouse in a lie, you might call him on it once. Making a big deal about it may be enough to stop the guilty spouse from continuing the affair, or at least may expedite the tapering off of the affair. This of course, will only work in a few circumstances. One, your behavior needs to change in a way that makes you seem like a better, nicer, more exciting spouse. Two, it might work if your spouse is one who feels constantly guilty and isn't really more than infatuated with the lover.

Don't Change Your Size and Look Dramatically

You don't need to look like a movie star or be as thin as a model in order to lessen the chances your spouse will have an affair. After all, your spouse married you and chose you, with whatever size and "look" you had when the two of you first were attracted to each other. However, too many spouses think it's not a big deal to allow themselves to get severely overweight, lose a lot of weight, or change their hair color/look entirely.

We think this is a mistake, because people are attracted to each other for a certain reason. If your spouse married you when you were thin, it's not like you have to maintain your 25-year-old body perfectly. However, your spouse may not be attracted to you sexually in the same way as before if you gain 50-60 extra pounds.

We know also that the reverse can be true—some spouses are attracted to a heavier weight/frame to begin with, and so losing a lot of weight might also be a turn-off. Drastically changing your hair color might also be a turn-off, as might be cutting long hair very short.

It's not that you can't change your weight or your look somewhat as you get older. The main thing is to realize that your spouse might care greatly about a dramatic change, and you want your spouse to be still attracted to you sexually.

Chapter 30. Concrete Steps Towards Healing

Diary

In the early days I used to write a feelings diary, which was helpful in order to see the progress made over time and to see if there are particular times of day that I struggled with negative thoughts. I also used to email my feelings that day to my husband so he could understand what I was going through in order to help me. This progress diary I have put in this book. When I was looking at ways to recover from his affair on the internet, I wanted to read real stories of people who have been betrayed, healed, and successfully stayed married. This prompted me to start my own website which in itself is therapy.

Counseling

At that time, before I knew the truth, when I was unable to function or process what was going on in my head, I insisted we went to a marriage counselor. It was helpful for me to be able to talk to someone as my husband didn't want anyone to know, which meant I could not talk to any friends or family. I felt like I was going crazy, every thought in my head was centered on the how's and why's of the affair. He didn't see the need to be at marriage counseling and I always came out feeling like a small part of the weight I was carrying had been dealt with. We stopped the counseling before I knew the entire truth of the affair and we never went back. The only reason the counselor was helpful for me was because it gave me someone to talk to, a few times in front of my husband. Counseling did not provide direction for me; I needed someone to tell me this is how you can deal with this.

Online Counseling

This I have found very helpful as the Internet has a vast amount of material to read. Instead of paying for a marriage counselor. This is straightforward and walks through the steps needed to get through the devastation an affair has on a marriage. This is for both the cheater and the betrayed, although my husband is not able to willingly pick this up to read, he does read things when I say you should read a certain paragraph. Googling also leads me to forums or other websites where I can read advice, explanations or see other comments on how affairs are affecting them. It is always helpful to feel like you are not alone.

I have also started marriage counseling online with Marriage Sherpa. This has been incredibly helpful and I love the fact I have someone who I can type an email with my thoughts and feelings. My counselor is superb and has made me think clearly and see a future, but this future is down to me and I should look to myself and do what makes me happy and strong. I let my husband into my life because I want him there, not because he is my life.

Anti-Depressants

As soon as the doctor had prescribed this medication I felt so much more positive and able to cope with the demands of having a young family, my emotions were generally more stable and the shock of the affair had less of an impact on my daily life, I was able to function. Come night time I would still be crying and asking questions about the affair, with everything going around in my head again and again and again. I would cry until I was so exhausted, I would sleep, my husband would cuddle me tightly. I needed this reassurance. The medication was a big help to me, I stopped neglecting my children, or thinking of suicide and I was able to stop crying so much during the day.

The anti-depressants were great for the short term; this I would say was 10 months with me. I would really like to come off them and I have been reading up on how to control depression through food. Those susceptible to depression are found to be lacking several vitamins and minerals; serotonin is depleted over time during increased stress, so I have been looking at ways that I can boost this naturally.

From what I have read so far, Vitamin C, Vitamin B's, Vitamin D, Omega 3, Chromium and Magnesium all play a great part. Omega 3 has been proven to lift people in depression successfully. Other natural remedies include St. John's Wort, 5-HTP and exercise; all are adrenalin and serotonin boosters.

Transparency

My husband has become completely accountable and transparent. I have access to his computer, work calendar and mobile phone and can check anything. He now emails all flight and hotel details to me, never goes out with the office socially and if he does, I am to be invited too. If there is a client dinner, he is to email proof and let me know times and restaurant. Everything he does, he now tells me and if I am worried, he reassures me. He leaves the office on time, calls me at lunch so I know who he is with and where he is going. I can also still track him if I am feeling insecure. He isn't trapped but is taking the necessary steps to rebuild the trust I used to have with him.

Talking

The saying, "a problem shared is a problem halved" is so true. As soon as I took the decision to start talking about the affair and our marriage, to carefully selected people, I immediately felt better, the more I talked the easier life became. I could not tell my family as they would encourage me to leave my husband, and if I chose to stay would make him feel awful and undeserving for the rest of his life. I chose someone in his family who I thought would be able to help, having been through a similar situation and who was perhaps close enough to my husband that he could then have someone to talk to. I also chose a good friend who was not judgmental and in fact was encouraging me to stay and work through this situation. She was trying to see the affair from his point of view and said it could happen to anyone, that feeling of being flattered by someone else's attention could lead all of us into similar scenarios.

Couple Time

One thing that has clearly helped is making time for us as a couple. The demands of children and work puts a strain on a marriage, so him working away and leaving me with the children and no one to help, meant there was little time for 'us' and our marriage. I was quite often tired from looking after the house and children by myself with no break and he was tired from travelling and stress. One good thing to come out of the affair is that he has realized that we need to be a couple sometimes not just a family. Up until now he has always refused a regular babysitter as it costs too much money, so we rarely got the chance to be alone. We have been on a week's holiday without children for the first time in ten years, taken weekends away, go out at least once a week when he is not travelling, making us happier by allowing us to be a couple.

Hypnotherapy

Now this isn't cheap and I am fortunate to be in a position where we could afford this therapy. Without it I am not sure we would be at the stage we are now or even be together at all. I had three sessions, the first eliminated the negative thoughts that were swirling around in my head constantly driving me crazy and making me unable to think clearly. The second session, I asked that I be able to believe my husband's story of the affair and to stop obsessing about details, I also asked that when my husband says he truly loves me and is sorry for what he has done' I am able to believe that. The third session, I asked that I no longer react when I see or hear her name. My husband still works in the same office as her and as I am checking all his emails and texts, her name quite often comes up, which I used to find upsetting. The therapist did some anger management treatment, so that the part of me that wants revenge on her can be tamed.

Books

Out of all the things I have tried, the books I have read have been informative and have provided direction and reasons. I have tried to get my husband to read some books I think are useful and although he starts them, he has not finished one yet.

Conclusion

There are so many factors that can contribute to cheating. Sometimes it's how a person is raised, selfishness, childhood experiences, narcissism, low self-esteem, many of us are insatiable when it comes to being pleasured, often needing a variety of different "flavors." These people look at infidelity as a great opportunity instead of a bad mistake. The only time this so-called opportunity becomes a mistake is when they get caught. Millions of men and women consider cheating a survival tactic, trigger patterns which are hardwired into their personality.

You could never have imagined yourself here, I know. We marry for life; we trust, we love, we believe that this is a done deal that's how it's supposed to work. We believe that there is no break too hard to fix. That's true but not always in the way we think. Healing relationships means letting go. If we want to have a better relationship with our spouse (or anyone else for that matter), then we have to let go of the past. Total forgiveness is the only way the relationship can move forward. These words sound glib, even matter of fact, they are not meant to be. This is painful and takes work and most of all, time. Also please understand that two people have to make these changes to heal a relationship; otherwise it will not work, and you will find yourself back in the very same boat you're trying to get out of now. As I continued to grow, my world was actually getting more volatile. My husband and I were no longer fighting, but the feeling in the room was never really good. There were things done and said that were purposely hurtful, cruel even. When real healing has not taken place, the void over time gets bigger, the lies we tell ourselves get bigger, and we find any way to avoid being together honestly. Time can be spent together, sex can happen, the "I love you" said...but if we really allow ourselves to feel, we feel empty, lonely, unappreciated, unloved. This is what happens when you don't have two people working on it and you don't feel safe to forgive deeply. Feeling safe enough to forgive had to start with me. Could I dig down deep enough to admit my hurts and my own needs? Where was I hurtful and distant with him? What was I asking of him that he had no capacity to give? What was I asking of myself that I was unable or unwilling to give? Diving into these questions helped me examine my own dark side, my own secrets and the lies I tell myself. Looking into your heart and shedding light on all the dark places lets you take a good look, and it's not always pretty. But, just sometimes, it's beautiful. I always had the vision of myself internally, as an over grown garden filled with wild flowers and weeds, all blooming at once. A beautiful mess. With time, I have begun to do some gardening, pull a weed here and there, plant some new things and allow the wild flowers to grow untouched. This beautiful mess is me: lovely, adventurous, quirky, funny, kind, joyful and a klutz. But it's me. You are your own garden. Maybe it's a rose garden – pristine and fragrant. Or an English garden, with rows of wild flowers and ivy wrapped around little white fences. Take the time to imagine what yours would look like; how beautiful it grows within you. You can't possibly hate yourself when you are a garden full of flowers, there is no need to compare your garden to anyone else. It's yours, unique, beautiful, one that you have created. Now, see that same beauty in your life. Look around. Smell the air. Cuddle with your kids. Hold hands with someone, hug often. In the midst of the chaos and hurt there loves to be found everywhere, if we know where to look. If you are having trouble seeing the beauty in your life, do this: stand still, breathe deeply, and find one thing you're grateful for, just one. Gratitude changes life. Life without gratitude is empty. Here are some final, overall thoughts. There will be hard days. Navigating those days will require being aware of your feelings, allowing those feelings, releasing those feelings. This requires honesty. The hardest thing is to be with one's self. Find it, and don't comprise it. Trust in the Universe, it will always guide you to the truth. Put up boundaries, everyone will respect you for knowing yourself. Love who you are, there is no one else like you.

PART 2

Divorcing and Healing from a Narcissist

Emotional and Narcissistic Abuse Recovery. a Workbook on Surviving Co-Parenting after Dealing with a Toxic Marriage, Splitting, Conflicts and Codependency.

Introduction

Imagine you have met him—he seems perfect. He is charming, funny, and seems entirely interested in listening to you. He brings you gifts months later that are related to little conversations that you have had before, such as bringing you that newly-in-season drink you had mentioned months prior. He seems like a great guy—until it seems like a light turned off.

The man who once was kind and caring, attentive, and aware, suddenly is demanding. You find yourself shifting from feeling like you were adored when you first met to feeling constantly guilty. You feel like you can't do anything right when he's around, and just the sight of him can be enough for you to feel like you cannot breathe. You are miserable—in love, desperately so, but you cannot deny that the love that you are feeling is also incredibly painful.

This man, even with the little given, is showing tendencies of narcissism. The proverbial you in that story is showing the telltale signs of narcissistic abuse—feeling madly in love, but like the love that is felt is miserable, draining, and painful.

Who is the Narcissist?

The narcissist, simply put, is someone who has a narcissistic personality disorder. These tend to be incredibly difficult to identify simply because they are always changing. The narcissist rarely has one particular personality type—they shift who they are constantly to show other people who they think they need to be to win over their targets.

Narcissists are predators—they hunt other people as their prey, searching for the right personality type to latch onto and draw from. They feed off of admiration and respect, and they seek to get it at any cost. They will find their targets, win them over with love, affection, and pleasantries, and then when they are confident that the other person is so deeply enamored with them that there is no reason or way they would ever make it a point to try to escape, the more sinister abuse and manipulation comes out.

Narcissists are particularly dangerous because the abuse of choice for a narcissist is entirely emotional. It exists within your head, leaving you feeling confused and hurting, while still having no idea why you feel the way you do. You are desperate for answers, and yet, those answers do not come. This is because the narcissist tends to have three distinct traits that make them incapable of giving those answers to you:

They lack empathy: Narcissists struggle with a lack of empathy—that primary component in basic human interaction. They do not empathize with other people, meaning they do not feel the emotions of other people in a sense that would allow for a connection. This means they do not particularly care about protecting the feelings of others, because unlike people without NPD, they do not care how they make people feel.

They are grandiose: Narcissists believe they are the best gift within the world—they are better than sliced bread and any other recent advancement that has changed the world for the better. They think they are better than everyone around them, and that idea of being better than other people leads them to act like they have the right to do whatever they want.

They feed off of attention: They do not just like attention and admiration—they need it. This need for attention is regularly referred to as a need for narcissistic supply, and they will do just about anything they need to to get that attention.

Narcissistic Personality Disorder

Narcissistic personality disorder (NPD) is quite pervasive—it is a Cluster-B personality disorder, meaning that it is primarily characterized by having dramatic, emotional, and unpredictable behavior. This sums up the narcissist greatly—those who are narcissistic are grandiose, believing that their self-worth is far better than it is, leading to that sense of dramatic behavior. They are emotional—when they do not get their way, they tend to be incredibly angry and lash out at anyone and everyone around them. Lastly, their thinking and behavior are unpredictable largely because it is so skewed. In particular, the narcissist has several characteristic behaviors that fit nicely into the three standard diagnostic criteria for Cluster-B personality types.

They are obsessed with power, beauty, and success. The narcissist is utterly convinced they are deserving of power, beauty, and success, and they will do just about anything to ensure they get it. They will fight to make it clear that they are deserving, and anyone who does not want to provide that for them is likely to be disregarded.

They tend to exaggerate. The narcissist will always tell other people they were more important to a situation than they were. The person who may have happened to hand over a rag to stop bleeding on someone who got hurt in a freak accident may then proclaim to all who will listen that he saved the life of someone today when really, all he did was offer up a rag to staunch the bleeding.

They believe they are superior and act like it. The narcissist tends to acknowledge himself as superior to everyone around him, and he will intentionally rub it into other people's faces. He may treat a waiter poorly because he perceives the waiter as being beneath him, or he may refuse to associate with certain people when he gets a new house, believing those friends who still live in apartments are not good enough for him anymore.

They are incredibly entitled. The narcissist, with that idea of superiority, also believes he is incredibly entitled to anything he wants. If he wants it, he should have it, especially because he believes he is so special. He is convinced he deserves what he wants just because he is him, and he will not spend the time to justify or earn it.

They care greatly about class and status. The narcissist is incredibly concerned with their ability to interact with other people, and in particular, may make it a point to pay special attention to who they perceive to be their equals and superiors (and there are very few people within this category) or they will ignore anyone they see as lesser.

They assume everyone else must be jealous of them. The narcissist, assuming he is perfect and so wonderful, also assumes that when people are looking at him, they are doing so because they are jealous. He feels like they are doing so because they are acknowledging his superiority, when in reality, they may be looking at him in annoyance. After all, he has done something to offend or annoy them.

They take credit for anything done within their families. Although narcissists rarely make good parents and are usually incredibly distant from any of the child-rearing work, they will not hesitate to declare to anyone who will listen that they are directly responsible for the successes of their children and their children's successes.

They expect to be praised. The narcissist refuses to acknowledge an instance in which people do not actively recognize their praises. If they do go ignored, the narcissist tends to become quite angry and offended.

They make unrealistic goals. The narcissist may declare he will be getting that promotion this year, even if he has none of the necessary skills actually to do well at the job. He assumes that, just because he is who he is, he will get it without needing to go through the process of getting the necessary education.

Beyond just that, however, the narcissist tends to take criticism incredibly poorly. He cannot possibly tolerate the idea of someone else calling him out on doing something because he assumes that he is right at all times. He struggles with the idea that people may try not to obey him or do what he is asking of them. Because of that, he tends to get incredibly angry at other people.

Ultimately, the narcissist has an incredibly distorted view of the world around him. His personality disorder skews his thinking so much that it no longer becomes realistic, and yet, he cannot help but force other people to obey his thinking schema. He assumes other people will do so without much argument or protest. If he is met with that protest, he will be infuriated. Anyone who denies his ideas is usually met with that anger that arises when one's truest beliefs are challenged.

Diagnosing NPD

Ultimately, diagnosing someone with true NPD is somewhat difficult—it involves rigorous questionnaires and interactions with a therapist that a narcissist may otherwise avoid or reject. Nevertheless, proper diagnostic criteria do exist for the disorder. Before the testing, however, a doctor will usually clear the individual from any physical causes for the behaviors. It is always possible that someone's physical body will be the root cause of their disordered thoughts. After all, many physical ailments can directly impact the mind's functioning. With the physical health cleared, ultimately, nine traits are determined to be diagnostic of narcissistic personality disorder.

To be deemed diagnosed with NPD, the individual must have at least five of the following symptoms:

An exaggerated sense of self-importance: The narcissist believes their importance is far more than is normally acceptable. They assume other people will recognize this.

They fantasize about gaining power: This power can vary from person to person, but most narcissists dream of being rich, famous, powerful, and having an attractive partner.

A belief of uniqueness that can only be understood by others who are as unique as they are: They assume the only people who can understand their genius are people who are equally as unique and that anyone else who may voice displeasure when being around them simply does not recognize perfection and superiority when they see it.

They are entitled: Narcissists are so entitled by nature that it is actually within their diagnostic criteria.

They need constant attention: Narcissists without attention tend to act out simply because they are not getting it. The narcissist is only able to feed their self-esteem and validate it through other people. They will do anything necessary to get that validation. This is where narcissistic abuse and manipulation comes in. Usually, the manipulation is in response to not getting the attention they need, and the abuse comes when they feel like that line of constant attention may be threatened.

They are exploitative: The narcissist will usually take advantage of the situation and other people if they have the chance to do so, especially if it will benefit them somehow. Usually, they prefer to exploit access to that narcissistic supply and will not go out of their way for more unless specifically quite sadistic.

Chapter 1. Understanding Narcissism

A lot of people believe, erroneously, that narcissism is as a result of having an overinflated sense of self. They think the narcissist is the way they are because of their ridiculously huge ego. The fact is that the display of seeming confidence is only that: A display, and nothing more. It's all smoke and mirrors. So, the idea that a sense of superiority is what makes the narcissist tick is not accurate. In truth, the root of narcissism is opposition to being open and vulnerable with other people, at all times.

The narcissist does not know the first thing about trusting others in relationships. Since she has no idea how to trust, she will do anything not to find herself in a situation where she needs to be vulnerable. Forget that show of how grand and above it all she puts on. The narcissist is ever anxious, and ever vigilant. They have no point at which they feel at ease with anyone.

Trying hard to feel good about themselves at all times, the narcissist fails woefully. If you stop to think about it, no one feels one hundred percent awesome all the time. It never happens. However, the narcissist worries that if he appears weak, or he gives any signal that could imply he's vulnerable, then he will be taken advantage of. The narcissist fears having to relinquish control or having someone else in charge of what becomes of her.

What the narcissist does to keep you thinking all is well, and to keep from feeling vulnerable or weak, is to make his performance more exaggerated than ever. You get the sense that he is the strongest and most powerful person on the planet. In all honesty, the narcissist does not truly feel like he is either of these things. He's just overcompensating for his vulnerability.

When we speak of the roots of narcissism, we do have the "superiority" component at play, but that is only secondary. The real root is the narcissist's aversion to having to trust. This is one of the reasons therapies never works for a true narc. For therapy to work, the client would have to be vulnerable, open, and trusting.

The Two Parts of Narcissism

The narcissist has two parts to herself: her extremely fragile ego, as well as her fake show of grandiosity. The fragile ego is usually on account of having been coddled a lot as a child and never being allowed to deal with her emotions healthily on her own. The show of grandiosity is on account of a need to be recognized as "better than everyone else." This happens as a result of the narc's parents telling him he's better than others and reinforcing this message with rewards.

The only way to develop a strong, authentic sense of self is by being self-aware, knowing your true value, being accepting of your strengths and weaknesses, and being okay with the fact that you are human. Your authentic self is molded into who you are now, over the years. This is a process that should ideally begin as early as when you were a toddler.

Here's a fact about toddlers: they're mostly narcissists. Cute ones, yes, but narcissists all the same. It's natural at this time of their lives for them to be this way. Also, it's not uncommon for teenagers to be narcissists, too. It's all part of that phase of life.

The problem emerges when you've grown past both stages, yet you've been unable to come up with an authentic viewpoint on who you are, and how you make meaning out of life. It's an issue when you haven't figured out how who you are and your purpose in life tie in with other people socially. This is the narcissist, essentially. An overgrown toddler, ever irrational, ever self-centered, ever ready and raring to go with a tantrum.

Unlike toddlers, there is nothing cute about the adult narcissist. The grown narcissist is dangerous, sinister, out to destroy. In the past, it was the widely held belief that the narcissist becomes the way they are on account of traumatic childhood experiences, which damaged them irreparably. While this can be the case, it's not the only cause of narcissism.

A lot of narcissists today also include those who always had things their way growing up. Their parents never bothered to get them to help out with chores at home. Their parents felt no need to call out the grown narcissist on their self-centeredness. As a kid, the grown narcissist was never given a timeout or some other sort of lesson for being cruel to his siblings. Their parents enabled them the whole time. In the worst of cases, the narcissist's parents put her on a pedestal.

The narc's parents made sure everyone knew just how beautiful or handsome their pre-narc child was, and drummed it into the little narc-to-be' head that she is better than everyone else. Each time the mini narc would get into some trouble, the parents would swoop in like the Avengers and save the day. They'd never bother with correcting their child.

If the narcissist was ever upset as a kid, the parents did all they could to appease them. If the narc felt frustrated, the parents made sure the frustration was gone, rather than teach the narc healthy ways to deal with things that he found disagreeable.

The narcissist's parents, more often than not, rendered their child emotionally handicapped. The narcissist grows up without knowing what it's like to be emotionally resilient.

The Line Between Good Parenting and Bad Parenting

I'm not suggesting that you subject your children to "tough love" by always denying them things, or emotionally ignoring their needs. That's just as bad as spoiling your kids rotten. I'd argue it's still spoiling your kids — just that they'll be a different kind of spoilt.

If you're a parent who constantly enables your child, and you felt like I was talking about you in the past few paragraphs, then you'd better watch out. You just might be raising a little narc. Don't ignore your kids, but don't coddle them either. It would be like being worried your child will fall flat on his face as she attempts to walk. To prevent that, you carry her around everywhere, rather than let her practice walking. Eventually, the muscles in her leg will be good for nothing, and she'll have to spend the rest of her life being carried or wheeled about in a chair.

The only way to avoid creating another narc for the world to deal with is to allow her to use their emotional legs. So, what if she falls, emotionally? This is how she will develop the resilience she needs to face whatever life and other people throw at her. If you keep coddling her, you'll teach her that people exist for the sole purpose of making her happy. That's not true, and she'll never be happy all the time in the real world. You're not doing her any favors.

Chapter 2. Codependency

Co-dependency is a term that describes the reliance, neediness and over-dependence of a party in a relationship on the other party. Co-dependency is beyond clinginess or the usual "wanting to be with" feeling present among partners in a relationship (either among lovers, family or friends). It is very much beyond that, a co-dependent partner relies totally on the partner for his or her happiness and survival, pleasure and purpose and eventually, the co-dependent person feels that his life is dependent on the partner.

Co-dependency in a relationship is not good for both the person and his partner, as constant display of affection, willingness to bend to every request or suggestion, not having a mind of one's own can exhaust the person always on the receiving end and cause friction in the relationship. A heavy reliance and the need to be needed is what characterizes co-dependent relationships.

Looking at it in another way, a co-dependent's partner in a relationship can get so used to the constant clinginess, sacrifice and care that it becomes a routine activity in the relationship that the showering of love, affection, attention, sacrifices is only done by one party in the relationship and all that the other party has to do is to be on the receiving end constantly; always expecting that particular kind of treatment all the time and not offering anything in particular. As bad as it is, the giver in the relationship could start to feel guilty anytime she thinks about herself instead of her partner. In this kind of relationship, they are both dependent on each other to survive. If one party fails or slacks in delivering the caring and sacrifices shower, not just the other party on the receiving end is severely affected (because he's accustomed to it). Still, even the benevolent partner feels guilty and sad for not doing what he or she is accustomed to doing for his or her partner. Here, it is evident that both parties are heavily and actively dependent on the other for survival and this kind of relationships are not healthy in the least. The cycle goes on and on.

Co-dependency in relationships causes a halt or neglect of other life duties or activities just to please one's partner, this neglect could be health-wise, relationship-wise, career-wise, fulfilment-wise or every other thing wise because the individual feels that he gets all the pleasure, fulfilment and happiness needed from extremely satisfying the partner. The co-dependent's self-worth and esteem is determined by the partner's approval of what it is, they only feel a sense of importance not with achieving any other thing but with the sole satisfaction of the partner.

Co-dependency most times comes with the belief that the other person is perfect. The individual in the relationship has to be the giver and must not fail in fulfilling that responsibility of satisfying; doesn't matter what it entails because that is what the survival is dependent upon, the other person's approval and how satisfied the partner is with what is being done, the other person in turn is dependent on the care being showered to the extent where he can't help but rely on it. It's an addiction, a cycle, an unhealthy one. An unhealthy addictive cycle.

Characteristics of a Co-Dependent Relationship

In a co-dependent relationship, certain traits will be noticed, pointing at the fact that the relationship is built on co-dependence.

- The relationship is usually characterized by physical or emotional abuse resulting from inadequacies in satisfying the partner. The partner always trying to satisfy the other party might get stuck up mid-lane while always trying to do everything revolving around the other partner. Having gotten accustomed to the treatment, the one on the receiving end might take advantage of the sacrifices and over-dependence of his partner and implement the use of physical and emotional abuse to get what he wants or just to manipulate and take control.

- There is a placement of priority on the partner over oneself and this puts the individual in a very compromising and vulnerable situation.

- The co-dependent's self-worth and esteem, happiness, purpose is dependent on the satisfaction and acceptance of the partner. Without the partner's acceptance, satisfaction and happiness, the co-dependent feels worthless.

- In a co-dependent relationship, the individual feels they must be needed by the other person for them to have any purpose

- A co-dependent doesn't have any identity, hobbies, interests, priorities outside the realm of anything that has to do with the partner

- A relationship built on co-dependence has a partner feeling bad for thinking about himself, he feels that his needs are unimportant and do not need to be attended to or at least not before the partner's needs, he feels the satisfaction of his partner is what automatically qualifies for his happiness and satisfaction.

- In a co-dependent relationship, abuse and hurt are most times endured perhaps because the co-dependent feels he or she has to please the partner after all or that it is the brunt that has to be faced for love. Also, because the person is heavily reliant on the partner's presence for happiness, the co-dependent evidently wouldn't want to leave. Lastly, he could feel that the partner's abusiveness would only last for a while. There is a high level of addictiveness and heavy reliance on the partner for a life. So the co-dependent tends to take whatever it is that comes with it.

- A co-dependence based relationship is very much one sided because it is only one partner that does the sacrificing and love giving and all of that but the partner on the receiving end only accepts all that is brought. That acceptance is what brings to the co-dependent satisfaction and happiness. The receiving party however accepts the love and sacrifices gladly or otherwise and he's as well dependent on that which his partner brings to him.

A co-dependent relationship has a faulty pillar and may not breed a happy, healthy and working relationship. In a healthy relationship, both parties have roles to play in making the other happy and making the relationship work. A relationship should not have one or both of the partners overly dependent on the other for survival or satisfaction, that's why it's a relationship, it's a collective effort. To have a healthy lifestyle overall, beyond relationships one has to self-prioritize too and not depend on another person wholly for happiness, satisfaction or even survival. A goal-oriented individual that gets into a co-dependent relationship can get his whole windscreen get blurry and messed up if not careful. It is therefore important that you get enlightened about this to avoid it like a plague and also help others to avoid it too as well as help those in it already too. After reading this book, you are expected to be fully rounded; An influential personality, a persuasive individual, a goal getter, an effective communicator and ultimately a goal-oriented individual. And so, it is expected that you help those around you to live a purposeful life too.

Causal Factors for Co-Dependence in Relationships

Co-dependence arises from a network of circumstances that form a learned psychological and behavioral pattern in the individual and makes him feel the need to embrace co-dependency consciously, sub-consciously or unconsciously.

Poor growing up experience: As a result of an unfavorable parental relationship some people had while growing up, they develop and adopt certain behavioral patterns that make them act how they do, depending on the situation. For co-dependency, a mother who is an alcoholic or drug addict or who is just self-centered and lacks proper child grooming skills neglects or overlooks the importance of catering to the needs of her children while they are growing might end up raising children that believe they do not matter, that their priority should be caring and catering to the needs of others around them first and should bother less about themselves.

So, when they find themselves in relationships as they grow further, they always feel the need to give their all and get back nothing in return because it is what they grew up with and what they deem as right. This behavioristic pattern is created in them because their mother always made them feel less important or undeserving of things for themselves by scolding them when they asked for things or made attempts to prioritize themselves.

She made them care only about her and not themselves. In their future relationships, they only find comfort and satisfaction in pleasing others and that's how they please themselves because that is how they grew up and that's the behavioristic pattern registered in their minds.

An abusive background: Related to the point mentioned above is the point of growing in an unsafe and unfavorable environment; Abuse is another large contributor to development of a co-dependent personality type.

An individual who grows up in a home of constant abusive activities; physical, sexual, emotional. He grows up with the weakness within, unable to voice out, to speak up or even to stand for himself and this in turn tells on how he relates with people later on in his life. He grows up with the feeling that he does not matter, he relies on other people heavily for his happiness and satisfaction and will do anything to make sure they get someone to need them and that is why they sacrifice so much to get someone to stay with them. That's how they know how to love and that is how they know how to live.

When he grows up and unfortunately gets into another abusive relationship later in life, he finds it hard to leave because after all he didn't have a choice but stay earlier in life. He lives on with the trauma and with the hurt. It is because he's been robbed of his pride, dignity and self-respect and made to feel like he had to accept whatever was thrown at him and live with it. Someone with an abusive history is most likely to want to seek comfort, love and "the need to be needed" from somebody else but himself because he thinks he cannot give it to himself judging from the trauma and pain within. So, he does all that's humanly possible of his abilities hoping in return to feel needed regardless of what comes with it.

Chapter 3. Dysfunctional Relationship

Experiencing Dissociation as a Survival Mechanism

An interesting thing about narcissists is that they feel emotionally and physically detached from their surroundings. They often have memory disruptions that alter their sense of self, consciousness, and perceptions. Often that causes an overwhelming experience that translates into a distortion of emotions, images, physical sensations, and thoughts, resulting in the person assuming a different form of life altogether.

It is this kind of dissociation that contributes to an emotional numbness especially when faced with a horrible situation. This way, mind-numbing activities that include addictions, obsessions, and repression become their way of life so that they can escape the reality in front of them. In other words, their brains find it necessary to block out such experiences as pain so that they do not have to deal with it.

In most cases, narcissists develop a more traumatized inner self that has no connection with their personality. It may include parts that were unnatured as a child, the anger that one feels towards those that abused them when they were helpless and those parts that you think you may not be able to express when you are among other people.

You Walk on Eggshells

One of the most common signs of trauma is staying away from anything that could serve to re-open the wound. It could be people, places or even activities that are thought to pose a considerable threat. It could also be your friend, family or boss among others. In their presence, you tend to watch what comes out of your mouth so that you do not end up being punished or becoming the subject of others' envy.

With time, you realize that this is not practical and you end up as a target for the abuser when they feel entitled to use you as their punching bag. You know that you have to be careful and feel some anxiety to deal with them in a way that avoids confrontation.

You will also find that when you are living with a narcissist, you may tend to extend people extra pleasing behavior outside the abusive relationship, hence losing a more natural and casual approach when it comes to navigating the world.

You find yourself putting aside your basic need and desires so that you can please your abuser

Being abused is something that may be happening to you before you have realized that that person you are living with is a narcissist. Well, you may once have been full of life and had dreams that you would have loved to achieve. But what happened to them? A narcissist came and took control of your life, and now you feel as if living is just so that you can meet their needs and help them achieve their dreams and goals instead. You now feel as though your life revolves around another's.

The truth is, you may have even gone to the extent of placing your goals, personal safety and friendship on standstill just so that you can make your partner feel fulfilled. One thing that you have to understand is that they will never get satisfied no matter what you do, and so they will keep sucking the life out of you until you are left high and dry. Watch out!

You are struggling with serious health issues indicating that you are in physiological turmoil

The other sign that you are living with a narcissist is if you have gained or lost too much weight and ended up developing severe health complications that you did not have initially. In most cases, there are physical symptoms of early or premature aging. You may be experiencing elevated levels of cortisol causing your immune system to take a severe hit and leaving you very vulnerable to so many diseases.

You may also be experiencing a lack of sleep, or when you go to sleep, you have nightmares that do not seem to go away. You also may be experiencing harsh flashbacks that take you to the very place that reminds you of your past mistakes, pain, and wounds.

Developing a Pervasive Lack of Trust

Does everyone around you signify a threat? Do you find yourself anxious about what others are about to do? If you have experienced malicious actions of other people in the past, especially one that you trust, it is highly likely that you have lost your sense of trust. In other words, hyper vigilance replaces normal caution. This is mainly because the narcissist in your life has convinced you that everything that you have experienced is invalid and hence causing you to withdraw your trust from the people that once meant so much to you.

Having Suicidal Ideations

Have you experienced self-harming tendencies before? What do you think triggered these ideations? So many of us feel a strong whim of depression and anxiety that comes on as a sense of hopelessness. It is true that your situation may have been unbearable and maybe even inescapable. You soon begin to feel as though you are helpless. This feeling is what drives you to the edge, wishing that you would not survive another day. So many people that have been abused at the hands of a narcissist often feel that harming themselves is the best way to cope with the painful experience.

In fact, according to research, there is evidence that shows that victims who have narcissistic partners are twice highly likely to commit suicide several times compared to those not in intimate relationships with a narcissist.

Self-Isolation

Did you know that many abusers isolate their victims? Did you also know that these victims also separate themselves from other people because they feel ashamed about the whole abusive experience? The truth is, so many victims blame themselves for their abuse, and what is even worse is that law enforcement, friends and family members make the whole experience even more traumatizing because they invalidate your perception of abuse.

The fear is that there will be no one that can understand or even believe what you are going through. Therefore, rather than reaching out for help, victims usually tend to withdraw from people in their surroundings so that they cannot undergo judgment and punishment from their abusers.

Comparing Yourself to Others

One thing that you have to be careful about is the fact that narcissists often demonstrate a high skillset when it comes to manufacturing love triangles. And the possibility of bringing other people into their relationship dynamics is exploited so that they can continue traumatizing their victims. The victims, on the other hand, tend to internalize that fear, believing that they are not enough. Hence, you will see them continually fighting to compete for the attention of their abusers.

There is also a high chance that the victims will want to compare themselves to other people who are in happier, healthier relationships. The main reason is that they wonder why their abusers treat them in a hurtful manner with no respect. They often get trapped in the thought that they are to blame for whatever is happening in their lives. Let me tell you one thing: quit blaming yourself for another person's actions. The only thing that you did was to trust them and love them for who they are, and that is not a crime. Your abuser is the person to blame for not appreciating you for you.

Self-Destruction

Are you a victim of abuse? Do you often find yourself ruminating about the mistreatment and hear the voice of your abuser right inside your head? Is it amplifying destructive self-talk and a high tendency to drive you into sabotaging your own life? Be very careful because that is what the narcissist in them is aiming to achieve. That person will not rest until they see you destroyed.

Most narcissists use verbal abuse just so that they can put their victims down. The victims, in turn, develop a tendency to punish themselves as a way of coping with their toxic shame. They end up sabotaging their goals and dreams just so that they can measure up to their abuser's needs and plan. In other words, the main aim of the abuser is to instill the feeling of worthlessness in their victims so that the victims feel as though they do not deserve anything good that this life has to offer.

Fear Doing the Things That You Love

The main reason why you are not running after your dreams and pursuing excellence is that that narcissist has instilled so much fear in you. The main reason for this may be because they are envious of you and take pride in punishing you because of your successes. Due to this victim tend to associate their talents and achievements with cruelty and callous treatment. In turn, it causes you to fear success lest you suffer for it.

The danger with this kind of fear is the fact that you end up with depression, anxiety and a lack of confidence, allowing your narcissistic friend to keep stripping you of your joy and happiness over and over again. One important thing that I want you to realize is that your abuser is not undercutting your successes and talents because they believe that you are inferior. Rather it is mainly because your gifts threaten them and their control over you. The sooner you realize this, the better you are at defending yourself and your sense of self-worth from these kinds of monsters.

Protecting Your Abuser and Putting Yourself on Fire

It is quite unfortunate that so many people see the need to rationalize and deny the abuse just so that they can survive their abusers. Most victims of violence will try as much as they can to convince themselves that the abuser loves them and they do not want to hurt them. They try to tell themselves that all is good when all there's is pain and hurt. They even go to the lengths of blaming themselves for provoking abuse.

The truth is, if you continue in this form of darkness not wanting to dissociate from this cognitive dissonance, that person will keep abusing you over and over again without necessarily waiting for you to give them a reason to because that is just who they are. The point is that your abuser will always aim at making you helpless enough so that you surrender to them and you eventually are surviving at their mercy. It is even sad that most victims will protect their abusers from legal consequences by lying to people that they have a happy relationship even when there is nothing but hate between them.

Chapter 4. Protect Yourself from the Narcissist

Self-esteem is critical if you wish to defend yourself against the narcissist. It is critical just about anywhere in your life. Still, in particular, the narcissist loves victims who have low self-esteem. When your self-esteem is low, you are going to find that you struggle to stand up for yourself in just about any context. No matter whether you were supposed to defend yourself from the narcissist's abuse or just to have the faith that you know best, having high self-esteem is critical.

Red Flags

When you learn to recognize red flags as they arise, you will be able to defend yourself simply by deciding to walk away when you see them. When you see these red flags, you can remind yourself the best thing to do is walk away—it is not your job, nor is it your responsibility to try to fix the narcissist. You do not have to figure out how to make things easier for the narcissist or feel guilty for walking away, no matter how hard he tries to make you feel guilty. He will almost definitely do exactly that—he wants you to feel guilty because if you feel guilty, you will give in to him. There are several red flags within relationships, but when dealing with the narcissist, you are likely to see the following five:

- He is self-centered: Remember, the entire world revolves around the narcissist in his book—he believes everyone else is an accessory to his own main story and refuses to acknowledge the three-dimensionality of everyone else in the world. If you notice the narcissist in your life is constantly falling for self-centered behaviors, such as talking about himself constantly without allowing you to recognize or feel like your own person, you have a problem that needs to be addressed as quickly as possible. This problem is only going to get worse if allowed to fester in any way.

- He is arrogant: Watch for how those that you date treat their cashiers and waiters—it is an incredibly telling method that can help you figure out whether or not the person that you are dating is good. If you find that, rather than making it a point to actively thank and recognize the waiter is trying his best, the individual that you are considering dating is making the situation worse, such as yelling at the cashier or belittling the cashier, you are effectively showing yourself exactly what you will be seeing in your relationship as soon as you have been left alone for a while.

- He is entitled: This is perhaps one of the most obvious on this list—when you are entitled, you simply expect you will be getting something, and that is the only option that exists. In this case, the entitlement comes from feeling like the narcissist being able to determine exactly what is going to happen when and how it will all go down at any given moment. Effectively, the narcissist attempts to control everything.

- Excessive bragging and need for attention: The narcissist will always make it a point to go for bragging as much as possible. He will brag about the game he just bought or the way he did one certain thing. Everything was always about comparing where they were in life

- He has to control everything; Perhaps the biggest red flag of them all, however, is that he feels an excessive need to control everything and anything. He feels like he has to take control because he knows that he is the most perfect person there is. As the most perfect person, he is entitled and responsible for us not perfect people. He effectively will constantly make it a point to chase after control of various situations.

Ultimately, the more defense mechanisms that you put up in play, the more likely you are to avoid having any sort of similar issues in the future. If you can protect yourself from harassment, such as making sure that you are willing to respect yourself and refuse to put up with abuse, you will be far less likely to find yourself stuck in abuse in the first place.

Remember Your Boundaries

Boundaries are critical against the narcissist. However, they are critical just about everywhere. If you had weak boundaries before and a narcissist has already gotten in, he will most likely be back at some point to harass you further. Keeping this in mind, you may find you are best served by remembering your boundaries from the beginning. Rather than feeling like you need to defend your standards and what you are doing, you should actively be stopping, reminding yourself that your boundaries are what they are, end of the story, and leaving behind anyone who refuses to acknowledge it.

Your boundaries, if remembered early on before you can get involved with other people, can be your greatest weapon.

Become Emotionally Intelligent

Emotional intelligence refers to one's ability to identify and regulate one's own emotions while also being able to understand and influence the emotions of other people. When you learn to become emotionally intelligent, you are developing the necessary tools to ensure you are more than capable of actively becoming the person who the narcissist fears—someone who is confident, in-tune with themselves, and ready to reject the notion of any sort of abuse altogether.

Effectively, when you are emotionally intelligent, you are ensuring you avoid the problems of abuse from the narcissist. You will be so good at reading and understanding the situations around you that you will into fall for the narcissist's antics. Instead of being abused, you will be able to avoid the narcissist instead. Instead of being harassed, you will find a way to avoid the narcissist's attempts. You may be able to ask questions that redirect the burden onto the narcissist, making the narcissist uncomfortable and that much less likely to ever attempt to get your attention again.

Emotional intelligence is primarily made up of four distinct skillsets known as pillars. These are:

• Self-awareness: The ability to understand and identify one's own emotions

• Self-regulation: The ability to control one's emotional impulses

• Social awareness: The ability to understand and identify the feelings of other people

- Relationship management: The ability to regulate the relationships between other people

This technique is incredibly useful when dealing with narcissists. When you are emotionally intelligent, you learn to see right through the narcissist once and for all.

Respect Yourself

Frequently way easier said than done, when you respect yourself, you are effectively able to remind yourself that you do not deserve the treatment that the narcissist is dishing out. You can tell yourself that, no matter what the narcissist says, you did not deserve to be abused. You were not destined to be alone if the narcissist rejected you. You are not the problem at hand, and if the narcissist continues to say that you are, then when you respect yourself, you can remind yourself that he is wrong.

Effectively, when you respect yourself enough, you can remind yourself that you do not care what the narcissist has to say. You remind yourself of whose opinions truly matter and remind yourself to reject what the narcissist has to say. You effectively remind yourself that it is your version of events that should be trusted—not the narcissist's. When you trust the narcissist's version of events instead of your own, you are granting the narcissist that power over you. Do not give up your self-respect too easily—you deserve to have that respect for yourself.

Chapter 5. Dating a Narcissist

As much as you might have heard or read about narcissists, you are not wrong to build a relationship with one. You also need to know that you are not deliberately setting yourself on the path of self-destruction. Narcissists are quite romantic and can be charming. They are great lovers and can be friends. The truth is they can be sensitive to how you feel and adjust to your needs.

However, narcissists can be very manipulative, and they are complicated people; therefore, being in any sort of relationship, whether romantic or not, spiritual or professional, you need to know that it can be confusing and be set for the situation. Narcissists are complicated and hard to understand because sometimes you will find them very helpful and dependable to point, they will seem to care about you. The truth is their devotion and kindness are mostly to benefit themselves and further put them in control of things.

Forming a relationship with a narcissist is not uncommon. Many people are in such a narcissistic relationship without even realizing it until they are far into it. A victim doesn't feel like leaving because his or her life is centered on the narcissist. It is difficult to let go of such a relationship. It could be because they are married and have kids. Also, at times, dealing with an ex who is a narcissist can be quite difficult.

Narcissists are potentially harmful in many ways. How do you simply make the relationship work? How is it possible to build a healthy relationship with a narcissist? It is indeed possible and maybe rewarding to have a relationship with someone who is a narcissist. Still, that relationship would be psychologically and emotionally draining. A narcissist usually lacks what it takes to build a strong relationship. They do not show consistent kindness, compassion, selflessness, reciprocity, compromise, and empathy. They drain the energy and spirit from their supposed partners, turning them to figurative punching bags.

What to Expect in a Relationship with a Narcissist?

Being in a relationship or having any link with a narcissist has many challenges like I have earlier said. Still, when you are aware of some of the things to expect, you should know how to handle the relationship better to build a healthy one.

You Will Need to Make Some Sacrifices

To be able to have a fairly good life or relationship with a narcissist, you need lots of sacrifices to keep the relationship going. You will sacrifice a part of you, especially your beliefs and what you stand for, and one of the expected constants is that you will be lied to over and over yet must accept it.

Narcissists are crafty and very manipulative. They are good at changing narratives and altering reality into the version that suits them, and in the end, they get you to agree to something that you didn't do. To keep narcissists happy, you will need to learn how to accept their version of reality as the truth of what has happened even when it is not. That way, you will always escape their fury and not be on the receiving end.

Part of the sacrifice is that you might never get praised for achieving something or rewarded for behaving well. Narcissists will at every opportunity try to undermine your effort. They are so manipulative to the point where they call all the shots yet in a very shrewd way that will seem as though you are in control. They will let you make decisions but will do something different, and you have to appreciate them for doing that.

Building healthy relationships with narcissists mean you have to play a secondary role. You need to make sacrifices that will drain you in a lot of ways.

To a Narcissist, No One is to Be Trusted

Narcissists wouldn't trust anybody except themselves. Even when you do everything right and have never given them any reason not to trust you, they would still not respect you enough to allow you to lead your life without interference and surveillance. They can go to the extent of spying and stalking you.

Narcissists have the habit of tracking their partners. In a romantic relationship, narcissists are likely to install trackers without the knowledge of their partners. It could be on their phone or computer, and they feel no remorse about it but rather proud of their action.

Regrettably, most narcissists abuse drugs and alcohol to the extreme. Their partners will have to endure and adapt to their lifestyle and live with the perpetual fear and expectation that they may take things too far with the drugs or alcohol and act unpredictably.

Most narcissists usually develop bad habits and, because of that, can become so irresponsible, missing their appointments, meetings, and work. Therefore, it puts their partners in situations where they have to clean up the mess they create and make up excuses to absolve them. The reason is that the partners have been conditioned to believe that they are a team and that it's them against the whole world.

Narcissists will never put their trust in anyone; therefore, they use words that will keep their victims spellbound like "You are my world" and "Without you, I'm nothing." That way, their victims are comforted with a false sense of security. Meanwhile, they are just cutting their partners from everyone and everything, pitching them against the world and using them.

Narcissists will say things and take actions that will be convincing enough to make you believe in them. Trust them and risk it all for them. You should be ready not to be trusted when in a relationship with a narcissist.

Although it is not clear if narcissists do things intending to hurt their partners to the level they do, they give the excuse of having a bad childhood. It is your duty to understand and forgive them for all their shortcomings and behaviors. They will explode, and you will face their rage if you don't forgive them of everything they have done, including the times they abused you.

You Will Be Drained and Tapped Out

Narcissists don't like taking the blame for anything. They look for someone else to take the blame, and you who have a relationship with one will likely be the one to fill that role. Therefore, to make your relationship work, you will have to come to terms with the fact that you are a scapegoat at every opportunity and probably be demeaned. And if you don't want to take the blame for them, the narcissistic traits will kick in, and they will accuse you of being crazy and inconsiderate. Mostly, all your feelings will be used against you to make you feel bad.

They Will Then Term You a Boring Person.

Some narcissists will rather have you keep your job so that you can help keep their lifestyle financed, milking you while you slave for their happiness.

Your time is one of the greatest gifts you can ever give to someone. This is a world where time is money and of the essence. We usually don't have the time to spend with our loved ones. But giving time and energy to someone you care about can hold the relationship together. That way, you will have time to fix all the problems that may arise even if you get blamed.

Tips and Tools to Maintain a Healthy Relationship

You are on the path of managing narcissists. The following tips should be incorporated into your daily dealings with narcissists. With time, narcissists should start getting used to the changes, and possibly, you will notice a change in them too.

"We" Should Be Used as Often as Possible

Whenever it is possible, try using the word "we," and then strongly emphasize relationships during communications. According to research from Rethinking Narcissism: The Bad—and Surprising Good—about Feeling Special, this simple method works well on narcissists. The research indicates that narcissists were given passages that are filled with words like "our," "we," and "us." When they were done with the passage, the narcissists were moved and were willing to help other people in need and also became less obsessed with their ideas of being the center of attention.

Reward Good Behavior

Make it a point to observe and compliment the narcissist when you notice they are warm. Give them compliments for their warmth. However, do not compliment them for their performance or their achievement. It only makes them want to manipulate and dominate you more.

When you notice they are warm, give them compliments? You can complement them for being warm, not for their performance or achievement. Be observant and look for moments that the narcissist demonstrates a better behavior and emphasize on it. Pushing a narcissist to the center means emphasizing on the moments that they show some kind of ability to collaborate, show interest in people, or concern and care for the people around them. Whenever they behave more communal, reward them.

Differentiate Good and Bad Behaviors

When you compliment, does it help? If it does, then you can take it up a notch. You should tactically contrast their good behavior with their bad behavior. Contrasting both behaviors is more or less like catching, except you are recounting the past and present the same time. If you do have any of such behavior, note it. It is far more effective when it is contrasted with some recollection of communal behavior.

Let Them Know How You Feel

First and foremost, tell the narcissist how you feel. As you feel unhappy, uneasy, and uncomfortable, use the word "I." For instance, "I am unhappy about your actions." You can use more impactful words like "scared," "afraid," and "sad," but if you are not in a romantic relationship with the narcissist, a less intense language might be better to use. Always go with your gut. The goal here is to describe your experience to narcissists and let them know their behavior that is causing it.

You can let narcissists know how they affect you and how they make you feel. Mention their bad behavior and the likely corrections you want to see.

Understand and Accept Differences

To build a healthy relationship, it is very important that we frankly accept our differences. We need to understand that everyone is unique and different in many ways. If we understand that we all perceive the world in different ways, then we might as well have crossed one of the greatest challenges in building relationships.

People often feel better when they feel other people understand them and are in tune with their point of view. On the other hand, however, life would generally be boring and dull if we all think and act the same. Understanding and accepting that we are all wired differently, making us unique, will be a very strong foundation on which we can build healthy relationships.

Listen and Pay Attention

The art of listening is a skill that improves relationships, perception, and understanding. When you listen and give attention, the other person will feel proud and confident. They will feel supported. They will feel heard. Responsive interactions can promote healthy relationships.

Chapter 6. Signs You Have Narcissist Victim Syndrome

These symptoms can be disheartened because victims of narcissistic relationships suffered from some if not all of these symptoms. You likely recognized yourself and your behaviors within these signs.

- Receiving just a few crumbs of affection, love, and validation from the narcissist makes your day. Receiving even a little bit of the validation and other positive emotions that the victim received in the first stage of the relationship puts them on cloud nine because the reward center is activated at the narcissist's will.

- Feeling stuck in the relationship and see no way out. Many times, it is not that the victim cannot physically leave. The intense longing to be close to the narcissist is what confines the woman to that relationship.

- Feeling that the narcissistic partner will be the only one who can fulfill your needs even though this person is not currently doing so.

- Worrying that your actions and words will set the narcissists off. Walking on eggshells around the narcissist is common and a great sign of trauma bonding.

- Your brush off or excuse the narcissist's bad behavior even when confronted by friends or family about it.

- You often feel that there is a level of "prey and predator" in the interaction of that relationship and that your vulnerabilities are being exploited

- You are aware that you are being deceived by the narcissist but still cannot say that the ties of the relationship.

- You feel shame at the things she had done, accepted and endured in this relationship.

Do not despair though. The trauma bond is hard to break but it is not a possible task. The rest of this book is dedicated to helping you do just that.

Tactics for Dealing with and Severing a Narcissistic Trauma Bond

A trauma bond is likened to a drug addiction because it gives feelings of euphoria and then sucks them away. We know of instances where persons have beaten drug addiction. Hence, women who suffer from a trauma bond developed from narcissistic relationships have the same hope.

The hope is only facilitated by taking action. There are a few tactics that you can employ to finally break free of that trauma bond that you have developed with your narcissistic husband. They include:

- Taking it one day at a time. It is easy to become overwhelmed when making decisions about your future and moving on from a narcissistic relationship. This overwhelm can make it seem easier to just stick with the status quo. You cannot allow that to happen. Therefore, to ensure that you move on for good, make one decision at a time and move on one day at a time.

- Committing to living in reality. The trauma bond is sustained by fantasies that things can be different and that a narcissistic partner can change. Remember that narcissism can only be dealt with by the narcissist. Therefore, you need to pull yourself out of the fantasies and deal with what is happening, and the reality is that this person is toxic to your health in all ways. The only reasonable response to that is getting rid of that toxicity.

- Living in the here and now. A lot of the fantasies that sustained a trauma are founded on what could be and what will be if you only just do what the narcissist outline. Stop that detrimental psychology by being aware of how you feel now and what is happening now. That is the only way that you will notice that this person is compromising your sense of self-worth and self-love. That will allow you to notice the obvious that can stop being obvious. Stop waiting for a change and act on what is happening now.

• Acknowledge your role in the narcissist relationship. The narcissist would have placed all the blame on your shoulders for the things that went wrong. However, you need to take a step back and put things in perspective. If you were as bad as this person said, then he would have walked away. The fact that he had not supports the fact that he was using you. Putting things in perspective allows you to see the obvious and break free of the emotional prison.

• Allowing yourself to feel. There are a lot of messy emotions involved in being in a toxic relationship and sometimes, it can seem easier just not to feel them. However, the only way you can get past them is to feel them and acknowledge them for what they are. Then you can develop the techniques necessary to manage them healthily.

• Allowing yourself to grieve. By severing your trauma bond with a narcissist, you allow this relationship to die. Grief is one of the necessary phases for getting over any death or loss.

• Committing to self-care. Self-care is not just a physical endeavor. It is about emotionally and mentally caring for yourself as well. A narcissist will teach his victim to discard such personal caring. Therefore, to counter this, start making decisions that focus on your needs and wants. It is time to think about what is best for you and the first step to doing that is being compassionate and understanding towards yourself. Stop beating yourself up about the decisions that you made in the past and start encouraging yourself to do better towards uplifting and empowering yourself.

- Making a list of personal boundaries that must be honored by the other party if you were to ever be in a romantic relationship again. These boundaries are meant for both you and the other party. Boundaries can be simple such as not entertaining a man who drinks heavily or not allowing someone else to take control of your finances no matter what. The point is that writing these will solidify them in your mind and therefore, allow you to recognize when these boundaries are being trespassed by another person.

- Developing a healthy support system. The narcissist may have achieved his goal of cutting the links that you had with other people but this is the time in your life where you must commit to rebuilding old connections or developing new ones that are not centered on drama and negative emotions. Healing from a trauma bond all the more difficult if you have no one around you to show you care and concern. If you do not have that ready support in your life, do not be afraid to reach out to a trained medical health professional.

- Allowing yourself to think of your life as bright and fulfilling without this person. Envision what it would be like to have a partner that is supportive and uplifting rather than one that displays behaviors that encourages the development of a trauma bond. Envision your life doing things as an individual so that even if your future does not have a romantic relationship, you will still be happy and fulfilled. Hold onto that vision and start implementing measures that will allow you to make it a reality. Such measures can include starting new hobbies, joining clubs, and furthering your education.

Chapter 7. Narcissist Abuse Syndrome

When a person is in a relationship with someone with a narcissistic personality disorder, what he goes through is known as narcissistic abuse. According to the DSM, narcissistic abuse can cause potentially lifelong, crippling effects on the mental health of a person. The group of symptoms is known as the narcissistic victim syndrome (Athena 2017).

Generally, narcissists are easily identified over time by the peculiar way they make use of language intending to captivate another person's mind and will. The term emotional manipulation best describes what the narcissist does to their victims. Avoid the risk of falling prey to the ploys that narcissists use to hide, shift blame, and mislabel those people whom they victimize.

Narcissists find it very easy to disguise. They are masters of disguise. The narcissistic abuse is a form of thought control with the use of a particular language that is designed to manipulate another person emotionally.

A narcissist takes control of a person's mind and will; therefore, the thoughts and desires of that person become a possession of the narcissist to use for his or her selfish gains.

The narcissist's language is aimed at getting his or her victims to do the following:

- question the authenticity of their sanity

- lose trust for those people who give them support, like their friends and family

- feel like it is only the narcissist who cares about them, so they feel abandoned

- work very hard but never give themselves credit for their hard work

- doubt their ability to come up with sane thoughts and make good decisions

- get disconnected from the things they want and need

- lose value for their contributions to things

- get obsessed with their faults and mistakes

- ignore the narcissist's wrongs and even make excuses for them

- try so hard to get the favor of the narcissist

- become obsessed with ways to make sure that the narcissist is happy

- begin to idealize the narcissist

These days, people with this personality disorder have advanced their ways of emotionally and mentally devastating other people. This happens most of the time by making the narcissist's relationship partner to have an altered state of mind and body. The person feels powerless and helpless for at least a temporary time until he or she is eventually able to wake up and get out of the fog.

People who have been victimized by narcissistic abuse often submit themselves for counseling therapy. Most of the time, they are not aware of their emotional pain and mental anguish as they are usually disconnected from them. Rather than taking their own emotions into cognizance, they concern themselves more with their failures and inadequacies as they go in a desperate search for ways to remedy some problems or flaws that narcissists have identified as the root cause of their misery.

There are cases when the abusive partner will hand over to the victim a set of expectations that he or she is meant to take with him to see a therapist. Most of the time, these expectations are centered on how they are not very attentive, how they pay too much attention to their family and children, as well as how they lack enough fantasy for sex.

The victims, however, keep their minds occupied with the search for ways to address the confusion, and this results in the use of some not-so-favorable tactics, like gaslighting and word salad in his mind, with hopes to distort their reality to accommodate the needs of the narcissist. Victims look for answers as to the reason why the narcissists are miserable and insecure, why they treat people the way they do, why they are unable to communicate, why the victims are yet to figure out what the narcissists are trying to tell them, and many more questions.

The thought pattern of a person who has been through narcissistic abuse is always laden with self-blame and condemnation of oneself. When they begin therapy, down to a later stage, they are found making statements like the following:

- "There are no problems, just some minor things."

- "We are happy because most of the time, we get along."

- "Please, is it possible for me to get help?"

- "Do I have any hope at all?"

- "It is all my fault."

- "Can I learn not to upset him?"

- "Is there a way to ask him to continue loving me after what I did to him?"

- "I cannot afford to lose him. Can you fix me?"

Aside from these repetitive statements that they make all the time, their thoughts and words describe their situations in a way that suggests an unbalanced sense of responsibility. For example, victims find themselves having these thoughts:

- They have "failed" or are failing to make the narcissist feel secure and loved.

- They are not able to fix themselves to stop upsetting the narcissist.

- They have done some things that "crushed the narcissist so much" and the narcissist will never get over it even though it is a minor thing.

- They are the reason why the narcissist is having an affair with another person.

- They cannot blame the narcissist for being interrogative, being punitive, yelling, ignoring them, moping, calling them names, and so on.

In a nutshell, the victims' self-image becomes exactly the way the narcissists want it to be. The victims see what the narcissists want them to see. They believe the things about themselves that the narcissists want them to believe. Narcissists also want their victims to feel the way they want them to feel.

It is in these ways that narcissists get to be emotionally manipulative. When one talks about emotional manipulation while discussing the narcissistic personality disorder, it involves guilting, shaming, threats, name-calling, and so on. When talking about being emotionally abused, most people like to include victims of narcissistic abuse, and many people have experienced it first-hand during childhood.

Emotional manipulation, on the other hand, in a very aggressive way, targets the conversion of another person's mind and will for one's selfish use. The use of emotionally abusive language, however, is rooted in an automatic reaction that is both defensive and protective. The distinction between emotional abuse and emotional manipulation is, however, important to disarm the narcissist's tactics (both overt and covert) of hiding their weaknesses and shifting the blame to the victims.

There are several symptoms of post-traumatic stress disorder in narcissism. These symptoms include the following:

- Having intrusive memories and thoughts

- A hypervigilant, irritable, and easily startled nature

- A distorted sense of blame, which is related to trauma

- Both physical and emotional reactions to whatever reminds them of trauma

- Negative thoughts about themselves and the world

- Detachment and isolation from other people

- Having nightmares and flashbacks with thoughts that tell them a bad event is taking place again

- Avoiding people, situations, or thoughts that are related to/with a certain trauma

- Difficulty to sleep or concentrate

Nature and the Side Effects of the Narcissistic Abuse

It is very important for a person who has suffered the narcissistic abuse to learn and understand the nature of the abuse and its effects, as well as the narcissistic abuse syndrome. This is a very critical aspect of healing and getting back the ability to care for oneself.

It is also very important to know the difference between the NPD and other personality disorders, such as antisocial personality disorder, which shares some similarities with narcissism. The difference between the NPD and APS is the fact that there are some lines that the narcissist does not cross. While both personalities do not show any remorse when they are exploiting or hurting the feelings of others, the sociopath crosses the line from being lawful to exploiting the other person in an unlawful way, such as abusing the victim physically, exploiting him or her financially, and so on.

In the minds of these people, a person who holds a position of authority needs to show a certain level of callousness. He or she must show no empathy so as not to be seen as a weak person. When in an intimate relationship, the narcissist and sociopath have a habit of inflicting pain on their partners in the same way that exclusive groups for men (e.g., fraternities, sports teams, or secret societies) have some hazing practices.

Both types of personality disorder are prone to hurting and taking advantage of other people for their selfish gains without showing any sense of remorse. They consider remorse as a thing for weak, inferior, and low-status personalities.

In the actual sense, narcissists are weak and fragile people who just have to prove that human love and mutual care are phony. This can go to a dangerous extent where narcissists begin to refuse to accept that they are human with resources and intelligence, just like every other human. They fail to understand the fact that it is almost impossible to gain control over another human being, even little children, without bearing a high cost to oneself.

The human brain contains mirror neurons that create neurochemical states of mind and body within oneself. Thus, when a person has feelings of scorn, hatred, or disdain for other people, that person mirrors the same feelings for himself or herself. Therefore, it is not possible for a person to intentionally seek to hurt another person without hurting himself or herself too. If a person decides, however, to go the other route of staying numb, it means that he or she is not living but merely existing.

In an odd and paradoxical way, codependents remain hooked in a way that is similar to being addicted to a drug. Codependents, most of the time, refuse to take the things that are capable of bringing them out of the fog and illusions into cognizance. They willingly refuse to acknowledge the fact that the narcissists whom they willfully fell in love with never had a conscience or had human feelings. They deny the fact that narcissists intentionally choose to drain the life out of their victims. To feel alive again, it is very important for the victims to get out of this fog and illusion.

Chapter 8. Marriage and the Narcissist

You will remember that just a month, week, or a few days earlier, your partner was so sweet and pleasant. Then suddenly, they have started to change. When you think about it, your brain will trick you into thinking that you might have done something wrong that made your partner start withdrawing.

The problem is not you or coming from you. You have not done anything wrong. If you are cocksure that you have not done anything wrong to your partner to deserve their recent change in attitude and behavior, then you should not apologize for a wrong you have not done. If you apologize, your narcissistic partner will most definitely use it against you.

You are not the reason why the relationship transitioned to the devaluation phase; the primary reason is that narcissists get bored easily. Once they get bored, a lot of thoughts start forming in their heads. Also, when they're bored, they begin to think or behave like a typical introvert. They will cut off communications with you and prefer to be alone.

Additionally, the void in them begins to emerge again. They have to look for the next activity or event or person to fill the void.

As the emptiness that they feel inside continues to deepen, they will start questioning your usefulness in their life. Their mind will start playing tricks with them and tell them that you weren't special after all. Their mind will begin telling them that you were not beautiful, rich, or powerful as they had thought. They will believe that if you were special, attractive, or influential as they thought earlier, then the void they feel inside shouldn't have resurfaced.

If you complain that they have been disappearing from your life and also giving you the silent treatment, they will call you a control freak. Anything you do at this moment will earn you negative words and criticisms. The narcissist will do everything within their powers to make you feel that the problem is you. At a time, you will start thinking that you are the one that's causing problems.

You will start doing a soul-search to pinpoint where you had gone wrong. Just a few days, weeks, or months back, your narcissistic partner was such a sweetheart. This thought will make you want to have that sweetness you enjoyed sometime back. You will start putting up your best behavior; you will even become clingier.

The irony is that the more you try to cling to this person, the more they withdraw from you. You will start looking for their attention more and begin to ask to understand what's truly happening. If you continue trying to know what you did wrong or why your narcissistic partner has been pulling away from you, they will accuse you of being controlling. The narcissist will continue to treat you like an emotional punching bag.

the narcissist takes joy in inflicting pain on others. The same way they feed on the attention and admiration they get from others; they also feed on the misery they cause others. If the narcissist is not getting admiration from you, which they can feed on, then they want to see you in distress. As long as they are the ones causing you the misery, it gives them the same high that getting admiration from you will give them.

It is this indifferent, cruel, sadistic, and unfeeling person that you fell in love with. You thought you found the love of your life, but that was a lie. The narcissist was wearing a mask, now, the mask has been taken off, and the true nature of the narcissist has been revealed. At this point in time, you will desperately want the person you fell in love with. However, since the character you fell in love with never existed, things will never be the same again. You will either learn to cope with this partner (not recommended) or find your exit.

Since the narcissist feeds on the misery they are causing you, they will never take responsibility for their actions. They will never apologize to you for anything or any reason whatsoever. They don't care about you – it had always been about them, but you didn't know, or you were tricked into believing that they loved you.

Remember, narcissism is a disorder, it makes the sufferer incapable of forming healthy long-term bonds with another ordinary person. If you don't understand how people with the disorder operate, you will be at a loss as to how cruel your partner or lover had become. During this devaluation of your relationship, the narcissist will only see you as an object whose value is on a continuous decline.

The interesting thing about the narcissist is that no matter how much they have devalued you, they will not easily ask you to leave or throw you out of their house. It is quite rare to see a narcissist that throws partners out that easily. Remember, they are often quite envious – they will think that throwing you out will mean that some other person will come in and treat you better.

Also, the narcissist feeds on the misery they are causing – so, they will not throw you away. They want to keep you close, make sure they cause you emotional torture and watch you be in misery. It gives them a form of emotional high.

Chapter 9. Divorcing a Narcissist

A divorce is a legal procedure that ends a marriage in the eye of the law and therefore ensures that assets can be divided up fairly and equally between partners. If you have children, they will also help you to come to a custody arrangement, which is fair for both partners and above all else, fair for the child/children.

However, in the situation that you find yourself in, it's important to look for specialist legal assistance if at all possible. This part is going to help you understand why specialist legal help, e.g., a divorce attorney who understands narcissistic behavior and the behavior and challenges that are likely to crop up during a divorce of this kind.

The Importance of Finding Out Information Beforehand

Before you say anything to your partner, make sure that you do your research and find out what you are entitled to. This is something we have already talked about, but it will give you confidence and also ensure that the route you have planned to be smoother than otherwise. If you simply jump in and expect everything to work out how you want it to, you might have a few surprises, and not particularly pleasant ones at that.

However, if you do your research and work out what you're entitled to, identify what you're going to do, and get all your plans organized, you'll find your route ahead will be far smoother as a result.

This also means doing your research into which particular professionals may be able to help you. Thankfully we have the Internet available to use 24/7 and this means you can find out useful and important information on anything you want to know, without really trying too hard.

A search of the local divorce attorneys in your area will give you plenty of options, but you can then narrow your search down by contacting the ones you think might be best for you and asking questions about anything you need to know. Many attorneys will offer you a consultation appointment and there may or may not be a fee for this. Again, this is something you need to find out beforehand.

The bottom line is that a divorce from a narcissist is a little different to a divorce from someone who doesn't have narcissistic tendencies. This is a divorce which has a very high likelihood of conflict, and one which may have twists and turns which probably wouldn't appear in what we could probably call a "regular" divorce. For that reason, you need to be confident in your future plan and have everything you want in front of you. This will help you to avoid going back on your decision, which is a very real possibility when a narcissist starts to turn on the charm, or even the abuse.

How a Specialist Divorce Attorney Can Help You

So, how can a divorce attorney who has specific experience in dealing with narcissists actually help you?

The bottom line is that they understand NPD, and that is a huge advantage in your court. They know that your partner is likely to try and say anything and as a result, they can be prepared for it and know how to deal with it. That's not to say an attorney who doesn't have experience of narcissism wouldn't be able to help you, but if you want the best chance of a successful outcome, and one which is less stressful and upsetting on you, a professional with this type of experience is a good idea.

This doesn't mean that this type of attorney has any other qualifications in the law field; it literally all comes down to experience and knowledge. It could be they have studied psychology or personality disorders as a separate line to their law-based work and that helps give them extra information about the situation you may find yourself in.

As we mentioned earlier, a divorce from a narcissist is also likely to be quite high in conflict, so looking for a divorce attorney who has experience in dealing with conflicts and resolving them in a fair and careful way is a plus point.

To summarize, the advantages of opting for a specialist divorce attorney are:

- They understand NPD and therefore understand the challenges you face and the treatment you have been subjected to over the year.

- They have experience in dealing with conflicts and they have specific skills to help resolve high conflict situations.

- They know what to expect from NPD, so can possibly help to predict the challenges that might lie ahead.

Of course, you also need to be sure that any divorce attorney you opt to work with is within your budget, and that means doing extra research. It's worthwhile going for what you really can afford in this situation, as your divorce attorney is the single best person to deal with this problem from the start, and therefore take the workload and the stress away from you. You have dealt with enough, and if you can reduce your own problems after the decision to walk away from your marriage, you should certainly do that.

Be Honest About Everything And Work Out Your Case

Once you've found a divorce attorney who can help you and someone you feel comfortable with, it is vital that you tell them as much as you possibly can. The more open and honest you are, the more your attorney can help you. If you hold anything back, your partner might decide to twist that detail in court and as a result you're left in the dark, because your attorney isn't able to help you on the spot.

It's likely to be painful having to open up about the abuse you have dealt with at the hands of your ex and it's very normal to feel perhaps even a little embarrassed, but you have to push this aside. You have nothing to be ashamed of, nothing to be embarrassed about, and you really just need to open up and give your attorney as much information to work with as possible. By doing this, they will be able to prepare themselves for whatever your ex throws at you during the divorce proceedings. As we've already mentioned, you should expect the worst and hope for the best, and you can help your attorney prepare for the worst by giving them as much information as possible, whether you struggle to give graphic details about it all or not.

From there, sit down with your attorney and work out your case. What do you want? What are your hard lines? If you have children, what are you prepared to do in terms of custody arrangements? Thinking about assets, how do you want to split things and how are you going to work out what goes to who?

At this stage, you're not deciding; this will be decided in the divorce courts, but you can lay out your offer and as a result your attorney can get to work on making sure that you have a case which has the best chance of giving you what you really want in the end.

It can be difficult to sit down and tell a relative stranger about what you have endured at the hands of your partner over the years, but it's something you have to try and be brave about and just do. The more information you can give, the better prepared your attorney will be, and that greater the chances of a quick and successful outcome for you.

Chapter 10. How to Start Responding

There comes a point in time when you need to cease thinking about what you are losing and begin to think about what you will get by leaving the relationship. This is because, the longer you stay in the relationship, the harder it will be for you to get your serenity.

If life was similar to romance movies, the one we fall in love with would be the one to make us happy. However, in reality, things tend to go differently. We fall in love, let our guard down, and someone takes advantage of this to hurt us multiple times. Yes, it is fine to fight for a relationship, but when the relationship is a toxic one, you need to learn when to say enough. This is because if you don't, the damage it will cause you down the line can be irreversible.

Love can seem like an addiction, and like all addictions, there are healthy and unhealthy ones. Relationships, are also the same. And harmful relationship addictions can break down a person in the most negative ways. A relationship that is toxic and filled with emotional abuse, hostility, danger to you, and other toxic behaviors, are the most difficult to leave. In theory, they should be easy to walk away from, but practically, this is not the case. And this is why it is essential for you to walk away as fast as possible, because the longer you stay, the harder it is to let go.

Knowing When to Say Enough and Walk Away

There are instances when the signs are apparent. These could range from cheating, physical, and emotional abuse, continuous criticism, among others. Sometimes the signs may be as mild as lack of intimacy, perpetual heartache, and loneliness.

It is hard to leave any relationship, including toxic ones. It requires a tremendous amount of strength and energy to say enough and let go of a toxic relationship. So, what do you need to do to help you through the process of saying enough? The steps we will be covering in this portion can be of help.

Stay in the Present

It is tempting to live in the memories of your relationship. For instance, how the relationship used to be. The same applies to living in the future. That is hoping that things in your relationship will get a lot better or fantastic. However, if you need to find the strength to leave a toxic relationship, you need to live in the now or present. To do this, experience the entire relationship for what it is at that moment. Doing this will help you see how damaged or toxic the relationship you are trying to save is.

When you constantly look at the relationship the way it once was or the way you hope it would be, to convince yourself to stay, then there is a problem. See the relationship for what it is presently, and it will be less complicated for you to make your choice.

Have a Record

Keeping track of how the relationship makes you feel can be another excellent means of helping you decide. Keep a journal which comprehensively states everything you feel in the relationship. You need to include the day to day events of the relationship over a specific period. If you don't enjoy writing, it is also possible to take advantage of pictures to help you with this. Take a photograph of every vital moment in a relationship that brought out either a bad or good reaction from you. Do it for a specific period which could be 1 -2 months, or weeks, depending on what is suitable for you.

After the set period, go through your records and answer the following questions:

- Are the feelings mostly good or bad?

- How often do these feelings take place?

- Is there a pattern?

- Is it a continuous or rare occasion?

- Do you love the person you have become?

If you used pictures:

- Do you look happy or lively or drained out in them?

- Do you seem sadder than usual?

Providing answers to these questions can let you view the relationship the way it is. Without the excuses and paddings, you use to make it more appealing to yourself. In the end, you will see things with more clarity and make the right decision.

Observe What Your Body Says

The mind and the body are interconnected. The connection they each share is one that is quite powerful. If you block off the messages and signs that your mind or gut tries to tell you, then your body takes up the role. You will observe some feelings and signs in your body like tension and heaviness, among others. Also, the way it works will change.

To determine what your body is saying, ask yourself the following:

- Do I feel physical pain in my body?

- Is there a feeling of heaviness in my body?

- Does my body ache?

- Does it look like I am losing weight?

Providing accurate answers to these can help you see the relationship for what it is.

What Is Your Coping Mechanism?

Look within yourself; do you have any coping mechanisms to ensure you don't feel terrible? Or what behaviors have you adopted to help you in the relationship?

As opposed to not dealing with the terrible feelings that arise, try to examine them. When you deal with the pain you are feeling; you will get the strength, bravery, and wisdom you require to be able to say enough.

Put a Deadline in Place

When you hope something to improve in the future, it is not difficult to forget how long you have been waiting. To place a deadline, select a specific period, be it a few weeks, months, or even a day. You need to pick a deadline that you feel is ideal for you. During this period, do all you can for your relationship. Put in as much energy as you can into it until you exceed the period you have set aside for yourself. Then observe the results, and you will find the answer you need.

Get Out of Your Role

In all relationships, each partner picks up a role over time. This is more like a pattern which keeps the relationship going and allows each partner to maintain their behavior. This does not imply that you are responsible for being treated the way you are being treated, especially if the relationship is one that is toxic. However, it does mean that you have picked up a particular way of behaving that makes it easy for you to bear the unhealthy relationship.

In toxic relationships, there is a victim, and there is an abuser. You need to determine what your exact role is. Are you the rescuer? Or the one who keeps giving excuses for the other? Determine your role and try to get out of it. By changing the dynamic this way, it will ensure the unhealthiness in your relationship is more apparent, making it less complicated for you to say enough, and leave the relationship. At the very least, you may trigger a positive change in your partner.

Leave the Imagination Behind

When you fantasize about the possibilities of the future, it can result in you being tied down to a relationship which is toxic. Holding on to fantasies will prevent you from seeing things as they really are. Because you believe things can get much better, as you have seen in your fantasies, you will keep trying until you can try no more.

The more you allow your imagination to rule you, the more you try to change your reality to match your fantasy. The same applies even if you are in an unhealthy relationship. Your imagination will push you to hold on longer than you usually should, even if the relationship is a toxic one. If the way you imagined your relationship was going to become a reality, it would have changed already. So, let go of the imagination, and you will see things for how they are, which in turn will give you the energy to say enough.

Defend Your Well-being

By prioritizing yourself, you will indirectly give yourself the energy to fight for you. Everyone, including you, deserve happiness, but in most instances, you will have to fight for the joy you actually want. Give yourself a priority and fight to get the best treatment for yourself in a relationship. When you observe it is not something your existing relationship will offer you, you will get enough energy to walk away.

Stop the Excuses

It is perfectly normal for us as humans to give excuses for those we love. This becomes particularly heightened when we are in a relationship with that person. However, doing this excessively does not make one see the relationship for what it is and can make you stay longer than you should in a toxic relationship.

Search within yourself. Have you ever gotten what you desired from this relationship? How does your desire differ from what you presently have? Does it feel like you are being loved or treated right?

In a healthy relationship, even when arguments arise and we say and do things out of anger, you can still feel the respect and love behind it even during the hard times. Once you stop making excuses for your partner, you will be able to see the relationship more clearly and see it for what it is.

Unhinge Your Mind

If in your mind, you genuinely believe you can't leave, then it will be difficult for you to do so. Do not limit yourself by constantly believing that you can't leave. Change your mindset and tell yourself you can leave when you want to. Make your choices based on what you want, not based on what you think you can't do. By changing your mindset, you will get the strength you desire to make a decision that you truly want.

Take Courage and Make a Decision

Lastly, take courage and make your decision. And whatever you choose to do, ensure you own the choice you make, knowing you were responsible for making this decision. If you don't make a decision now, it may seem fine for a while; however, over time, it will keep you tied down, and without the strength you require to say enough and leave this toxic relationship.

Besides, note that if a relationship feels toxic and unhealthy for you, then it probably is. At this point, you can fight as hard as you can to fix your relationship. However, when you have no more energy to keep on fighting, you will see things clearly, as they are.

Chapter 11. How to Deal with a Narcissist in Court

This only applies if you are dealing with an extreme or malignant narcissist who truly wants to gaslight you and destroy your world. As you may have learned by now, there are people like this in existence. Some narcissists really do have zero empathy and enjoy inflicting severe chaos and intended suffering on others. If you find yourself needing to take your ex to court, therefore, it is wise to become knowledgeable on how to do so.

First let's briefly explore the reasons why you would need to beat or expose a narcissist in the court system.

• Financial manipulation, theft or monetary losses as the result of their narcissism.

• Family and domestic disputes with children involved.

• Question of resources, assets, shared business or joint ventures.

• In extreme cases, physical abuse as a devolution of their mental, emotional and psychological abuse inflicted.

• Any consequence of their 'evil' and cruel nature. Remember, malignant narcissists can be truly heartless.

❏ What you should know: They've found your wound. They have infected your wound with negativity! Your wounds are what feeds them, so find healing and put boundaries up. Focus on yourself and not them. This enables you to stay connected to your story and not dragged into theirs.

❏ Deflect! Deflect their 'evil' (unbelievably sadistic and harmful) intentions. Don't allow them to get into your personal boundaries. Be wise and take preventative measures for your protection. Engaging in some meditative or mindful activity leading up to court can really help with this.

❏ Don't expect them to play fair. Assume the worst-case scenarios- put yourself in their shoes and see all perspectives. How would the worst person in the world word things and try and play it? What angles do they have on you? Take a step back and see the big picture, including all the negative, shadow and dark parts. You may be kind, decent and a lovely human being but the narcissist will pick the tiniest negative and amplify it for their own gain (and your destruction). Be in the know and wise.

❏ Recognize their arrogance and misplaced confidence. Remember, the narcissist is feeding and playing off some distorted truths and out of place perspectives. Their reality is made from these distortions and elements which can potentially destroy you and your world. Recognizing that a lot of what they say, perceive and attempt stems from some delusion, illusion or false belief can help you overcome the effects effectively and efficiently.

❑ Do not try to expose them as a narcissist! This is vital and crucial to your success. Trying to expose them or label them just looks like 'finger- pointing.' Instead, be humble and actively practice humility, staying centered in your own reality and truth. Trying to expose them in a negative light is essentially attracting negativity to yourself (where awareness goes, energy flows.)

❑ People will be susceptible to kindness and seeing the positive. Respect is given to those who respect others and choose to act with kindness, not engaging in negative talk. Being sophisticated, courteous and completely truthful in your words and dealings ultimately makes you appear as the best version of yourself, and naturally exposes the narcissist.

❑ Adopt the principle: "respond, don't react." Allow him or her to lie and remain calm yourself. Maintaining calm even when the narcissist is blatantly lying or speaking badly about you, trying to represent you in a false light, is the best and most powerful way to get your message across. The words and actions of a narcissist are never on the same page- allow it play out. Allow them to speak untrue. Focus on the facts and actions, as real actions speak louder than any mistruths or manipulations. In other words, do not resist or react to your partner's story and intended mistruths, as the facts will come to light.

❏　　Put the abuse, neglect and manipulations in the spotlight, not the fact that he or she is a narcissist. Again, facts are very important and as much as an emotionally loving and compassionate- insightful society and court system would be ideal, the emotional layers and undertone are overlooked. Do not explain narcissism in any way! The style of manipulating truth from the narcissist can be so effective that it is more significant than truth itself.

❏　　There is great power in silence. Silence provides space for truth and hidden things to come to light. Regardless of what is being said against you, the most effective thing you could do for yourself is to be silent simply. All of your partner's darkness, shadow, lies and buried anger will come powerfully to the forefront. Quite simply, the narcissist cannot stay silent in the midst of truth. They get worked up into anger and self-rage as a result of their lies and manipulations being exposed. The calmer you are the more they will fall apart. This cannot be stressed enough.

Chapter 12. Mourning, Grieving and Letting Go

One of the most challenging types of relationships to end is one with a narcissist, and there are numerous reasons for this. For many individuals, the kindness, loyalty, and desire to keep the promises they have made along the line, make it extremely difficult to do so. The narcissist can also make leaving a problematic process because he wants to be the one to call the shots in the relationship, including when it has to do with ending it. So long as the victim believes keeping the relationship going is a vital element to their lives, the narcissist will have the freedom to control them and the choices they make.

For many individuals in a relationship with a narcissist, the breaking point is when the narcissist performs a specific action that they won't tolerate. However, for many victims, this breaking point differs. However, male victims of a narcissistic relationship are not as likely to leave in comparison to female victims. This may be due to the additional weight of responsibility culturally felt by men to see to the needs of women.

Notwithstanding, when a victim of a narcissistic relationship does take the step to leave, they find it hard to stick to the choice they made. This is mostly a result of pity and guilt they feel for the narcissist. Besides, if the narcissist fails to let the victim leave, they will continuously pressure the victim to have a change of heart, frequently with the typical promise to change and do better, which is often not true. The narcissist can make the life of the victim trying to leave the relationship very stressful so as to keep dominating them alongside the relationship.

Do Narcissists Ever End the Relationship First?

There are situations where a particular circumstance will urge the narcissist to end the relationship. These may include events which change the way life is for either the narcissist or the victim. If the victim falls severely sick, unable to move or not able or willing to go on with the life that has been created by the narcissist any longer, this may urge the narcissist to end the relationship. There are times where good events like having a new kid can change the power dynamics in the relationship. This is common in instances where the narcissist has to show more empathy or become more responsible. Some factors that can make the narcissist end the relationship abruptly with a victim include loss of a job, old age, illness, or a promotion at work.

However, for many victims, the narcissist never leaves and sticks like glue, continuing to dominate the victim as he or she so pleases. How then do you leave the relationship in this instance? Below, we will be looking into a few helpful things that can help make this process a seamless one.

Complete Detachment

The first step, of course, will be to end the relationship, and once you do this, you need to ensure you do not remain in contact. This is extremely crucial because, at this point, you are still in search of closure and want answers to what went wrong. This applies even if you know deep down that no response will arise, and this individual still makes you vulnerable.

You need to remember how you found yourself in the position you are in the first place. Do not put yourself through the process of abuse and incessant pain once again. You need to behave like this individual is not on the same planet as you, which in a way is correct. The individual you are yearning for now is only a smokescreen. Stick to that and make sure you keep them closed out totally.

The narcissist will certainly make efforts to reach out by every means possible. Block their numbers and divert all emails to the junk folder. You need to ensure they do not have access to you at their bidding anymore, as the narcissist will try everything possible to get you back.

If there are kids in the equation, you may need to get the help of a third party who will act as an intermediary if you can. If this is not possible, remember to exercise caution and never meet up by yourself with the narcissist you just barely escaped from. You can get the assistance of a qualified therapist to help you put a parenting plan in place. This is a document which is legally binding and has information about financial responsibilities, time-sharing for the kids, and means of reaching out allowed by both parties involved. This can further help ease the process.

Unfriend Mutual Friends

A friend of your narcissistic partner may not be aware of his lifestyle, and they may tell you that you're making a mistake by leaving him. They'll begin to tell you all he has accomplished and why you should have stayed. To prevent hearing about your partner and how he's doing, cut ties with anyone that keeps discussing him even after you made it clear you don't want to hear anything about them. Unfriend them to keep your sanity and if possible, go somewhere far. Narcissists are very good at persuasion and pretense, and they can send a close friend to make you change your mind, knowing the friend does not know them as much as you do.

Write Down the Things that Made You Leave

Due to the deceitful nature of narcissists, you may find yourself reminiscing on the good times you spent with them.

This is why you need always to remember the bad times too. The times that the narcissist made you feel worthless and guilty about what he's supposed to be blamed for.

Remember the times that they made you cut ties with your family and the times you question your sanity because you believed you were going crazy. Most notably, remember when you were manipulated and lied to even when you knew it was all lying, and the narcissist told you it was your mind playing tricks on you. Put all these down in a diary and keep safe. Whenever you start remembering the good times in the relationship, get the journal, and read it.

Remember That Narcissists Heal in a Short Period

Narcissists are very good at getting someone new as soon as you leave. They do not waste time before healing from breakups, and sometimes, they already have a preplanned exit strategy. This is how the narcissists believe they can win the game - since the relationship is a game to them.

Avoid Being Tempted to Stay

Narcissists always try to win back their victim by telling them sweet things. They'll leverage on the fact that they're aware of your weaknesses and use this to sweet talk you into coming back to them. Spend time alone and have a serious reflection about past events. This will enable you to understand yourself better, and you'll recognize any form of deceit when you see it.

Avoid being coerced into changing your mind, as narcissists are very good at coercion. They'll tell you what you want to hear at that moment, but it's all part of their game plan. As soon as you accept and go back to them, be ready for another dose of mistreatment, abuse, and emotional blackmail. It's best not to bother going back when you leave, even if you need to pick an essential item you left behind. If you must visit again, do so with caution and don't be deceived by the kind words you'll hear. Ensure you let them know you've moved on and they should do the same. Wish them the best and block their number. If you can't face them because you're not sure of yourself, do it by calling or texting them.

Forgive a Narcissistic Partner or Friend

Rather than feelings of hatred and anger towards a narcissist, look beyond the picture and understand that narcissism is a disorder. A narcissist is a weak person who devalues, degrades, and abuses their target in order to fill a void. Understanding this will enable you to leave a narcissistic person in peace without further drama. You can then easily forgive them and forgive yourself. Quit blaming yourself, as narcissists are known to be perfect manipulators and it's challenging to differentiate between reality and illusion when you're dealing with them. Yes, they're that good!

Take Time to Heal and Grieve

Yes, you need time to heal completely and grieve about who you thought your partner was. As soon as the narcissist's schemes aren't working again, you're able to really know the person you're dealing with. It may come to you as a big shock because of the kindness and affection shown to you at the early stage of your relationship. By the time you become attached and form an emotional bond with this person, you've already gone far into the relationship. However, always thank yourself and be proud of yourself for taking the bold step by leaving because the emotional abuse would have been worse if you remained with them.

Get Busy

Keeping yourself busy will help you heal faster and move on with your life. If you're not sure of what to do, you can write down a list of exciting things to do and get yourself occupied with this. You can exercise, take a walk, visit the zoo, go on a tour, learn something new or anything that makes you happy. Strive to get better at what you do and learn more. Grow as you learn and concentrate on things that'll make you happy. Ensure you move with people that share the same views and ideas with you. You can join groups on social media platforms to make this easier.

Concentrate on the Future

As soon as you leave a narcissistic person, it is essential that you concentrate on positive thoughts and energy on doing great things for yourself and people around you. Forget the past and focus more on the present. Thoughts of how to be a better you and heal faster should be your major focus at this point.

Love Yourself

You must have suffered lots of emotional trauma by living with a narcissist for months or years, and you may even have come to the conclusion that you don't deserve to be loved. That's what the narcissist has planned, and you shouldn't let it happen. Be kind to yourself and love yourself. Once you do everything to ensure you love yourself, any other person that comes your way will have to reciprocate. Self-love will help you build confidence in yourself and find love again. Don't flog yourself for too long, and ensure you always set proper boundaries.

Believe in Yourself

From time to time, you may find yourself thinking about your experience in the relationship, trying to figure out where you went wrong. This is not right! No one deserves to be mistreated as you were. Don't try to justify their actions. Believe in yourself and know the right thing for you. With time, you'll understand that you deserve a lot better than being stuck in a relationship with a narcissist. You'll regain your self-esteem and have a true understanding of who you are. Soon, you'll be compassionate to yourself and move on to healthy and happy relationships.

Chapter 13. Overcoming Loneliness After Narcissist Abuse

One of the things that you have to realize is that a narcissist does not see the need to seek help from a therapist because after all, they think that there is nothing wrong with them. Recovery is for those who have been through abuse. If you have been or are in a relationship with a narcissist, it is high time that you left and sought help for a professional. It is this kind of support that you need to rebuild your self-confidence and bounce back your self-esteem.

Trust me; you are better than you have ever thought possible. The narcissist might have managed to puncture your self-confidence and even crushed your self-esteem, but most importantly you are just a victim. You are not unworthy like they want you to believe. Finding a health professional that has a specialty in trauma recovery will help you journey through the healing process to recovery. If you are not able to leave the relationship, a therapist can also help you to learn the best ways in which you can communicate effectively with your abuser so that you can set boundaries that they will respect and hence, protect you so that they will no longer take advantage of you.

Here are some of the steps that you will have to go through to help you journey through healing to recovery.

Step 1: Cut contact

Once you have left the relationship, keep at that! Stop maintaining contact with your abuser. The main reason why you went is that the affair was not working for you. Therefore, there is nothing that will happen that makes things feel better. The best way to recover from abuse is for you to block all forms of communications.

If you have joint custody of the children, the truth is, you may not be able to wipe this person entirely from your life. It is therefore advisable to create a strict custom contact. And can only communicate on matters regarding your children using third-party channels only! Otherwise, ensure that you have set up court orders for all forms of agreements.

Think about the extreme trauma bonding, the gross abuse and the addiction that you had to the narcissist. Sometimes the best way is for you to accept that the only way you can recover from such damage is to pull away and cut your losses once and for all. Think of abstaining as a way of protecting yourself from hurt. In other words, each time you initiate contact with your abuser, you are handing them the ammunition to blow you off.

Remember that you lived with them and so they know what your weak points are and how they can wound you even more profound. It is until we heal that you will stop forcing yourself on the narcissist for love or craving them or even justifying to ourselves to give them a second chance when we completely stop contact that we can begin to heal.

Step 2: Release That Trauma So That You Begin Functioning Again

If we are going to heal, we have to be willing to reclaim our power. We have to do the exact opposite of what we used to believe; 'I can fix him/her, I will feel better.' Your power belongs inside you. The moment you take your focus away from your abuser that you will be able to channel that power into rebuilding your self-love and paying closer attention to making yourself whole again.

At first, it might seem like understanding who a narcissist is and what they do is essential. But the real truth is that these things cannot heal your internal trauma. What you need to do is to decide to let go of that horrific experience so that you can be. You will begin to rise, get relief and balance again once you have decided to take your power where it belongs-inside you.

Step 3: Forgive Yourself For What You Have Been Through

When the insecure and wounded parts of us are still in pain, we often are pushed into behaving like children who are damaged. We are often looking for people's approval and especially from our abuser, we hand our abuser the power to treat us as they see fit. And that's the time you will realize that you have given them all your resources-money, time and health. The most unfortunate thing is that while doing that, you end up hurting the people that matter the most in your life-your children, siblings, parents, and friends.

Yes, it might be hard to forgive yourself from this, but you can do that if you want to rebuild your life and everything that you lost to your abuser. By working through your healing process, you will soon find resolution and acceptance. You can move away from lacking self-love and respect to living a life full of truth and responsibility for our well-being.

You will realize that, when you forgive yourself, you acknowledge that this was all a learning curve and this is the experience you learned, and hence, you are going to use that to reclaim your life. It is when you release your regrets and self-judgments that you can start setting yourself free to realize greatness in your life irrespective of what stage we are. The point when you will begin to feel hope again, hope that will steer you forward into fulfillment and a life full of purpose.

Step 4: Release Everything and Heal All Your Fears of the Abuser and all They Might Do Next

Do you know what bait to a narcissist is? Anxiety, pain, and distress. One of the things that can perpetuate another cycle of abuse no matter how we tell ourselves that we have separated from them. It is indeed true that abusers can be relentless. In most cases, they do not like being losers. But one thing that you have to understand is that they are not that powerful and impactful as you may have thought them to be.

They need you to fear and go through pain so that they can function. Once you have healed your emotional trauma, they fall apart. Therefore, it is crucial that you become grounded and stoic by not feeding into their drama; this way they will soon wither away along with their power and credibility with them.

Step 5: Release the Connection to Your Abuser

So many people have likened their freedom from a narcissist to that of exorcism. When we liberate ourselves from the darkness that filled our beings, we are allowing ourselves to detox and let light and life to come in. If that light has to take over the shade, the darkness has to leave so that there is space for something new to come in. In the same manner, it is essential that you release all the parts that were trapped by your abuser so that you can tap into a more supernatural power, the power of pure creativity.

When you disentangle yourself from the narcissist, it is not just about cutting the cord; it is also about releasing all the belief systems that you might have associated yourself with unconsciously. It is only then that you can break free to being a new person and not a target of a narcissist.

Even though it might be tempting to seek revenge on your abuser, this is something that you have to try hard to avoid. Rage has the power of pulling you back into deeper darkness and a game that your abuser is an expert at in the first place. The best form of revenge is one in which you decide to take back your freedom and render your abuser irrelevant.

And is likely going to crush their ego, and they will be powerless that they cannot even affect you. Often are in despair when it hits that you are a constant reminder of their extinction. It is at this point that this ends and your soul contracts to allow love and healing in so that you can be whole again.

Step 6: Realize Your Liberation, Truth, and Freedom

Traditionally, we learn that loving ourselves is a very selfish act. However, when it comes to finding liberation and freedom from the hands of our abusers, it is a very critical step that allows us to take in the truth and let it set us free from captivity. Yes, it is something incredibly difficult to do, but it is a necessary step to achieving liberation.

Often, society has taught us that we are treated by others the same way we treat them. However, this is a false premise because we get treatment according to the way we treat ourselves. In other words, the measure of love that we get from others is equivalent to that we feel about ourselves.

Therefore, when we open up to healing and recovery, we are opening the doors for others to love us in reality and more healthy ways than ever before. It is this act that serves as a template by which we teach our children so that they do not carry around unconscious patterns of abuse that were passed to them by our ancestors. Only starts when we decide to take responsibility for our happiness and freedom. We slowly become the change that we would wish to see so that we can let go of being someone's victim and stop handing other people our power.

In other words, we take back our lives by doing everything necessary to aid our inner healing irrespective of what the narcissist does or does not do, something irrelevant either way. It is at this point that we can thrive despite what we have been through and what has happened to us.

Chapter 14. A Road to Recovery from Narcissistic and Psychopathy Abuse

What happens after you leave a narcissistic spouse? In time, the retaliation attempts to win you back and punitive actions will slow down or cease altogether. He/she may find a new love interest and begin the whole process with them, as they did with you. While you may be relieved to be free of their abuse, it is disheartening to see them with a new partner, and one who will most likely suffer the same fate. During this time, it's important to manage your expectations of the present and the future and take notice of your emotions and feelings as well, as they can remain strong for some time.

- Understand that it may take a long time to heal from a broken relationship, even where you no longer have regrets, and you are confident that leaving a narcissistic spouse was the correct decision. The emotional residue will linger for some time, even years, especially if you believed they were a completely different type of person at one time.

- A separation or divorce from anyone can trigger the stages of grief, whether they were toxic or not. They become a fixture in our life that is no longer there, and this is a loss that we must learn to cope with. Counseling or therapy is a good option if you find the breakup unbearable.

- Avoid getting involved in a new relationship at all costs. If you happen to meet someone who seems like an ideal match, become familiar with them as a friend first, and manage your time carefully. Starting a new relationship or dating too quickly will not resolve the feelings for your former spouse, and you may find your ability to make a sound judgment is not at its best form after a traumatic split. Take time to live with yourself and enjoy this freedom for a while before dating. In time, you'll find that you can gain a better sense of what you want and make a better decision once there are options available.

- Don't stress yourself too much, or place too many goals on your plate at once. For some people, diving into a new career, moving away or changing their life in a major way can help them move on past a painful relationship. While this may be an ideal situation, depending on individual opportunity and circumstances, it can also be the cause of new stress and worries. If you choose to move away and start a new job, stay in contact with your friends and family. Let them know how you are progressing and keep them in the loop about updates in your life. This will help alleviate the stress of stepping into unfamiliar territory and help boost your confidence.

- You do not have to prove yourself to anyone but you. Your ex-spouse may have mistreated and bullied you into losing too much weight or doing more when they said you weren't good enough. Sometimes, these hurtful words stay with us, and we carry them internally as an inner voice that pains us every time. It's important to recognize this side effect and ignore it as much as possible. You have no need to prove your worth to anyone, especially someone who is mean and abusive. It's also important to keep this in mind for future relationships, friendships, and family, who may be narcissistic or toxic in nature.

Make commitments to you. Give yourself the priority label, and if you have children, do the same with them. It's important to engage in self-care so that you feel worthy enough to make a better life for yourself and your family. Don't be too hard on yourself and take time from your daily schedule to simply relax and do nothing. Often, we weigh ourselves down with more stress than we realize, to escape from the negativity in our life.

Dating After Leaving the Narcissist

At some point in the future, when you have re-established your life and feel a renewed sense of confidence, you'll be ready to date again. This isn't always the case, as some people remain happy single, though dating can be fun, yet challenging, in a world full of online options and the ability to meet many people within a short time frame. As with any relationship, whether you have recovered from past abuse, or simply looking to avoid the likelihood of future problems, it's important to take a long, slow assessment of who you are looking for, and what you represent to them. This is a vital step to finding a healthy, strong relationship for the long-term.

- Begin with friendship. Some relationships start with passion and lots of energy, which is exciting and entrancing, though getting to know someone as a friend is more important, especially if you plan to spend a lot of time with them in the future. If they are uncomfortable with this approach, it may be a warning sign that they lack the ability to communicate well and can't hold a meaningful conversation. On the other hand, if they are eager to communicate and spend time getting to know you, it's a good sign.

- Take it slow, and don't commit too quickly. Dating is a good opportunity to get to know someone and understanding their likes, hobbies, concerns, and views on many aspects of life. You may eventually meet their family and friends as well. During this time, there should be no pressure to commit to a steady relationship, unless you are both ready. A relationship should also be fair, in that you both share and respect each other's viewpoints, even if they are different. Working through this process is further progression and shows the ability to respect boundaries and form a deeper bond over time.

- If your partner proposes marriage or wants to move in together, you may not see this as a red flag where the relationship has been strong for at least one year or longer. This also depends on the nature of how you know them: do you work together or come into contact regularly? Did you meet as complete strangers, or through friends in common? In some relationships, marriage or moving in may come early, after several months, which can be problematic. If you don't know much about them at this point, living with someone new can be an unknown path that you should avoid completely. Often, people who are codependent or unable to live alone comfortably will try to move in quickly, to "secure" their relationship with you early, before you find any faults with them. At this stage, it's best to ask them the following questions:

o Why do you want to live together so soon? We've only started dating three months ago.

o Have you thought this through? How long have you been out of a relationship before meeting me?

o I like where our relationship is going, and I'm very happy. Can we wait until we know each other better before taking this big step?

o This is a major decision. Have you thought this through? Do you have your finances in order?

o Is there anything I should know about before we move in together?

If they cannot answer any of these questions, or dismiss them as unimportant, this is a good reason to reevaluate the seriousness of their commitment. Some people may want to secure a living space because they have financial problems, or they can't cope with living in their current situation. In some cases, they may already be in a relationship with someone else and want to "escape" into a new situation because they are unable to fulfill their current responsibilities. This can lead to all kinds of nightmares, from discovering they have a spouse and kids with whom they still live, or they may have a number of other problems, even if not of their own doing, that they do not wish to divulge out of fear. You deserve to have as much information about someone before you increase the level of commitment to marriage or cohabitation. This means determining if your partner is willing to be direct and honest with you and not mislead you into false stories and lies, only to find out later they are a fraud.

Chapter 15. Finding Real Love

This can be utterly terrifying due to the fact that you were fooled once, and you will never want to be fooled in that way again. There are a lot of different things that you will need to learn, but there are also things that you will need to unlearn after being the victim of narcissistic abuse.

More often than not, people that have suffered from the hands of someone that has a personality disorder will want to learn about it.

Obviously, knowledge is power, so learning about personality disorders can help keep you safe from falling into a relationship with someone that has one.

You must understand that there are varying degrees of personality disorders and just because someone has 1 does not mean that they will not be a suitable fit for you. However, recognizing the signs of a serious personality disorder that will cause you to harm is a good way to ensure that you don't go back through the torture that was being in a relationship with a narcissist.

Not only will you have to learn a variety of different things before being comfortable stepping into a new relationship, but you are also going to need to unlearn some things. The narcissist in your life probably did a pretty good job at twisting and warping your reality. Undoing the damage that they have done will take time, but it is completely possible. You will likely need to take a step back from yourself and look at each experience with the narcissist individually so that you can see the truth of what actually happened. It is quite likely that you have already worked through that process if you are considering looking for a new partner at all.

Deciding to date after leaving a narcissistic relationship is something that can be extremely difficult as it can take years to truly heal and work through all of the obstacles that come along with narcissistic abuse. Don't be afraid to discuss what is on your mind with your friends, family, and therapist. It is fairly likely that your thoughts and ideas about love and relationships are still a little bit skewed and getting other's opinions on the situation can make it clearer as to what the right choice for you is.

When you are starting to consider dating again, you should take the time to brush up on the red flags that help you easily see that someone is a narcissist. You should also take the time to remember what your relationship with the narcissist was like in the beginning. More often than not, the beginning is a time that felt positive with your ex and examining it can show you some of the early signs pinpointing a person as a narcissist.

Let's take a look at a variety of different red flags that try to clue you in that someone is a narcissist. If you see these traits in someone you are considering dating, you are better off to run for the Hills rather than think it is a fluke or that you can change them.

One of the first red flags that you should watch out for is people that have a showy, flashy, or larger than life attitude. If you would make this statement about someone that you have never met anyone like them or it's like they are a magnet, you should be leery. If you genuinely like someone, you will be able to explain what it is about them that you like. So, the inability to explain what it is that draws you to a person is a red flag that they may not be relationship material.

Another huge red flag is when someone expresses their love for you after a short amount of time. If you have not been dating someone for very long, you should be concerned if they are committing themselves to you. It takes time for love and serious feelings to develop, so if you see that somebody is rushing in and telling you that they love you quickly, it is a pretty good clue that it will lead to an unhealthy relationship.

Love bombing is another major red flag that you absolutely need to pay attention to. If someone is showing you in an overwhelming amount of adoration or attraction without a core that is emotional, you should be concerned. Many narcissists use love bombing to manipulate and gain control over a person. It is actually quite surprising how often it works. If an alarm bell is setoff inside of you because someone is paying you an overwhelming amount of attention, you should listen to what your intuition is telling you and stay away from that person.

All of us have at least a few stories about our crazy ex-relationships. If the person you are interested in only has stories that are negative or expresses that they have only been in relationships that are toxic, you should see this as a red flag. More often than not, when people talk this way about their past relationships, they will take no accountability for the problems that or present. As you know, narcissists are unable to take responsibility or accountability for their actions, so if they don't have any positive things to say about the former relationships, and you need to distance yourself from them right away.

The last red flag can easily be observed if you sit back and take a look at how your prospective partner treats other people. Pay attention to how he treats waiters and waitresses at restaurants. You should also take notice of how they speak about the opposite sex. If they show disrespect for those around them, it can be a great warning sign that you are dealing with a narcissist.

This is a pretty decent look at the different red flags that you need to get familiar with to determine whether or not your prospective mate is a narcissist. There is a plethora of different traits that you may witness.

The best thing you can do to ensure that you don't end up in another relationship with a narcissist is to be mindful of your experiences. Try and stay present at the moment so that you have a good understanding of what is actually transpiring in front of you.

Making sure that you are connected with your mind, body, and soul will also help you avoid entering into another narcissistic relationship. There is a massive amount of intuition stored inside of us. When we learn to listen to what our bodies are telling us, it can seriously help us avoid the negative consequences of getting into a toxic relationship.

Getting in touch with your inner self is not a difficult process, but it will take a bit of time. Most people find that meditation is one of the best ways to find that connection and provide yourself with the ability to interpret what your body is telling you. Your subtle body will notice red flags and negative traits in a person well before your conscious mind will be able to. This makes it pretty easy to see why connecting with yourself is so important in making sure that you are choosing a healthy person to be in a relationship with.

You should always keep in mind that intuition works in both directions.

It can alert you when you are in a situation or around a person that is unsafe, and it can also clue you in when you are in front of a great match. When you are in tune with your body, recognizing the signals that it provides you with is relatively easy. You then simply need to remember to listen to what it is saying.

When you are in a relationship with a narcissist, it tends to do a lot of damage to a person's sense of reality and sense of self. You may not be able to easily recognize your personal feelings, preferences, or even your own opinions after leaving a narcissist. So, you will need to spend a lot of time reflecting on who you actually are. As you sit back and remember the things that you like and the things that you enjoy, you will start to remember who you actually are. You have to let go of the manipulation that was used to change all of your opinions so that they matched the desires of the narcissist.

When you are trying to reclaim your life, it is incredibly important that you take the time to remember who you are. There is no preference too small for a narcissist to try and change so, relearning all of the things about you that you used to know may be a difficult task, but it is necessary so that you can move on.

One of the best ways to find your true self and reconnect with your true thoughts, feelings, and ideas is to meditate and ask yourself some very basic questions. You want to ask yourself things like:

- What are the things that I truly enjoy doing?

- What things in life Do I dislike?

- What is my favorite food?

- Which season is my favorite?

- What is my favorite color?

- What are the things in life that I am truly good at?

These are only a few examples of the basic questions that you should start to ask yourself so that you can re-identify the person that you truly are. It may seem ridiculous to ask yourself such basic questions, but realistically, your narcissistic abuser could have easily warped your opinions so that they matched their own personal thoughts. It is really quite amazing how many things you can rediscover about yourself once you have stepped away from the narcissistic abuser that was in your life.

Creating a Healthy Relationship

Creating and maintaining a healthy relationship is not quite as hard as everyone makes it out to be. If you have suffered from narcissistic abuse, you may have very little faith in the fact that you can enter in and sustain a healthy relationship. It is totally normal to feel this way, but if you take the time to grieve and heal, eventually, you'll be able to see that healthy relationships are not a thing of fallacy.

We are going to look over the different elements that will help you create a healthy and long-lasting relationship. Some of these things are quite basic, but they're also extremely important. It is very likely that the things on this list will all be the opposite of what you have experienced while in a relationship with a narcissist.

This can make it hard to believe, but somewhere inside of you, you will know that it is true.

One of the first steps in creating a healthy relationship is to learn how to love yourself. When you are comfortable with the person that you are, you will lead a happier life, and this will impact your relationship in a positive way. Learning how to love yourself after experiencing narcissistic abuse takes time and patience.

Chapter 16. Personal Growth and Healing

Approve of yourself: True freedom comes in realizing that it is no one's job to approve of us or understand us. Rather, it is our own job to approve of us, appreciate us, and motivate us constantly. One of the major reasons why we are unable to love ourselves unconditionally is that we give other people too much power to have a say in our lives. We believe in their voices as the truth of who we are. We keep our hearts wide open for other people's judgment of us, yet we hold the greatest power to explore our deepest worth and stick on this. Therefore, realize that everyone has their own opinion of who you are but that it is your own opinion that counts. You are who you believe you are.

Do not be too hard on yourself: If you are too hard on yourself, you will always justify your personal criticism. You will always think like a perfectionist who tends to have no rooms for mistakes. You will even beat yourself up for the errors that have insignificant consequences on you. Even after correcting a mistake, you will always punish yourself. Also, you will always prioritize other tasks ahead of your self-care. Also, you will justify other people's actions when they treat you poorly because you think you deserved that treatment.

Therefore, do not be too hard on yourself. Learn to let your past mistakes go. You probably did not know the best techniques with which to handle things, you probably did the best you could, or you feel you could have done better. However, the past is in the past. That is where it belongs, and this is where you are now. You have grown, you have learned more, and you can start living differently now. Forgiving yourself will teach you to forgive others also. You will be able to eliminate negativity and low self-esteem and have meaningful relationships with others.

Love others and be kind to them: Do not turn people down or downplay their efforts. Seize criticizing others because you will realize that they are doing better, and this will deny you happiness. Be kind to others because you do not understand their struggles. As the universe has it, your life is a reflection of what you give out. Give out love, and you will be able to appreciate and love yourself more.

Do your mirror work: It might look inconsequential, but looking at yourself in the mirror to get in contact with your own eyes allows you to appreciate yourself more than anyone else can. It opens the gate into your heart because it is at this moment you are able to appreciate your beauty and speak life into yourself.

Nourish your mind with knowledge and wisdom: Seek to equip yourself with knowledge and wisdom, and you will become unbeatable. Research on anything you want to understand. In the world today, learning materials have become so close to us through the internet. Instead of using the internet and social networking sites for just fun and filling your mind with things that only turn you down, use it for the benefit of yourself and become knowledgeable. You will understand more things, and you will become more confident in the person that you are.

Daily affirmations: "I am wonderful," "I am able," "I am blessed," "I can do it"—these phrases can do magic in your life and turn everything for your favor. If there is someone who talks to you more than any other person in the world, it is you. Why not take this chance to love yourself and improve yourself? Make sure that the words you tell yourself speak life to your soul.

Also, remember that the mouth speaks whatever is abundant in your heart. Therefore, ensure that your heart harbors positive thoughts even though the outside environment feels tough. Whatever you can speak, believe that you can achieve, and you will. The power of the tongue has it that whatever comes out of your mouth determines how things turn out in your life.

Do something that you are good at often: One of the things that discourage us most is the failure to achieve anything that we set out to do. Although it is good to challenge ourselves with big goals and achieve far much higher than our expectations, it is also good to balance such goals with doing things in which we are very good at.

Therefore, set achievable goals that will make you proud. Sometimes goals that are challenging get us exhausted, and there is no chance or willpower for self-love. Consequently, our burdens and exhaustion reflect on how we treat people we relate with frequently and mostly our partners. Also, it lowers our self-esteem, and we begin to envy people who have already achieved such big goals, forgetting that it took them a lot of time and consistent efforts to get there.

Collect the good stuff: Self-love is a result of consistent efforts to create a storehouse of positivity. If something is good and it makes you feel good, keep it. The essential meaning behind this is to have a place you can always go and find the symbols of the things that make you feel good. Be it a notebook, a personal box, or a folder in your computer, have a place where you can point out all the stuff that makes you proud in your life. These can be as minor as the smallest gifts you have received, certificates of merit, nice messages you have received, pieces of writing that you feel good about, or pictures that give you good memories.

Surround yourself with positive energy: Once you declutter your life as explained above, you should seek to establish strategic connections (such as a mentor), create more time for family and friends, and be with a partner who loves you for you. Such are the things that keep you motivated and lead you into exploring your higher potential. It is directly linked to feeling happy and valued. Being exposed to criticism and often looked down upon is not healthy for our souls, after all. Therefore, you should learn to surround yourself with people who love you for who you are.

Essentially, make sure you love yourself unconditionally and at all times. By loving yourself, you will become more confident, and you will not be prone to unnecessary triggers for jealousy, and you will be more powerful to overcome jealous emotions whenever they attack you.

Chapter 17. Self-Love and Self-Care Recovery Plan for Healing and Moving Forward

Breaking up with a narcissist does not mean it is over. In fact, the pain begins. Being intimate with an individual whose only goal is to dominate you, lie to you, and manipulate you at every turn leaves a lot of negative mental impacts down the road. These are abusive attitudes which can leave behind effects that can last for numerous years. In worse situations, the victim never recovers from the impact.

Lots of individuals who have never come across a narcissist before, usually do not understand how they operate. Narcissists, as we learned earlier, can quickly move from intense love to hate continuously till they no longer have any feelings for their prior partners. This is in contrast to normal individuals like the victim who will require time to get over a breakup and perhaps a healing process.

For individuals who have gone through this kind of abuse consistently, their mental well-being can change drastically.

Normal individuals in a relationship may try all they can to fix the relationship, even at their detriment. This is the actual behavior of one who is in love. However, when it comes to narcissists, these are not applicable as many of them do not feel any form of empathy. That is why it is difficult for victims when the relationship ends. For this reason, it is vital to know how to get over this painful stage and get your life back on track.

Getting Your Life Back

When you break up with a narcissist, it usually does not end well. And in many cases, it is the narcissist who breaks off the relationship, leaving the victim to nurse their wounds. Below, we will be looking into some of the core things that make it difficult to move on when your relationship with a narcissist ends. They are the areas you need to focus on if you want to get your life back on track.

Many times, the narcissists tell the victims that they were responsible for everything that took place in the relationship. This was probably the same case in your relationship, and you must have believed this. Having thought that the relationship ending was your fault, you then breed the notion that it is your responsibility to correct them. Then, you start making efforts to alter your entire being, all in a bid to become who your narcissist ex wants you to be so you can get them back.

However, this couldn't be more wrong. Regardless of who you try to be, it will never be enough for the narcissist. Your first goal should be to get back your energy and your being so that you can let go and get into a healthy relationship.

Ridding The Narcissist from Your Being

Having made the decision to let go and move on, you need to get rid of the version of yourself you created to satisfy the narcissist. You may have created this version of you believing that this is the best you can be. This means it is fine to put in lots of efforts in healing from the relationship initially. However, do not let it consume you. To do this, the first thing you need to do is take back your time.

Take Back Your Time

In a relationship with a narcissist filled with emotional abuse, time is the common element used to hold down the attention and affection of the victim. Time is valuable, and abusers know this, so they do all they can to ensure their victim does not have it.

Regardless of how regularly the abuser manipulated or gaslighted the victim, or continuously took charge or questioned the victim on the way they used their time, it may sometimes feel scarier for victims when they finally leave the relationship. The goal of abusers is to make you feel like you have no one, and you are lost and scared. They want you to believe that their absence will cause a massive hole in your heart, but this is not the truth. The truth is that it wasn't. But this is just the first piece of the puzzle. Over the course of your narcissist relationship, your boundaries would have been trampled on multiple times, and you will need to create them once more.

Recreate Boundaries Once More

Boundaries are vital when practicing self-love and love with others. With boundaries, you are able to state your limits, where these boundaries start and where they end. It also includes a few conditions that are applicable when you communicate with other individuals in your vicinity.

When you communicate regularly, you create healthy boundaries. These boundaries are what you use to hold the individuals who are a part of the interaction with compassion and accountability. Narcissists do not respect boundaries, and over the course of your relationship, they must have crossed your boundaries as they pleased numerous times.

However, when the relationship with your abusive narcissistic ex ends, you may feel extremely hurt. It may not immediately feel so, but now, your power to create boundaries is back. And the moment you think it is time, you can create your boundaries once more while giving yourself a priority. After creating your boundaries again, you need to remember to forgive yourself if you genuinely want to get your life back.

Absolve Yourself of Any Blame

After a relationship with an abusive narcissist ends, many victims tend to blame themselves for being the problem.

However, this is not the case as you are not to be blamed for what the narcissist did to you. Narcissists are masters of making victims feel they are all that is wrong in a relationship, which is what brings about the guilt when it ends.

But you need to remember that all the fear, shame, and guilt you are presently dealing with, is not where you should be focused on, now or even in the future. Now, you should be learning to forgive yourself for what happened as it was not your fault.

Get Knowledge

When a victim leaves a narcissist ex, it may seem very tasking to determine the next step. This is partly because, during the entire course of the relationship with a narcissist, every aspect of the victim's life was controlled by the abuser. And depending on how long a victim was forced to view the world through the perspective of the abuser or do everything the way the abuser wants; it is not abnormal to deal with confusion as to the next step to take.

For many victims, a great choice may be to go into therapy, as this is known to be a great way to heal from abuse. If this is not an option for you as a victim, there may be a lot of other resources you can take advantage of close to you. These could include seminars, classes, and workshops you can participate in which are relevant to your present situation. By doing a quick search on the internet, you can find various support groups and communities close to you. If it is not possible for you to find any of these resources that you can attend physically, there is a range of comprehensive and helpful information on the internet. There are numerous websites that offer you information on what to do after emotional abuse. Regardless of the information you pick up, it will be a vital tool that would be of help to you in the future. Now that you have the information you need; you need to remember the person you once were before the narcissist manipulated you into changing to what they wanted you to be.

Remember Who You Used to Be

Like we explained before, dating a narcissist can alter the person you are in addition to destroying your self-esteem. The goal of a narcissist is to control a person completely, and in doing that, they will make efforts to prevail over a number of the victim's feelings, desires, hobbies, and so on.

For instance, let's assume a victim always had a thing for strawberry drinks. But over the course of the relationship, the narcissist has continuously told the victim how they actually like vanilla drinks instead. Then, the narcissist goes ahead to buy these orange drinks anytime they are out and takes it further to let anyone who cares to listen that the favorite drink of the victim is indeed vanilla. Now, after a while, this may become confusing, especially with the number of manipulation and gaslighting techniques the narcissist has in their arsenal. With time, the victim may start to wonder and doubt their own preference and sanity and start to buy into the idea that perhaps he or she does love vanilla.

Even though getting rid of all these views, opinions, and methods of thinking which have been methodically ingrained in you can be quite tough, it is possible. In addition, it is very imperative you do it if you want to get your life on track. It may take a long time, but no matter what, you need to find yourself once more. How do you do this? It is not complicated in any way. You need to ask yourself a few questions like:

- What activities do I enjoy and what do I dislike?

- What is my favorite drink?

- What is my favorite show?

These and many more similar questions are needed to get you back on track. By the time you determine those things you really like and engage in them once more, you will begin to find the person you once were. With time, you will slowly get your life together and find someone else who will accept you for whom you are. The instant you remember the person you used to be, the final step will be to create your story one more time, the way you want.

Recreate Your Story

The moment you have managed to break free from your narcissistic relationship, you get the opportunity to take your story once more. Undoing the lies, the narcissist has built-in your head over the years can bring you a lot of clarity. However, it is not very easy to process emotionally.

Recreating your story should be how you want it and at your pace. If you don't feel like doing something, you don't have to force it. Just go through this process the way you want and at your pace. Remember that the narcissist abuser is no longer your priority, and only you matter now.

Recovering from emotional abuse and the damage it leaves behind is not particularly easy. The reason is that you are healing from the damage that has taken place over a long time. For some people, it could be damage through weeks or months. For others, it could be damage built over many years, and it is not abnormal for it to feel like a battle. Being emotionally abused can do that to a victim.

Chapter 18. Considerations for Children

After you have divorced a narcissist, you are still going to be facing many challenges. When children are involved, those challenges become even more difficult. Your children will need help learning how to cope with divorce and dealing with the damage their narcissistic parent has caused. Things with a narcissist are never easy, and it causes a detrimental impact on your children. Learning different strategies to help them heal and cope is going to be necessary for ensuring they lead healthy and fulfilling lives.

There is a lot of common advice that is given to parents that have gone through a divorce and have children involved; unfortunately, this advice is not going to work or apply to those of you that divorced a narcissist. Trying to co-parent with a narcissist is almost impossible. You will, more often than not, be working on reducing conflict. At this point, you realize that narcissists love drama and will do anything they can to provoke you and even your children so that they can keep playing their games of control and manipulation.

Obviously, you want to protect your children from the abuse that narcissists dish out. One of the best ways to do this is to refuse to engage with them, especially when their behavior is inappropriate. The narcissist will try for any and all attention, and whether it is negative or positive, it does not matter. So, shutting down the opportunity by disengaging is going to work well in favor of both you and your children.

Disengaging with a narcissist can be a scary thing. In theory, it should be easy, but as you well know, there is nothing easy when you have a narcissist to deal with. When they realize what you are doing, it could escalate. They may become volatile. The best thing you can do is stand your ground. Eventually, the narcissist will realize that they cannot provoke you into a battle and they will move on to another target. This can take a great amount of time so you must be patient and strong through the process.

When you are trying to disengage and keep the peace between you and the narcissistic parent, you need to remember that conversations with them need to be at a minimum. Obviously, you are going to need to talk to them about matters concerning the kids, but that does not mean that you need to talk about anything else. You must also remember that communicating with your ex does not mean you actually need to talk to them.

In today's world, there are a variety of ways to contact someone without ever speaking a word. Between text messaging, email, and social media, there are plenty of ways to communicate about the children without talking. When you speak to a narcissist, they will do their best to manipulate you through their words. This is why avoiding actual conversations is going to be advantageous. It helps to protect you and allows you time to work through your emotions instead of flying off the handle when they say something awful or outrageous.

The narcissistic parent will need to have at least one phone number that can be used when they are reaching out to the children. That is pretty much the only phone number they need. Save yourself some extra trouble and keep your private number to yourself. You can even set up an alternate email address so that they are only contacting you in one specific spot. This can cut down on the drama that the narcissist is always trying to cause.

Using email as the main source of contact between you and your ex is good for a variety of different reasons. If the narcissist decides to get nasty in an email, it gives you time to process the information before reacting to it. Additionally, it gives you hard evidence of what your ex is saying, and this could be helpful if you end up back in court for any reason.

On top of all that, it also provides you with a record of any agreements, changes to schedules, or other information that a court may need if your ex tries to start major problems.

Limiting communication between you and the narcissistic parent is going to be advantageous for your children. They will not be privy to the non-sense that your ex spews, and it won't hurt them hear you fight. So, keeping them at a distance as much as possible is good for everyone involved.

When you need to parent wounded children and help them heal, one of the main focuses you should have is on your own health. If you have survived the abuse that a narcissist causes in a relationship, you will certainly need to work on healing. The healthier you are internally, the stronger you will be able to be for your children.

Support groups and counselors should be utilized. When looking for a support group, you want to find one that specifically talks about the abuse that narcissists delve out. Support groups can help you understand how to set boundaries and stick to them. This can help you keep the focus on your personal healing and the healing of your children.

As a parent, keeping conflict at a minimum should be the main focus.

A close second is going to be making sure your children are empowered and validated. A narcissist will treat their children just as they treat everyone else. You are not going to be able to put a stop to this unless the court decides that the environment is not safe for the children.

It is almost impossible to shield your children from the toxic behaviors of their narcissistic parents.

You may think that keeping them away from the other parent is the best course of action, but realistically kids need both of their parents. Your children love both of you even if one doesn't give it back to them in healthy ways. They need to see their other parent and make decisions regarding them for themselves. It is very difficult to watch your children go through the trauma that a narcissist can cause, but you have to take a step back. If you interfere, you will likely do more harm than good. You may even end up with children that resent you because they can't understand why you would put a stop to their relationship with their other parent. So, as hard as it is, you must sit back and allow them to figure out their narcissistic parent on their own.

Even though you don't have a lot of power when it comes to your children and their other parent, you do hold power for you and your children's relationship.

When you want to do something, choose to be their biggest fan and supporter. Allow them to talk to you about anything and validate the things that they are saying and facing. Their narcissistic parent will tell them lies and manipulate them, it distorts their reality, and you need to be the one that helps keep them grounded.

When you are listening to your children and learning about their experiences, you will need to be careful not to talk badly about their other parent. Instead, try to use neutral statements like, "I'm sure it doesn't feel good to hear that" or "I'm sorry you experienced that." You can keep things neutral and simple but still support your children in the way they need to be supported and validated. You should also dote on the fact that none of the behaviors the other parent shows have anything to do with them. They are not to blame.

Structure is also going to be very helpful for children who are trying to heal from divorce and from the abuse that the narcissistic parent hands down. When you structure their lives, it can help keep them to stay in this reality.

The emotions they will go through while dealing with their narcissistic parent will be like riding a roller coaster. So, the more structure they have with you, the better off they will be. You can provide them with a sense of safety and balance, which they will need to continue to lead healthy lives.

You also want to be careful about how you handle your children, and you should do your best not to feel sorry for them. Sure, growing up with a narcissistic parent is not going to be an easy thing, but there are definitely worse situations that they could find themselves in. When we pity our children, it helps enable them to take on a victim complex and this can be detrimental to them as they grow. When you have the mentality that you are a victim, it tends to stop you in your tracks which can make moving past the problem insanely difficult. Additionally, they are more apt to end up in toxic relationships rather than searching for healthy ones.

It is likely that your narcissistic ex will become emotionally intense from time to time. They will try and goad you into getting on this ride with them, but you must refrain and take into consideration the impact all of this has on their children. Instead of playing the narcissist's game, you need to stay calm, non-emotional, and pleasant. This is going to be an extremely difficult thing to do, but you have to do your best. Practicing things like mindfulness, deep breathing, and meditation can help you find balance and calmness more easily.

When you are trying to make sure your children can traverse this tumultuous past, you are going to have to let go a little bit. This means you should limit the amount of texting and contact you have with your kids while they are with their other parent, and your ex should do the same when they are with you. Obviously, if there is an emergency, you should both feel free to reach out but other than that, you should both allow uninterrupted time with the children.

If one or more of your children are contacting you about each and every little thing that your ex is doing it is going to cause you a lot of stress and make the situation even more difficult.

When you allow your children to assert themselves to their narcissistic parent, it helps them to cope with the situation and learn how to deal with difficult people throughout their entire lives.

You will definitely be benefiting your kids in a great way if you teach them about emotional intelligence. Additionally, you should practice what you preach as it will help them understand and learn it even more. When you can give them examples of some successful single-family households that they can use to understand how the situation they are currently in should be. Helping your kids understand how to regulate their emotions and cope with the difficult things in life early is a good thing.

Chapter 19. Custody Evaluation

If you are seeking permanent custody of your children, your case will be stronger if you have custody when you file for divorce. The laws of most states say that whoever has custody when the divorce papers are filed keeps custody until the court orders something different. This is to avoid parents stealing the children back and forth from each other.

In most states, there are two kinds of custody, often called Physical Custody and Legal Custody. Physical Custody is where the children are, which parent they live with most of the time. Legal Custody involves the right to make or participate in decisions such as medical care for the child or which school a child will attend. Most states also have the concept of Joint Custody, in which each parent exercises some custody rights over the child after the divorce. The alternative to Joint Custody may be called Separate Custody.

I'll discuss different kinds of custody in more detail because they usually come into play when the final custody order is entered by the court. When I speak about "custody," unless the context indicates otherwise, I'm talking about Physical Custody—which parent the child is living with, where the child's principal residence is.

In contentious situations, to make sure there is no question of who has custody at the time of filing, I've had my client take the children and a friend with him to the courthouse. The friend sits with the kids in the car outside the courthouse while my client goes inside to file the divorce papers I prepared. However, if you plan to ask for custody, don't allow your wife to take care of the kids for six months of separation, then snatch the kids the day before you file.

One final warning: While it is best for you to have custody when you file, if you effectively try to kidnap the children or do anything that will seriously upset them to gain early custody, that will come back to bite you later. Talk to your attorney before you plan anything tricky.

You should not do the following, unless your attorney approves before you take any of these steps:

1. Move the children out of a school they have been attending

2. Start the children with a new day care provider

3. Take or send the children across a state line

Divorce is very upsetting for children. For the benefit of the children and also to demonstrate that you are a careful parent, pay close attention to their emotional reactions. Phone their teachers and day care providers and tell them about the family situation so these people are in a better position to assist your child.

If you have custody of your children and have any reason to believe your spouse might try to snatch them, school and daycare are one of the most common locations for a snatch. You need to notify the school principal, your children's teachers and day care provider about the situation and make certain it is clear who is to pick up the children. Deliver a letter stating you are in a divorce proceeding and instructing the school or day care center to release your child only to you or someone you designate in writing.

If the events leading up to the divorce have been nasty and that nastiness has affected any of your children, you will want to consider professional counseling for them. Your attorney can recommend possible counselors.

Quite frankly, some of the counseling is for the benefit of the children, but some is also to inoculate yourself against accusations that you're a careless and negligent parent.

If the laws of your state are that whichever parent has custody when the divorce papers are filed keeps custody until trial and you have such custody, you're not going to be asking the judge to change that. On the other hand, if your spouse has custody and that's not what you want, your attorney will need to file a Motion for Temporary Custody.

The Motion for Temporary Custody will state reasons why custody should be changed, so this is often the start of mud being thrown in the divorce trial.

After a motion is filed, the motion will be set for a hearing. A temporary custody hearing is no different than a permanent custody hearing. Each side presents evidence relevant to what custody arrangements are in the best interests of the children and the judge makes a decision. After a temporary custody hearing, the judge's custody order is temporary, however, and continues only until the judge enters a permanent order at the end of the case.

Usually, an attorney will want to file a motion for temporary custody quickly. If the children have been living with one parent for three months after the separation, the parent with temporary custody has a powerful argument that switching temporary custody after so long will upset the children and if the final custody order switches them back, this will cause unnecessary emotional burdens.

Many judges are not excited about hearing custody testimony twice, once for temporary custody and a second time for permanent custody. (They like the idea of multiple temporary custody hearings even less.) Sometimes, a judge will respond to a motion for temporary custody by moving the entire divorce proceeding to an earlier date on her trial docket so permanent custody can be determined. Sometimes, a judge will respond to a motion for temporary custody by ignoring it, or setting and postponing a hearing several times.

If the judge sets a temporary custody hearing quickly, it's not easy to organize compelling evidence within a few days. If you're asking for temporary custody, you want to have a good chance of winning because losing a temporary custody hearing may put you in a disadvantageous position in a later permanent custody trial.

On the other hand, a quick temporary custody hearing is just as hard for the other side to deal with. If you have some smoking gun evidence—a cell phone video of your wife in bed with her lover with your five-year-old daughter lying between them, for example, or testimony from your wife's landlord that he is evicting her because the kitchen is full of rotting garbage—you stand a better chance of ambushing your wife's lawyer at a temporary custody hearing when he is unprepared to respond to such evidence. He has had much less time to discuss damaging evidence with his client than he will have before a trial on permanent custody.

Sometimes, a Motion for Temporary Custody provides a basis for negotiation between attorneys for the parties. A hearing is going to cost both parties some significant attorney's fees and make the entire divorce more expensive. Maybe the custodial parent is discovering he doesn't like being the sole caretaker of the children as much as he thought he would. Maybe the parties can agree on a temporary custody arrangement that puts the spouse who started out without custody of the children in a better position to ask for permanent custody later. Maybe the wife will give up custody of the children if husband agrees to pay a bunch of credit card bills.

As a general proposition, more Motions for Temporary Custody are settled by negotiation than by trial, but you can't be certain that will be the outcome in your case.

You can see why beginning your divorce with custody can be so important. While each parent has an equal right to custody under the law, if the children have been living with a parent for a year and nothing terrible has happened to them, it's hard for the non-custodial parent to make a case that leaving the children in that situation permanently is a bad idea. It's also easy for the custodial parent to argue that the children have already gone through enough trauma already without adding another move and, perhaps, different schools or daycare providers and different friends in a new neighborhood to that mix.

If you want to have permanent custody of your children, starting your case with custody is important enough to defer formal filing of papers until you have custody. Usually, it's safer if you file first than waiting for your spouse to file. Your spouse can drive to the courthouse with the kids in the car just as easily as you can.

If you anticipate a disagreement with your spouse about custody, your best bet is to keep quiet about any ideas of divorcing and hire a good lawyer to help you plan a strategy that will maximize your chances of a good custody outcome.

Chapter 20. Step-by-Step Through Your Divorce

The divorce process and the entire court system can appear intimidating, but it doesn't have to be. There is an order to the way things will progress in your case, and understanding this can make you more comfortable with the process. Understanding what to expect will make the entire process easier, and you will find you have fewer questions for your attorney.

The System and the Way It Works

Because the court system can be complicated and the documents are usually written in confusing language, it's easy to feel as if you are in over your head. Once you understand what the court papers mean and how your case is going to proceed, you'll feel more organized and in control.

Initial Papers

Your divorce will begin with a petition, summons, or application for divorce filed by the plaintiff, the spouse who is bringing the case to court. The petition lists what the plaintiff is asking for (such as custody, alimony, child support, and property and debt distribution) and explains the reason for the divorce (the grounds, or indicates if it is a no-fault divorce that's being asked for). This document has to be served on the other party, meaning given to them in a way that meets the state requirements. This is often done by a process server. If you're the plaintiff, you will go over this with your attorney prior to filing.

If you're not the plaintiff (which means you are the defendant) and you are served with this kind of document, keep it in a safe place because your attorney will need it. Store all of your court documents in your accordion folder, or if you receive an electronic copy, in the appropriate folder on your computer. If you are served with this kind of document it is very important you talk to an attorney as soon as possible because there is a short time limit on your opportunity to respond. If you do not respond, the case will move forward without you.

After the petition (note that your state might call these initial papers by a different name) has been filed, the defendant has a chance to respond by filing a document called an appearance, a response, or an answer. Then the plaintiff will likely file more papers that give additional details about the divorce. These papers may be served by a process server, but if your attorney is in contact with your spouse's attorney, it is often arranged that service will be handled by the attorneys.

If you receive a petition or summons, read it over and make some notes using the form at the end of this narrative. Your spouse may be asking for things you do not agree with so make a list so you can discuss this with your attorney.

Appealing Decisions

An appeal asks a higher, more powerful court to assess the decision made by the trial court. An appellate court tackles only issues of law, not issues of fact. This means that it decides only whether or not the trial court applied the law properly correctly in the case. The appellate court does not hear any new evidence or testimony, and there are no witnesses. It is purely an assessment of the legal decision made by the trial judge.

Appeals are most common at the end of the case —after the judge has issued a final judgment. However, your attorney can appeal temporary, initial, and interim orders and decisions at any point in the case.

If you feel that the decision made in your case is wrong or unfair, discuss it with your attorney. You have only a certain period of time to begin an appeal, and if you miss the window, there's nothing you can do.

If you decide to appeal, understand that it can be a lengthy (and expensive) process. You will not need to appear at any time. Your attorney will prepare a written brief, or argument, and send it to the appellate court. Your attorney may also appear in court to give an oral argument. Because the brief focuses completely on how the law was applied in your case, there is nothing you can do to assist your attorney in preparing it.

Initial Court Appearance

A date will be set for an initial appearance, when both parties in the case must come to court. Your attorney will send you a copy of the notice or call you with the information. Make sure you keep the notice and record the date on your calendar because it is mandatory that you appear. The initial appearance may occur soon after the initial papers are filed if one of the parties is asking the court for a temporary order. A temporary order is a preliminary court order that decides certain issues on a temporary basis, such as where the children will live, whether child support will be paid, and who will remain in the marital residence while the case is pending. A short hearing may be held to decide about temporary orders.

If there are no requests for temporary orders, the initial appearance is usually a settlement conference, where the lawyers meet with someone from the judge's staff and try to reach a settlement. There may be several such pretrial conferences, and the court might suggest mediation as an alternative.

Discovery

The next stage of the process is discovery, when each side gathers information in preparation for the trial. You may have to produce documents or answer written questions (with the assistance of your lawyer). In hotly contested cases, depositions are sometimes taken. A deposition is sworn testimony that is given in an attorney's office and transcribed by a stenographer. The attorney uses this opportunity to ask the opposing party questions that will help the attorney plan for the trial. If a deposition will be needed in your case, your attorney will help you prepare. Depositions sound like a duplication of the trial, but often they are a useful way to reach a settlement.

Settlement Meetings

All throughout the process, your attorney will be working to try to settle your case. He or she will speak with the other attorney and there be a meeting with all attorneys and spouses. If a settlement is close, another settlement conference may be held at the courthouse.

Trial

If your case does not settle, a trial will be scheduled (however note that most cases do settle and do not go to trial, although settlement might not happen until the moments before the scheduled trial). The trial is not usually completed in one day; it may be held in bits and pieces over several days.

When a trial is held, each side gives an opening statement, or brief summary of the case. Afterward, the plaintiff's attorney calls witnesses and presents evidence. The defendant has a chance to cross-examine those witnesses. Then the defendant then presents witnesses and evidence and the plaintiff can cross-examine. The trial ends with closing statements in which each attorney states what he or she is asking for and how he or she wants the judge to rule.

The divorce will not be final until the judge's decision is rendered in writing. Most judges won't tell you what they've decided while you are in court. They make their decisions only in writing, and that can take several weeks. Once you get the decision, your attorney may have some paperwork to complete to finalize the divorce.

Court Papers

Throughout your divorce, your attorney will collect many documents about your case, and you will receive copies of many of them. Keep them in a separate file with the most recent documents at the front. If your attorney emails your digital copies, keep them organized in a file on your computer. Then, if you need to double-check on a court date, you can easily find the most recent notice.

Your attorney will prepare all the documents to file in your case, and you will be required to sign them (physically or electronically) and swear that they are true. Because of this, it is important that you take the time to read them and make sure they are accurate before signing them. Double-check numbers on financial statements if they don't look right to you, and make sure the papers ask for everything you want to ask for. It is much harder to change things after they have been filed, so you want these to be accurate. Do not assume your attorney has gotten everything right!

Your attorney will also give you copies documents filed by your spouse. Read them carefully and point out things that are not true or that you do not agree with. It can be helpful to make a list to give to your attorney (use Response to Spouse's Divorce Papers). Remember to save venting for friends and family. Use your time with your attorney to get down to business.

Here are some terms you might encounter when dealing with court papers:

Affiant: person signing an affidavit

Affidavit: a sworn written statement

Allegations: things a person claims to be true

Amend: to change a court paper

Answer: a paper filed by a defendant in response to the plaintiff's papers

Complaint: a form that lists specific reasons for divorce

Default: to not appear in court or to fail to respond to court papers

Docket number: case number

Ex parte: without the other party present; sometimes a judge will make an emergency decision with only one party in the courtroom

Jurisdiction: a court's ability to hear certain cases

Litigants: parties involved in the case (plaintiff and defendant)

Motion: a formal way of asking the court to decide something

Notary: licensed official who verifies signatures on papers

Pleadings: initial court papers

Pro se: without an attorney

Stipulation: an agreement or settlement

Most legal papers are sprinkled with legalese—words like "witnesseth," "hereby," "adjudged," "decreed," "therefore," "in accordance with," "pursuant," and so on. These words are often just formalities without much meaning. Don't get bogged down by the language. You don't need to know the exact definition of each word; you just need a sense of what the document says. If there is something substantial you don't understand, ask your attorney. To save money, if your attorney has a paralegal that is working on your case, ask him or her instead of your attorney (they bill at a lower hourly rate).

Chapter 21. Co-parenting

If you're dealing with a narcissist, there is no co-parenting, and there's nothing you can do about it. Every time you get the kids back, you're going to be starting over from scratch, and your whole goal is trying to minimize the impact of this on the kids. Most ex-spouses that cause a lot of parent alienation are narcissists. For this reason, it is your goal to disengage from your narcissistic ex and engage only with your children.

The first step in doing that is minimizing contact with the narcissist. Now in many books, there's the catchphrase of "going no-contact." If the narcissist is your kids' mother, you have to interact with her, but you can still minimize that contact with her.

Narcissistic exes' first goal is to bait you, to get you to engage with them because they thrive on causing drama, and the minute that you re-engage with your ex-spouse is the minute that you are going on a journey of destruction. Do not respond to their emails; do not respond to their texts, do not engage with them in their effort to draw you back in the drama.

You will often see that there are times when your ex will come back and try to re-engage in the drama. It occurs because something happened, and they feel helpless. When they feel helpless, they are going to start re-engaging and going back to old patterns with you. So, once again, stay away from the drama, because once they get you in that again, you are trapped. What you need to do is not engage but instead disengage, and when you disengage from the narcissist's game, you are gaining power over them.

You must reply to their emails about the kids, events, or things like that, but keep it very simple and to the point. If they come at you with nasty words, do not respond to them with a nasty reply. Your leverage is focusing on what you can do and making a plan that will benefit you and your children.

Work with your children's teachers. You don't necessarily want to get the teachers in the middle of it, but you need to communicate enough in order for them to understand what's going on and work with you. Once they realize what is going on, they start sending you the information directly. Be careful what you say to your children's teacher, don't drag them in the conflict but let them know that you want to be part of it and work with them to help your kids.

Model good behavior with the kids, try to show them how healthy relationships are supposed to work, and make sure that you're sharing information. Make sure that you're not doing anything that falls into that narcissistic way of behaving or even a codependent way of behaving and try to help your kids set good boundaries with you, learn good communication and help them. Model what a good relationship is. Try to demonstrate to your kids a different way of living, interacting and communicating.

Don't talk about this in front of the kids. If you need to talk about some things regarding your family situation, do it far from your children. If they start talking to you and asking you questions, that's a different story. If they have a therapist or you're dealing with a therapist, then you might find an appropriate way to deal with that. But generally speaking, try to provide a good environment for your kids.

Don't try to reason with the narcissist; don't engage in conversations with her. It is bad for the kids, and it's not going to work. A normal healthy person can put their issues aside for the best interest of their kids, but if they're not able to do that, stop because you're falling into the narcissistic trap. You're trying to build a calm and solid environment for yourself and your kids with your support system, and once you have that, it makes it so much easier.

Alienated Children

Try to understand why your kids don't want to talk to you anymore and ignore you. It happened because your ex is alienating your children. How does she do it? It is not a quick process; actually, it begins slowly, and then over time it gets worse and worse.

First of all, your ex's goal is to isolate your kids from you, and they do it in the following ways: they start making requests of you. For instance, if your children are scheduled to be at your ex's house for a certain number of days, they will say they want to stay a couple more days. So, your response to that should be "no, we are going to follow the court," because once you give some leverage, they will take advantage of it.

Second of all, they tell the kids that they are the superior parent, that they are in control, that they are still making all of the decisions. Third, your ex begins to play the role of the victim to your children. She will say things to your children like "daddy has put us in this position, I don't understand why he is doing this now" and if your child hears this too many times they will start to believe that it is true. They want the kids to feel sorry for them, and once they get them to feel sorry for them, they are more in their control.

Next, they want to remove everything from the kids' world that they can't control, and the most important thing they want to remove from the kids' life is you! If you are sending a text to your children, they may erase it; if you are sending an email to them, they may erase that too. So, it's very important that you don't send an email and don't follow up with it early on with your kids moving along. She will use threats with your children, and the threats are subtle in the beginning, such as "if you don't do this for me then I'm not going to let you get the videogame that you want" so they start playing the game with the alienator because they want those things and kids are very impressionable, and so they become controlled by the alienator.

Frequently, the alienator will indulge your children, so that they don't appear as all good or all bad in front of them and because they want to keep their child as close to them as possible. She might say to the kid "you know what mommy is not all bad, she does good things for you" and so that clouds the fact that they're trying to brainwash them. You have all these factors involved in terms of why your kids do not want to talk to you.

The main issue for you to recognize is that your children begin to identify with your ex, who is the alienator, and that is why they push you away. They don't see you as a protective parent, but rather they see the alienator as that.

My first suggestion is that early on, when you start seeing signs of this taking place, don't let it prolong. If your narcissistic ex wants to keep the kids longer, don't let her show up at any of their activities, let your kids see that you are present and that you want to be with them, and that what the alienating parent is saying is not true about you.

I also want to encourage you to try to change their thought pattern. One thing that works a lot is when you refer to your child as "our child." The alienator is referring to your child as her child, but if you can refer to your children as "our children," it shows that you're not splitting them between you and your ex.

Other advice is doing the opposite of what the alienator is claiming about you. If the alienator is saying "you're not giving money, you're doing nothing," then send clothes and do things that allow your children to see that you are not what the alienator is saying about you. That is how you change how somebody thinks of and perceives you. Don't say anything negative about the alienating parent but challenge their thinking, asking your kids "what do you think about this? What do you think about what happened at daddy's this week?" and so on. Your kids know what is going on, so ask open-ended questions, and I hope that you get some of the answers that you need to rebind with your children.

Chapter 22. Dealing with Decisions

Part of being a parent's many responsibilities is coming up with decisions that will be best for the children. This is easy when both parents mutually approve of each other's opinions and have no ill-feelings towards each other. But when the parents just came out of a bitter and unpleasant separation or divorce, this may be a challenge.

Having irreconcilable differences is one of the common answers that divorced couples provide when asked what caused their separation. Change of religious views, political opinions or even the choice of lifestyle are just some of the differences that couples find it hard to resolve so they end up getting divorced. But these should be kept back when there are children involved and their welfare is at stake. Having legal child custody rights over the children means exercising the privilege of making parental decisions and even if it seems hard to work with an ex, one will just have to do so for his children's benefit.

Sheltering the Children

It is a given that one parent would inevitably move out from the family home but the question of who stays with the kids is always a tricky matter. Most courts have decided that the children should stay with their mothers until they are old enough to decide to whom they want to live with; until then, the father shall settle with visiting dates. Nonetheless, it is important to point that although one parent will be staying with the children, it is crucial that the other parent live not too far away. The reason behind this is for regular visitation and to avoid straining the relationship between the children and the other parent. As much as possible, the living arrangement that the parents should agree on would cater to and focus on maintaining a healthy relationship among the family.

When a parent is living with the children, it does not necessarily mean that the other has no say with the living arrangements. The "non-custodial" parent has the right to concern himself with house matters involving his kids. For instance, if the non-custodial parent finds that the neighborhood that his children are living in is not safe, he can voice out his apprehensions as it involves the welfare of his children. Another instance would be if the "custodial parent", as what we shall call the parent who actually lives with the children, starts dating again and this relationship is potentially harmful to the children. In cases like this, the non-custodial parent can also express his concern without necessarily meddling with his ex's affairs.

Despite living separately from each other, both parents still have the correlative duty to care for their children and to see that the latter are in a safe and comfortable environment.

Where the children will live, how their lifestyles will be and who they will be living with are just some of the many living arrangement matters that both parents should decide on, together. If there be any arguments relating to these things, it is advised that they are to include a professional to mediate.

Education and Medical Care

Having the obligation to provide for their children, both parents have the discretion in deciding which school is best. Some parents usually let their children stay where they used to study prior to the divorce to lessen the need of their children to adapt. But there are also those who transfer their children for various reasons, the two most common of which are: there is a great distance between the school and the new house; or there is a need to transfer so as to avoid the ridicule that the children will experience in school due to their parents' failed marriage. The latter situation is the usual reason why children transfer schools after their parents get divorced.

The same can easily be said about the medical care of children. Just like education, the children's medical care is a crucial topic that both parents need to discuss. What medical care plan they should get and what benefits are most appropriate for their children are just two of the things that parents should intently work on. In times of emergency, it will come in handy that the parents have already prepared a set-up so that there will be no unnecessary delay in providing for the kids' needs;

how the bills should get paid, who is the child's emergency contact and of course, who gets to primarily care for the child in times of sickness or injuries are some of the things to consider as regards medical care.

Where the children should study, and how the parents will provide for their medical care are two of the most significant matters that both parents should agree on because they are for the well-being of the children. Although seriously important, these matters are not usual sources of fights between divorced parents because both of them only want the best for their children so they compromise. Most parents deal with this situation maturely and every so often, they even let their children express their preferences.

But there are always situations when one parent does not agree with the other, as for instance when one's choice does not favor the other. When this occurs, both parents should remember that it is not their lives that they are dealing with but that of their children's – it is not their interests that are being explained. It is not an issue of what is advantageous to one or to both of them; what is important is that the decision is best for their children.

Financial Matters

One delicate part of raising children from divorce is that the household funds are no longer conjugal; therefore, the kids tend to receive financial support from both the mother and the father. Some divorced families handle this aspect really well, with parents convening and agreeing that they should divide every expense into half so no parent will give less or more than the other. However, this is not what is happening in most divorced families. Most parents are competitive when it comes to money, as they believe they can "buy" their children's affections. Yes, the mutual obligations such as educational funds, medical bills are settled accordingly, but when it comes to giving allowances or gifts, then it can turn into a contest.

Whoever gives the child a better present or a bigger amount of money earns the kid's fondness, especially when the children are still quite young and do not understand the concept of bribery. This is a prevalent situation whenever the non-custodial parent wishes to somehow connect with the child – he will be buying expensive gifts or splurging on grand vacations to make up for his absence. Although there is nothing wrong with spending money for the happiness of a child, parents should not make the situation a competition of who gets to be the better parent.

Also, parents should always remind their children that the things they receive from them are tokens of love, and there are no strings attached to them. If children are left without an explanation when it comes to these things, they tend to become spoiled. It is not the gifts that mend the relationship, it is the presence and active participation of the parent in his children's lives that actually counts.

When parents separate, they should keep in mind that though their finances are divided, they should nevertheless maintain that sense of impartiality when spending for their child. Whenever the topic of expenses come up, both parents should discuss the appropriate amount to be spent while taking into consideration the capacity of both to pay and the necessity of such expense. It is vital for divorced couples to acknowledge the fact that there is no rivalry, especially when it concerns finances. As in other things concerning their children, divorce couples should work together as a team.

Chapter 23. Inside the Mind
of a Narcissist

Narcissists are always mistaken to be strong people. Yet they are weak individuals who lack the sense of self. They build their image and reputation around others, and lack self-identity when alone.

Narcissists are often afraid of taking a real examination of themselves because the results would be discouraging. Most of them are emotionally dead, that is why they must seek validation from other people. When left to think about a narcissist, you will create a picture of a person that is arrogant and one who has an inflated ego. In essence, narcissist cannot exist in the absence of their victims. That is because narcissists depend on others to exercise their mindsets and behaviors.

Their mindset is characterized by fear, doubt and illusions. The negative mindset possessed by most narcissists tends to leave them fragile, vulnerable and wounded. They keep imagining themselves as superior even when it is obvious that they are not.

Narcissistic behaviors are often based on certain mindsets and beliefs that associate power with the ill treatment of other people. This belief system is what makes narcissists view their peers as weak and inferior people that do not need to be given any attention. A narcissist person also believes that a person's worth is derived from his level of superiority or inferiority. These attributes are exhibited through certain emotions like rage and anger.

The mentality of a narcissist can cause him to detach from the feelings of others. This explains why most narcissists will never connect with the pain and challenges of their peers or relations. It also explains why they will always dismiss complaints arising about them.

In the mind of a narcissist, partnership does not need to exist in relationships. To him, any relationship must have a top dog and an underdog. The narcissist will constantly fight to be superior, or the top dog. The general belief is that human beings can either rule or be ruled. Such a mentality causes narcissists to feel entitled to a certain kind of treatment.

Another mindset assumed by narcissists is that people are only there to serve their needs. That's why they ignore the needs of others because they think others do not need comfort and assistance. To them, it is the responsibility of their partners to serve and provide comfort. The narcissist wants to be adored, praised and valued all the time.

In a nutshell, life to a narcissist is all about competition. Narcissists will compete with their colleagues, family members and partners just to ensure that they remain in control. Due to this, narcissists never rest. They ensure to remain on the offensive side so as to keep others admiring their courage. Their behavior revolves around building their status and building their interests.

Narcissists will avoid every activity or behavior that can make their codependents feel appreciated. Their strategies are fashioned towards tearing others down. For them, there is only one way of winning – controlling the mind of other people. Sadly, with all the attention and admiration they receive, they rarely get pleased. They can only feel good for a short while, then get back to doing hurtful things to remain in dominance. That is why most of them remain miserable for a good part of their lives.

The thought pattern of a narcissist is always wired differently. Let us look at some of the common thoughts that keep running through their mind:

1. 'Why am I not getting the attention I need?'

2. 'I only need to concentrate on myself and take care of my own needs'

3. 'I need to get out of this relationship because I do not feel in control'

4. 'I am always right; you are always wrong and you can do nothing about this fact'

5. 'Why do I need to feel bad for someone else?'

6. 'I deserve some appreciation, why have I not received it?'

7. 'I feel bored, it's time to stir things up'

8. 'Why do you think you are to cause me shame?'

Manipulation Strategies Used By Narcissists

One of the tactics used by narcissists to degrade others is manipulation. Here are some of the manipulation strategies you need to beware of.

• Gaslighting

Gaslighting is a psychological concept where an individual attempts to make you doubt your sanity, perception or memory. It is one of the most common tactics because it makes you lose your sense of reality. It breaks your self-belief and shields you from reacting towards any form of physical and emotional abuse. To resist any form of gaslighting, it is essential that you stick to your reality. You can do this by telling the truth to a friend, or writing the experience down. If you do not do this, you may get to a point of gaslighting yourself and this can be detrimental to your sanity.

• Projection

Projection occurs when a narcissist refuses to admit his weakness. Instead, the person uses every possible way to avoid admitting his shortcomings. Narcissists often use this strategy to defend themselves from failed responsibilities. The tactic allows them to shift blame onto someone else, thus avoiding any form of accountability. One disadvantage of projection is that it comes out as abuse. Instead of a narcissist admitting his imperfections and weaknesses, he will pin this to unsuspecting individuals in a disrespectful way. That explains why narcissistic people never improve on their weaknesses. The solution to this is that you avoid projecting the mistakes of a narcissist back to him. If possible, cut ties with such a person.

- Ill conversations

If you have ever interacted with a narcissist, you admit how difficult it is to strike a meaningful discussion with such a person. When engaging a narcissist, prepare for any kind of language. This is because narcissistic people rarely mind the words, they use to address their peers. If you are not careful, most of your conversations will end in an argument or disagreement. Narcissists will use words to confuse you and make you feel less important. You need to understand that your thoughts and perceptions will never match with theirs. This will help you avoid any problems that may arise during your conversation.

- Generalization

A good number of narcissists are intellectually lazy. Instead of considering what you say in deep perspective, they will always seek to generalize all the information they receive. The generalization makes them come up with some blanket statements that cannot justify their arguments. Even when you raise several perspectives into an issue, they will only pick one and use it to make general conclusions about the situation at hand. Doing this results in invalid assumptions that can be used to destroy the place for justice. Generalizations and blank statements are very common in toxic relationships. Once you attempt to bring the abusive person to accept his negative behavior, he will convert your statements into general opinions instead of addressing the underlying issue. To overcome such, you need to hold on the truth and avoid getting blackmailed by the abuser.

- Misinterpretation of thoughts

A narcissist can twist your feelings, thoughts and complains to make you appear irrational. He will completely reframe your words against you to ensure that you end up defeated. By doing this, he makes your arguments invalid and instils some guilt in your reactions. Narcissists use this strategy to divert your mind from the current situation. They read your feelings and thoughts, then they use these to come up with intimidating conclusions about you.

As much as you may feel bad about such manipulation, the narcissist will not apologize for his action. Instead, he will continue accusing you of having bad thoughts of him. To avoid such, you may need to walk away from the person. So long as the toxic person knows that you can bow to their misinterpretation, they will continue manipulating your feelings. But if they see you creating a strong boundary around them, they will stop depicting such manipulative traits.

- Shifting goal posts

This is another strategy common among toxic individuals, also known as narcissists. However much you try to prove a narcissists misconduct, it may be difficult for you to win over him. Even when you have all the necessary evidence required to implicate narcissists, they will keep setting new expectations that require you to provide more proof. For instance, even if you are successful in your career, a narcissist will keep asking why you are not a millionaire, or why you have not reached the peak of your career. Instead of the narcissist appreciating you, he will do his best to show you that what you have achieved nothing compared to where you ought to be. This is a form of shifting goal posts that you need to watch out for.

- Evading the subject

Narcissists are fond of changing the subject in a way that suits their need for attention. They will digress from the main topic by raising a totally different subject for discussion. The reason why they will do this is to get the attention from you or any other person in the room. When a discussion is started that challenges the narcissist's status quo, evading the subject should be expected. To overcome this, you may decide to continue with the discussion without focusing on the distractions. Redirect the audience back to the main topic and encourage them to focus on the issue at hand.

- The use of threats

Narcissists always feel challenged when their sense of superiority diminishes. They always make demands that are unreasonable and may punish you for not meeting their expectations. They also rob you of your right to give opinions or perspectives on certain matters of importance. Their aim is to make you fearful so that you cannot challenge their demands. If you sense that such a person is threatening you into submitting to their plans, show the person that you are not ready to bend low to their demands. If the threat concerns your wellbeing you may need to report the person to relevant authorities.

- Use of abusive names

When narcissistic people identify a threat around them, they will ensure that they frustrate the threat until it ceases to exit. In their mindset, no one should dare challenge their power. One-way narcissists use to showcase their rage is by calling you nasty names. Through this, they know that they can easily manipulate your emotions and cause you to follow their demands.

By insulting your character, abilities and level of intelligence, they will make other people to doubt your personality as well. Name-calling is very common among toxic people and the target is always you, the victim. If an interaction gets to the point of name calling, it is crucial that you end it if you know that you cannot tolerate the insults. As much as the action may be hurtful, make sure that you do not internalize the words. Understand that they are coming from a frustrated individual and that you need not pay attention to them.

Chapter 24. Why the Narcissist Chose You

It can be very hard for you to walk away from a relationship with a Narcissist, and one that you have built for a very long time. Well, many people feel that it is good for them to fight for their relationship and their partner, but at times it is good for you to walk away.

When it comes to a person that abuses you, it becomes hard for you to know what to do, narcissists aren't the best people to be with in a relationship. They have this uncanny behavior of coming up with story after story just to get you hooked, while they play with your self-esteem.

But what made you the perfect victim for the narcissist? Remember that the person didn't just choose you randomly – how he took his time to get you into his loop. The narcissist knows what they want in a partner, and it might turn out that you were the perfect partner for them.

Usually, the victims almost seem that they didn't get involved with the person, rather, the person got involved with them. One day you are harmlessly flirting with this guy and then next instant you are so deep in love with him that you even cannot remember what happened for you to reach such a stage.

This is because narcissists have been carved out to be masters of survival. They have this ability to identify the people that will fall in their loop and listen to them. They know that the person will stick around and take care of their needs even when they have revealed their inner destructive habits.

So, who is the perfect target for a narcissist?

You Have What They Want

A narcissist is looking for what they call "narcissistic supply." Here, the person is looking for that one thing that will feed his ego and then keep them pumped up and protect them from the fragile view that they have about themselves.

What they want is admiration, fame, money, compliments, and good looks, an image of a perfect family and a prestigious career and more.

If you have an issue about the way they behave for one reason or another, then they won't be interested in you at all.

When you are planning to get into a relationship with the narcissist, then they might be looking for physical stimulation and for you to praise their performance after a sexual encounter, even if they don't deserve it at all.

They want to be with you because you will praise them when they do something to you. They aren't concerned about how you feel or what you feel during the act – all they need is for you to praise their ability. If they find out that you can be controlled sexually, they will want you so much because they know that they hold the reigns over you.

What Does a Narcissist Want in a Woman?

You will get swept off your feet with fancy dinners, compliments and gifts that you never thought will come your way – you will think that you have got Mr. Right, when in real sense you are the pawn in a chess game.

The romance will be out of this world, and you will feel as if you are in a movie, but this only lasts long enough for you to realize that everything that happens in the relationship is all about him, and you are always on the fringes.

He constantly talks about what he is about, what he does and puts all his needs over yours in all situations. He is sensitive to any form of criticism, and is always obsessed on what he does because it is all about status. You will now realize that the fancy dinner dates at high and restaurants were just part of the game.

Let us look at the top traits that the narcissist looks for in a woman.

You are Successful, but Insecure

You might not admit it, but if you are an insecure person and you keep on admitting it, even if you are attractive, then you might be advertising yourself to be fit for the narcissist.

The narcissist is looking for a person that fits the description of someone that will make them look good. And if you have the looks and a good job but you always feel as if you don't belong, then they will easily make you feel like a hero.

They are attracted to you not because you are beautiful and so accomplished – no, instead, they want your appearance and the achievements that you have to fuel their ego.

However, they don't want to be with a woman that is too confident because they know that she might be in control – something that they don't want. Instead, they want to be the ones to run the show all the time.

If he senses that you are insecure, he will be more attracted to you because you won't be in the way of his success, whether fake or real. If the narcissist senses that you have a high level of self-confidence, he will turn and walk away.

So, how does an insecure person behave? If you have any of the following traits, then you need to know that you are insecure:

- You undervalue yourself. Your self-worth determines how much you value yourself. If you always accept less every time, then you will feel worthy and you will never think that you deserve more. You will accept less than what a normal person will accept.

- They put other people down. Due to their insecurities, people that are insecure tend to resort to putting other people down so that they can feel good about themselves. They have put themselves down for so long that they feel that they also need to treat others the same way. They want to put others down so that the other person can be at their level.

- You copy other people. Insecure people lack the self-belief to come up with something on their own. They feel that if they come up with something on their own, it won't be good enough to work for them, or they might end up being judged for the poor show. They therefore stick to their comfort zone and then copy other people that are more successful.

You are a Pleaser

Well, we all desire the person that we date to be happy, but if this comes at the cost of your own happiness and wellbeing, then it has become unhealthy.

The narcissist is looking for that person that will give him the attention that he yearns for and a level of emotional validation that he desires. If you don't have a strong sense of what you want, then the narcissist will take over so fast.

The narcissist is interested in monopolizing the relationship and one that will never compromise on what he wants. He always demands what he needs. If he realizes that you have boundaries that you follow, he will get away so fast that you will be surprised.

Signs you are a people pleaser:

- You pretend that you agree with everyone. When you are a person pleaser, you will listen in to other peoples' opinions even when you aren't in agreement with them. You are pretending to agree with them just because you want them to like you even if it means what they represent don't go along with you.

- You feel responsible for what people do. Well, it is always good to understand how your behavior can influence other people, but thinking that you have all the power to make them happy becomes a huge problem. It remains up to you to be in charge of your own emotions. Don't always be responsible for what people do, because it makes them take advantage of you.

- You are always sorry. If you find that you always blame yourself even for things that you haven't done, or you fear that other people are always blaming you for things that you haven't done, then you need to be cautious. Frequent apologies are always a sign that you are weak and you have a bigger problem. Don't always apologize for being you.

- Your always do things for other people. If you are a pleaser, you will always have a schedule that is full of activities that you do for other people, even when they aren't necessary at all.

- You never say no. Do you know that you have been given the power to say no to things that don't make a lot of sense to you? The sad thing is that many people don't know when to say no. They will end up accepting anything that comes their way and they say yes to things that they know they aren't able to do.

- Feel bad when someone is angry at them. Just because someone is mad doesn't mean that you are the one on the wrong. If you cannot stand the thought of seeing someone angry at you, then you are more likely to go back on your values.

- You copy the people around you. If you find that you are doing something so that the other person is happy, you will end up attracting a narcissist.

- You value praise. While a little praise and some kind words will make anyone feel so good, pleasers are out to get a lot of validation for anything that they do. If you believe that your own value depends wholly on what other people think about you, then you will only feel good when you are complimented for any thing you do.

- You avoid conflict at all costs. It is one thing for you not to want to start a conflict, but if you are always avoiding conflicts at all costs, it means that you are struggling hard to stand up for the things that you believe in.

- You don't admit it when you get hurt. If you have been hurt many times and all the times you aren't willing to tell the person that hurt you of your feelings, then you are the perfect target for a narcissist. If you can't stand up and say that you are sad, embarrassed and angry after someone has done something to you, then the narcissist will take advantage of this to hurt you more.

You Avoid Conflict at All Costs

There are a few people that love conflict. If, on the other hand you tend to avoid any conflict totally, then you are becoming more attractive to the narcissist. A narcissist is looking for someone that will cooperate with them even during times of conflict. If you are one to give in easily to their demands or wishes either at work or in your personal life, then you are the ideal partner for the narcissist.

If you are always putting your needs to the side just to make things work in the face of conflict, then you will easily fall for the narcissist who thrives when you give them the attention and empathy that they seek. Well, being compromising in a relationship is good, but when you are a doormat, you receive the negatives only.

Chapter 25. Are You Still Codependent?

It is possible to relapse into codependency no matter what recovery stage you are in the process of. When someone is in recovery from codependency, they may hit a problem in life in which they feel they can't or don't want to deal with. So, they get stuck. That can trigger a bit of a crisis, especially for someone who has been in recovery for a while.

The crisis may be the result of pride and not wanting to admit that there's a problem. Denial has kicked in again at that point, and that's a really big issue that can have a lasting effect on their recovery. This means that they are heading towards additional problems. In denial, they may start to use other things to distract... like painkillers, getting on the internet, playing games endlessly, or watching Netflix all weekend. These are examples of other ways of acting out to avoid your primary attention.

The trigger event may not even be that big. There can be a very small thing like a problem with your vehicle or a bill and it becomes a trigger for internal chaos. A very uncomfortable sense of self becomes a reality. Internal self-talk which is undermining in nature and physically painful to endure, becomes a habit. The dysfunction on the inside can only lead to dysfunction on the outside.

The old addict starts to resurface and they begin thinking that recovery is not going to work with the sort of person that they are. They become overwhelmed with the trigger and fail to comprehend the situation and let go of themselves. They start thinking about their pre-recovery times, the places they frequently visited, such as a favorite hangout place. They begin to use substances or develop problems in relationships... projecting stuff on other people, creating the crisis, etc., as a way of avoiding looking at themselves.

Substance misuse, food disorders, sexual issues... regardless of the choice of self-inflicted addiction, they lose further control. At some point, because they have been in recovery, they might reach a point of awareness of their actions and feel shocked, seeing it as a deviation from the steps they have been taking for their well-being. They may get back to a point of recognizing that they need help. That sort of brings back a shock to the system, and they restart the recovery process.

That's one route. The other route is the opposite extreme, where their behaviors continue to go on for some time, or the person may choose to end their life because they can no longer bear the shame and internal pain. There are various points in the relapse where you can pull yourself back and get into the recovery system. A relapse prevention plan is necessary, one that can chalk out the process that the person can adapt in case they are triggered.

Recovery makes codependents take charge of their lives as they're learning to value their feelings, needs, and opinions. As their self-esteem gets better, codependents find the determination to question their mistaken childhood beliefs. This then sets them free to know more about healthy relationship skills. This requires thorough practice.

Codependents normally fear that in their early recovery, they might become selfish. This is not true. Recovering codependents remain much more caring than most people. Recovery simply extends the abundant compassion of codependents towards themselves. They vow to become people respecters rather than people pleasers, and unconditionally respect their feelings and emotions.

To change a dysfunctional childhood, behavior, or beliefs takes practice, mindfulness, self-introspection, and time. The challenge to make such major changes comes from within. Life provides us with various opportunities to learn the lessons that we need in order to live a healthy, fulfilling and meaningful life. You need to know and understand that mental illness is not your fault. It is nothing to be ashamed of. It's a chemical imbalance and not personal.

Loneliness will always be a part of recovery, but it is a necessary part, because in truth, you are working on yourself, and no one can do that for you. Relapses can sometimes feel like the worst points in your life, because we often perceive relapses as failures. It is only a matter of changing your outlook on how you view these relapses. Even though you suffer greatly, you gain something from it. You gain empathy.

What is it Like to Live with Codependency?

Most of the time, you can't see on your own how much your loved one's care about you. When you take the steps to recovery, you discover what the illness is taking away from you, but you also see what you can gain from it. Finally, relapse is a crucial part of recovery. You may fall over and over again, but the important thing is to be proactive about relapse and not be reactive to it.

You need to stay vigilant and take care of yourself. Your relapses and struggles make you what you are. If you don't struggle, you don't find the true essence of your true self—like what your passions are. Relapses may occur in all areas of our lives. They can occur in your career, relationships, or society, in general. There can be a relapse in identity when you start to think that you don't know who you are anymore. Whenever you feel you have hit rock bottom, there is only one way to go, and that is up. You are going to get stronger and better.

There is a need for transformational behavior change. The underlying behavior of the codependent needs to be targeted and cured. They need to be taught and become well versed in regards to the gaps they had in their life, and the need to fill these gaps for a full recovery. They need to know they are capable of living their lives with integrity, accountability, and love for others. In order to be able to make a full recovery, and bid farewell to codependency, you have to follow a few simple steps.

The first step is actually to want to change. You need to keep in mind that life will get better when you leave your current situation and move to a healthier mind space.

The second step is to learn to act in a way where you are open to situations. It means that even if you don't want to be decent or codependent anymore, you act that way until it becomes you. You practice being a healthier person over and over until you become that person.

You know the kind of person you want to be like—perhaps how you don't want to get back into manipulating your partner, acting needy, etc. Envision yourself as already becoming that person. This is a very important step and action to take, and can't be achieved within a day. This practice needs to happen over a long period of time.

The next point to remember is to help others. When a person helps another, the helper becomes better. The way to save your life is saving another's life. You need to give responsibility to those who surround you, to hold you accountable for your actions. They need to be brutally honest with you when you mess up. This is where learning happens.

Sometimes when someone points out a fault in your behavior, you don't believe it to be true. If more than one person tells you the same, it will get you thinking. Recognizing your destructive flaws can help change you for a better person, when you are willing to accept and work on them. These people in your life are the ones who love and care about you and will want to see positive changes in you.

The next step is to have immediate consequences for bad behavior. Immediate consequences are necessary to your own expectations, so that you never feel it is right to come back to the pre-recovery stage.

Chapter 26. Create a Sense of Urgency

Cut off the narcissist

Cutting off the narcissist involves taking a step back from the situation altogether. However, unlike a time-out, cutting off is typically a permanent severance of the relationship. The only way to truly avoid any more harm, whether emotionally or physically, is to refuse to engage or associate with the narcissist completely. By never being near the narcissist or never acknowledging the narcissist, the narcissist never has the opportunity to hurt you.

Refusing to engage with the narcissist also comes with a secondary benefit: you have cut off the narcissist's strongest motivator. By refusing to be a source of the narcissistic supply he craves, the narcissist eventually loses interest in you and instead will move onto someone else who will provide him with his fix.

Disengage Emotionally

Recognize that NPD is a personality disorder; the narcissist literally has a disordered way of thinking, and therefore, the narcissist's perceptions about the world around him should not be used as a measure of the truth. Remember that the narcissist seeks to manipulate others to get what he wants and cannot see the world in a realistic manner. He will say things and believe things that are untrue so that it fits his own paradigms of the world around him. Just because his way of seeing the world is skewed and disordered does not mean you have to accept it.

By disengaging emotionally, you hear what he says and briefly acknowledge it, but do not take it seriously. Just as you would not care much when an angry child calls you a doo-doo head, you should not care much when the narcissist screams that you are a horribly selfish person that would be better off dead because at least then, more than one person would benefit from your life insurance or estate. While it can be hard to ignore what the narcissist says, especially if the narcissist is someone you have held in high regard in the past, such as a spouse or a parent, you must remember that it is not true. By refusing to become upset at the narcissist's accusations, you protect your self-esteem, and when you refuse to fall victim to the narcissist's tactics, the narcissist slowly loses interest in you as well.

Studying Them

You need to study the narcissist, not from the perspective of a loved one, but from that of an outsider. If you cannot do this, then none of the other tips tackled in this part will work. When you objectively start studying the narcissist, you will better be able to learn how to detach yourself mentally and emotionally. If you can analyze the behavior of a narcissist in a dispassionate manner, then it will give you the clarity you need to restore your emotional balance.

Call Out

Most narcissists tend to be quite proud of their narcissism and think of it as a positive personality trait. You must call out the narcissist for their narcissistic ways. This will only work if the narcissist also values and cherishes the relationship you share. If that's the case, then use a measured and non-sarcastic tone to tell the narcissist that their narcissism is showing.

Feed Their Ego

A narcissist needs a lot of attention, affection, praise, and adoration to thrive. So, by complimenting him and feeding his fragile ego, you can easily handle living with a narcissist. You must be prepared to keep feeding his ego, if not, be prepared to deal with his tantrums. This is something you will need to get used to if leaving the narcissist is not an option for you. A couple of simple compliments can go a long way while trying to deal with a narcissist. This is not manipulation. Instead, it is about understanding his personality disorder and using it to help smooth things out.

Manage Your Expectations

Narcissists lack empathy. They certainly expect sympathy from others, but will seldom reciprocate. This absence of empathy makes it difficult for a narcissist to develop close and intimate bonds with others. You need to learn to accept and make peace with this. So, stop seeking empathy or compassion from the narcissist and instead try to manage your expectations.

Find Yourself

To find yourself again, you need to step back and view yourself from afar. This means evaluating your current state in detail and then looking at that evaluation from an objective distance.

The best way to do this is to remove your thoughts and emotions from your own mind and put them somewhere else, where you can examine them more clearly. A great way to do this is to begin a daily journal, pouring all your emotions and the thoughts you've had onto paper. Make sure to concentrate on how you feel, not just on the events that made you feel that way.

Other alternatives include painting or drawing or writing your feelings in the form of poetry. Choose a medium that you feel suits you and will allow you to take what's happening on your head and put it on paper instead. It can take practice, especially if you're not used to giving voice to your emotions, but it's very important that you put every last piece of you onto that paper.

Take time every day for this activity. Close yourself into a private space where you won't be interrupted and where nobody else can see what you are creating. This is just for you – keep the results somewhere secure, so you don't have to worry that anyone else will ever see them.

Creating a mirror of yourself in this way not only allows you to pour out all the damaging emotions in a safe way, it also allows you to see them outside yourself. It allows you to see the true you, and the progress you are making, and the progress you still need to make.

Rebalance Your Life

A more formal version of this rediscovery of who you are and what you want is to reintroduce balance into your life. This is about what you need as well as what you want and involves rebuilding a balance that may have been toppled by your abuser's actions.

Your abuser may have removed your connection to friends, they may have insisted you live and work in places that weren't really your choice, they may have chosen your hobbies for you by demanding you do the things they wanted to do. One or more areas of your life may currently be lacking equilibrium, and it's time to bring that back.

The areas you will need to look at include:

- Your career (or future career if you are still in school)
- Your relationships
- Your living situation
- Your hobbies and interests
- Your beliefs

First, you will need to look at each of these areas in turn and ask yourself how the abuse affected them. Did, for example, your abuser mock your spiritual beliefs and make you feel guilty for wanting to attend services? Did they choose the apartment you rented because it was more convenient to them or suited their tastes and make you feel obliged to agree?

Once you have determined what changed in these areas of your life thanks to the abuse, you can think about what you want instead – and then make those changes happen. As you do, think about the boundaries you want to set.

Tell yourself what you will and won't accept from outside influence in the future. For instance, you might say you will never again allow someone to stop you from attending your horse riding classes because they are important to your happiness and your sense of self. Perhaps you will pledge to yourself that you will always attend Thanksgiving with your family and that there would need to be genuine negotiation before you broke that pledge.

How to Protect Yourself and Your Children from a Narcissist

There are several ways to shield yourself and your kids from the narcissist in your life. The most important thing is for you to implement each one and stop that self-absorbed person.

You can convince yourself that you are actually safe in a narcissist's hands. However, their good person facade wouldn't last long, so you better brace yourself using a few strategies.

- Set boundaries. Know when you are at your limit in dealing with all the sarcastic remarks or hurtful things from a narcissist. At least you would know when to react after simply smiling and nodding to everything that a narcissist is saying or doing. By letting that person know your boundaries, he or she might at least be aware of it and possibly try to control their behavior.

- Determine the behaviors that are too much for you and tell them about these behaviors. While you're busy setting boundaries, you should not forget to tell the narcissist about excessive behaviors that you can no longer tolerate. List them and express why you don't like each one.

- Enjoy your down time more. Incorporate more rest into your daily schedule, especially a chance to get away from the narcissist for a breather. No matter how much you love that person, you might naturally feel suffocated too. Stay away from the negative vibes that a narcissist is emitting at home. Even the kids should be shielded from that person to avoid ruining their lives.

- Find a strong support group for yourself. While you might not be able to resist the need to whine and complain about your rotten, bad luck for being with a narcissist, support sessions should be spent more on renewing your energy and getting a fresh perspective on things. Take these times as your time to recharge and face the narcissist as a confident and self-assured individual after being ruined by their constant bullying and put-downs.

- Prepare a reserve. Aside from determining your boundaries, you should know when to strengthen them after years of being together with a narcissist. Take the time to repair the cracks in the foundation of your self-confidence.

- Stay strong and steady. Remain steadfast in your decision, whether to continue handling the narcissist, or staying away from the narcissistic relationship. Being neutral will also help.

- Be keen on spotting deceptions. Avoid being fooled into believing that you will still thrive with a narcissistic person. Tell your children about it too. Instead, try to look for real love, a love with no conditions and no self-centered behavior.

Chapter 27. Co-parenting Approach

There are a variety of ways that co-parents can relate to one another after a divorce. Some parents find that they can be supportive friends. Others find that they can be pleasant and cooperative, but with some emotional distance. Still others find that they cannot tolerate interaction, but they can provide good parenting when the children are with them, and they can allow the other parent to do the same. There are many ways to make co-parenting work, which is fortunate because not every pair of co-parents can do it the same way.

Post-divorce co-parenting relationships can be viewed as falling along a broad continuum in terms of their degree of conflict. Some may have almost no conflict while others may have vast amounts. Your post-divorce relationship may fall squarely in one of these categories or it may fall in between two of them, but most co-parents are able to identify which category is closest to their own experience.

Low Conflict

Co-parenting relationships with low conflict are those in which the parents are able to drop their guard, to communicate honestly, and to adjust to accommodate reasonable requests from each other readily. The interactions may or may not be warm and friendly, but at the very least, for the vast majority of the time, the interactions are at least civil and cordial. The parents in this category view the important undertaking of raising their children as a joint effort. There may be brief periods of more pronounced conflict, but these parents are able to rationally approach that conflict and find ways to resolve it or contain it.

Moderate-to-High Conflict

Co-parents who experience moderate-to-high conflict have a less predictable relationship. They may go long periods of time operating with moderate conflict only to find that, for reasons they do not fully understand, they suddenly experience weeks or months of higher conflict. What tends to be consistent is that negative emotions arise easily and the parents are frequently locked in a power struggle. This impairs their communication, and one or both parents are less willing to accommodate requests. There is typically some degree of anger and hostility in these relationships, at least on the part of one of the parents.

Severe Conflict

Finally, there are co-parents with such severe conflict that they fall at the far end of the spectrum. Their relationships are characterized by the consistent presence of open hostility and a desire of one or both parents either to ignore completely or to antagonize the other. At least one of the parents has a corrosive effect on the other. Even when they appear to be tolerating one another, there is usually a sense of dread that bad things might happen soon.

The first approach, cooperative co-parenting, is the approach that best fits for co-parents with low-conflict relationships. The second approach, parallel co-parenting, is the better match for relationships with moderate-to-high conflict, while encapsulated co-parenting is the right match for relationships with severe conflict. We will assess each of these approaches in detail and explain when they fit, why they fit, and how you can use them to guide you toward a more functional co-parenting interaction that is suited to your circumstances.

Cooperative Co-parenting

In cooperative co-parenting, children are allowed reasonable freedom to adjust their schedules and to travel between the homes to pick up their sports equipment, school items, or favorite articles of clothing. When a dispute arises, parents resolve it through calm discussion and avoid stonewalling or verbal attacks, thereby insulating the children from their disagreements. Parents who use cooperative co-parenting are also good at respecting boundaries and following rules, so they respect each other's time with the children and stay within the lines when an agreement is reached.

There are obvious advantages to cooperative co-parenting over other approaches. The lack of tension creates a more normal family environment for children. In addition, the high level of flexibility makes it easier to accommodate the needs of both the children and their parents. Finally, this approach is more efficient, with little or no time, energy, or money wasted on conflict. Parents work together as a team, helping each other in the shared life project of raising their children to adulthood.

Parallel Co-parenting

The second co-parenting approach is parallel co-parenting, which is geared toward co-parents who fall in the moderate-to-high conflict category. Because parents in this category are not able to sustain a sufficiently positive and coordinated relationship to make the cooperative approach work, it is essential that they have a way to navigate their conflicts with the least amount of stress and strain between them. Asking parents with greater conflict to use a cooperative co-parenting method is likely to do more harm than good, so we strongly recommend that parents with a moderate-to-high level of conflict consider a parallel co-parenting approach. This is also a preferable method for parents with poorer boundaries, dysfunctional communication, or inflexibility.

With parallel co-parenting, co-parents interact on a limited and controlled basis. Communication takes place only when it is needed, and it typically occurs via email or text to avoid the conflicts that arise in spoken exchanges. Parents make joint decisions only for major decisions, such as which school the children will attend or whether a child will have a serious medical procedure. Each parent handles daily life with the children separately, with minimal interaction between one another. They are still required to inform each other when school reports are received or when the children have medical appointments, but the communication is limited to notification, with little or no discussion taking place. When using a parallel co-parenting approach, parents follow the timesharing schedule4 with few alterations, and they learn to make accommodations within their own lives to deal with scheduling challenges without involving each other. For example, if a father has a work conflict that prevents him from picking up his son from soccer practice, he might have his sister or a close family friend pick up the child rather than arranging for the mother to step in.

In some ways, one might think of parallel co-parenting as two single parents sharing responsibility for a child, with interaction only in regard to major decisions. Another way to describe this approach is to imagine the parallel rails of a railroad track. Picture the children moving down one rail of a railroad track when with one parent and down the other rail when with the other parent. Either way, they are moving in the same direction toward the same destination, but each rail is independent of the other. Hopefully, the parents are both working in the same direction in terms of fostering their children's health and well-being, their academic progress, and their social and emotional development, but the way that they go about achieving those ends may differ from one another.

While parallel co-parenting may not be the ideal way to raise children, it is much better than engaging in ongoing conflict. By reducing interaction, there are fewer opportunities for friction between parents, and less friction means less stress for everyone. Children do not have to see their parents argue, nor do they have to overhear confrontational phone conversations. They also avoid the negative effects of being around a parent who just had an angry interaction with the other parent and may be stewing about it. All of these factors help to protect the children from exposure to hostility between their parents. Finally, parallel co-parenting is helpful to some parents as they move on with their own lives, as it allows each parent to live with less intrusion from the other parent.

Encapsulated Co-parenting

When the parenting conflict is severe, or there is a history of angry outbursts or threats of violence, we recommend a third approach to co-parenting that we call encapsulated co-parenting. Some divorce professionals see this approach as being an extension of parallel co-parenting, but we think that there are enough unique aspects to encapsulated co-parenting that it is best explained and understood as its own distinct approach. The encapsulated approach takes the chaos and volatility of severe conflict and contains it so that it does not escalate, thereby minimizing the fallout on the children. This approach applies specific guidelines to buffer the children from parental conflict and to protect the parents themselves from explosive interactions. The following types of provisions are generally recommended:

- The co-parents rigidly follow the timesharing schedule and make special requests only in the presence of a third party, such as a parenting coordinator or a family therapist.

- Both parents do not attend any special events without a specific, detailed arrangement that is worked out in advance to assure that no negative interaction will occur. When an arrangement cannot be made that allows both parents to attend the same event in a safe manner, then one parent must miss that event. While disappointing to that parent, and possibly to a child as well, some co-parenting relationships require this restriction in order to protect the children.

- Parents use phone communication (calls or texts) for emergencies only.

- Email communication is monitored by a professional and is conducted via a website that is designed to help high-conflict parents

439

communicate. Many of these sites provide a calendar for communicating about children's activities, allowing both parents to know what is going on in the lives of their children without requiring direct communication between the parents.

There are significant downsides to encapsulated co-parenting. One downside is that it creates a family environment that may feel polarized and unnatural. Another is that there is minimal flexibility in adjusting schedules and other matters, and that can feel overly restrictive to the children. While these downsides are unfortunate, an encapsulated approach is a necessary choice for families in which the co-parenting conflict is severe.

Hybrid Approaches

There are hybrid approaches that combine elements of the three co-parenting approaches explained above. For example, Annie and George are co-parents who use a parallel co-parenting approach for the most part, but they find that they are able to incorporate some aspects of a cooperative approach successfully. They will often accommodate each other when it comes to trading days in the timesharing schedule, and they are generally open to arranging for George to provide childcare while Annie works. In a pure parallel approach, these activities would not typically occur. On the other hand, Charles and Samantha, who use a cooperative co-parenting approach in general, have found the need to apply a parallel approach to certain aspects of their co-parenting. When their communication began to slip into bickering, they agreed to restrict themselves to emails and texts. They also decided to follow a rule that any requests for trading parenting time must be made at least two weeks in advance. These are examples of how hybrid approaches can allow for the tailoring of the co-parenting approach to the needs of a particular family.

Chapter 28. Protecting Your Children

When you divorce a spouse, you forget that your kids are a part of both of you. Together, you created the miracle that is your child. For all the animosity, anger and bitterness towards your spouse, your child should not suffer. There are certain steps that you can take to protect the mental health of your child, which is already fragile, and which is blasted into smithereens upon hearing the news.

Your Child's Emotional Health

This is the biggest concern with regards to divorce. Just because you and your spouse aren't living together anymore means naught to raising your child. You might hate your ex, but you did create a child with him or her. Keep that in mind every time you get mad at your ex. Your child's emotional safety is of utmost concern.

Act Like an Adult

Keep you calm at all times when you talk to your ex or iron out a deal with him or her. Remember, you're the adult here. Your child looks up to you. Avoid fighting with your ex, especially in the presence of the child.

Remain Involved with Your Child

Even in a shared custody, the child will live with one parent and visit the other periodically. That does not mean that you neglect the child when you're not visiting him or her. Both the parents should be actively involved in the child's life. Even if you think you make a great single parent and take on the roles of both mom and dad, it rarely ever works out. To maintain your child's emotional health, ensure that you and your ex are as involved with the kid as possible.

Your Child Did Not Get Divorced

Remember this- you got divorced because you couldn't stand the stress of the marriage anymore. Your child did not. He or she was created by both of you and will always be a part of you, no matter what. It's quite natural for a child to love one parent more than the other. Do not make him or her feel guilty about this fact. You need to keep nurturing your relationship with your child, without creating undue guilt in the child.

Announcing the Divorce

Before you announce your decision, make a plan with your spouse as to how you're both going to break the news to the child. You need to be extremely clear, yet gentle when you tell them. Answer the questions with honesty and don't sugar coat the facts. Also, both you and your spouse need to break the news together. Sit them down and tell them gently. Keep your child's life as normal as possible. His or her daily routines- be it morning, school, play activities, projects; meeting with friends- should be the same. Tell the kids you did everything to save your marriage and never, ever blame the other partner for the split. Your child will be bewildered, hurt, angry or just plain unemotional. Understand these feelings and back off when the child wants you to.

Reassure the Children That They Are Not Responsible

Often, when the parents decide to separate, the child somehow gets it into his head that he must have done something wrong to have caused the split. Reassure the child, as many times as necessary, that this is simply not true. Explain to them, in a simple language, that you tried everything to keep the marriage together, but it just wouldn't work out any more. Children respond more easily to honesty and can see through you when you try and make stuff up. Be open, be direct and tell them it's no one's fault and that both of you will love the child just as much. Nothing will ever change in that department.

Don't Restrict Visits with the Other Parent

Tell your kids they can see and visit the other parent whenever they wish to. Do not restrict them from doing so. Your goal now should be your child's stability, which has been torn apart by the divorce. Get them their personal cell phones. Have them spend as much time with the other parent as possible. Keep things as normal for the child as is acceptable by both parties.

Don't Over Promise

As it is, the child's life is confusing and messy right now. Don't compound it with false promises you can't possibly keep. If you say you're going to pick him or her up from hockey practice and have an ice cream together, make sure you find time for that. If you keep forgetting your promise or your time with your child, he or she will slowly glide out of your life, feeling ignored.

Give Your Child Some Time

The sudden news of a divorce will no doubt, feel like a calamity to the child. Different children will react in different ways. Some might shout, cry, break things, go into a shell, adopt a sullen silence, turn hostile etc. Whatever the case might be, give your child some time to get over the news and to heal. He or she will soon become normal.

No Talks About Your Ex

Do not talk ill about your ex even on the phone. Kids are smart; they will hear every word and wonder about it the next time they're with that particular parent. If you can't be civil to your spouse, keep your mouth shut.

Maintain Appropriate Boundaries

Your kids are just that- kids. Do not look to them as substitutes or friends. They need your support to deal with the situation. Do not let the child take care of you. Find some other adults who can do that for you. Let your child remain a child- not grow up overnight.

Be There for Your Child

Not just physically, emotionally as well. You will, no doubt, be drained and exhausted mentally due to the stress of the divorce, but understand the fact that your child needs to talk to you. To understand, to get over the situation, to vent- he needs his parent. Be there for him when he needs to talk to you.

Get Your Child to Develop a Positive Attitude

You never know when your hidden animosity or anger towards your ex might affect your child's thought processes. To avoid this, keep emphasizing on how much you love your child and that no matter what, both you and your ex will be available for the child at any time of the day or night. Help your child deal with his emotions in a healthy manner.

Get Professional Help

Sometimes, children need the ears of someone other than their parents to deal with their stress and situation. Go to a mental health professional, like a psychologist or therapist to get your child to talk and express his or her emotions. Very young children will benefit immensely by play therapy.

Maintain Your Routine

Just because you're divorced doesn't mean everything goes for a toss. Especially when children are involved. To help them get back on their feet and deal with the situation better, maintain the same kind of social life prior to the divorce. There should be as fewer changes as possible to outings, picnics, family gatherings, friendly visits, sightseeing trips etc. Make your child feel as normal as possible.

Make the Transition Easy

After the divorce, one parent gets the kids; the other receives visitation rights. The children keep shuttling from one home to the other. It is imperative that both the homes have similar and comfortable surroundings, like, a bedroom for the child in each home, decorated the way the child wants it to be. Each parent can indulge in certain activities with the child, which he or she might associate with "My time with dad" or "My time with mom".

Take New Relationships into Account

It's quite possible that your ex might find someone else to share his or her life with. Make sure that this does not affect your ex's relationship with your child. The child still is your priority. Children view the new relationship as threatening. They don't want anyone to take the place of their mom or dad. Help your child understand that no matter what, you and your ex will be the parents. The new person in your spouse's life should also be included in your child's life, but gradually, and that person should be sensitive to the needs of the child.

Be Morally Upright

Do not do or say anything about your spouse that might have negative repercussions later on. If your ex is behaving irresponsibly, that does not mean you ape him or her. Take the moral high ground and keep your sanity intact.

Refrain from Dating for a While

Take some time to heal from the bitterness and stress of divorce. Even if you are dating someone, do not be in a rush to introduce him or her to the children. If things keep going well with your new flame, there might come a time when you will introduce him or her to your kids and let them form a bond. But do this only if you're sure that the relationship will culminate in marriage. If your kids form a good bond with the new stepparent, only to lose them to a break-up, they will take it much harder than the actual divorce. So, exercise proper caution.

Dealing with Abandonment

It's a cruel thing to do, but sometimes, a parent is so fed up of the responsibilities thrust upon him or her, that he or she may simply abandon the child and take off to greener pastures, without giving a second's thought about how this will affect the child. This is a kind of loss that leaves an indelible impression on the child and stays with him or her forever. When this happens, you can step in and fill the emotional hole in your child's heart. Do not go on badmouthing your ex for doing so, but instead, use this opportunity to keep your child as sane and normal as possible. Tell him or her that the other parent is having a hard time dealing with this mess and needs time to sort everything out. If the abandonment is prolonged or permanent, do whatever you can to create a positive mental attitude in the child and keep the hope alive that someday, the other parent might return.

Chapter 29.   Consider Things Practically

Division of Assets

Decide What You Must Have (Not What You Don't Want Your Partner to Have)

When making decisions around division of assets, including homes, furniture, pets, and personal effects, take time to think of what you need and what you can live without. Don't make decisions based on what you don't want your ex to have. Think about your limits and what you are willing to compromise. Then be mindful that you are not trying to punish or retaliate through division of the items you have acquired together. It might be helpful to make a list of items with categories of what you need, what you want, and what you prefer, but could live without. This will help you negotiate more easily if your partner has a strong desire for an item that you only have as a preference. Often, the things you think you want now you will get rid of following the divorce, especially if you acquired it only to keep your partner from having it. Items come and go, and most can and will be replaced in time. One way to assist you in thinking about what you value most is to imagine you only have fifteen minutes to grab your most valued, shared possessions from the home. What would you take? This visualization can be helpful in initiating your detachment from your possessions.

Another consideration here is the emotional meaning you have attached to certain objects. There are some items that have such sentimental attachment or strong memories associated with them that you will not be able to use or see them without thinking of your partner anyway. This is also true regarding the decision to remain in the family home. You may want to consider whether you wish to "start over," or be tied to the memories certain items will hold. So, while you may like the item or consider it functional for future use, you may actually find you do not wish to have it around later due to the feelings it brings up for you. I think an excellent technique to use in this case is the KonMari Method. The KonMari Method was developed by the professional organizer and renowned author of the book The Life-Changing Magic of Tidying Up, Marie Kondo (2014). I used this method upon moving out of the home I shared with my spouse and found it tremendously helpful. While going through all of our household items is a lengthy process, divorce requires we sort through most of our possessions anyway.

Personally, I found it a cathartic task that allowed me to be mindful in the moment while doing something productive. The simple technique of this particular concept in the book (which is certainly worth the read) is to handle or touch each item in your home and notice intently how you feel and what images and emotions arise. Whatever item does not bring you peace or joy is to be let go. Thus, the beautiful leather jacket I obtained on our last trip to Europe as a couple, with tags still attached, awaiting cooler weather, was let go. Ample art, decorations, towels, and bedding were also removed. Lucky for me, my ex did not want many household items from our shared home and was happy to take many of the items I did not want and asked for very few items that I did want. Although I was sad to let some favored items go, I felt it was fair and reasonable that he selected the items he did, since I was keeping so much of what brought me peace and joy.

This may not be the case for you. You and your partner may want many of the same things, or you may not have the option to handle the items in question, particularly if you are not residing in the space where they are housed. You may also decide that while you will ultimately release something (like wedding photos), you may not be ready to do so just yet. Be gentle with yourself in these moments. To the best of your ability, meditate to gain clarity about the items that matter and those that do not. In the end, material items are just "things," and things have a funny way of breaking, getting lost, wearing out, or otherwise leaving our life unexpectedly. Try to keep this in mind when you are sorting through and negotiating over your "things."

How to Handle Family and Friends

It is important to consider ahead of time how you intend to communicate during the separation and divorce process with the people in your lives. It's best if you can come to a mutually agreed-upon understanding with your partner. If it is possible to jointly discuss your individual needs for support and your concerns around each other's disclosures, you may be able to reach an agreement you can both honors. However, as this may not be possible, you can also decide for yourself what will best serve your post-divorce vision, while still allowing you to feel supported. In other words, it is important to have a support system and a few trusted confidants to help you manage emotional upheaval and big decisions you might want to talk through. But, bending the ear of just anyone is neither wise nor beneficial.

Divorce is hard. We are often in the position of feeling anxious and conflicted when we are faced with difficult, life-altering choices. During these times, I have found myself seeking (consciously and unconsciously) the support and validation of others that my decision is the "right one." The truth is, no one has the right decision for me, and no one else can really know what is best for you on your journey. However, it is true that selective counsel from trusted friends and other wise individuals may help you consider options and alternate perspectives. But it's worth being selective in whom you choose to confide. Building a case against your partner by vilifying them to others may make you feel better in the moment, but ultimately, it may not be in your best interest. Try to keep in mind that others are often going to say something supportive because they love you and not because you are actually "right." In fact, if your partner gave their version of the story to someone (which may feel true for them and fabricated to you), they would often be given the same kind of support. No one actually wins by pulling more people to their side.

While pulling people to your side during the separation and divorce may make you feel better in the moment, it often creates more significant conflict as people are now involved in your business (even if you don't want them to be). Keep this in mind when seeking support from friends, family, neighbors, work associates, and others. Be particular about where you seek support and wise regarding who you choose to involve in your relationship struggles. Using caution with social media is also important. In this age, anything you put out on social media may be there forever. Making emotionally driven decisions to post on your social sites for support can create problems for you now and later. Social media posts are used by employers, attorneys and thus judges (in divorce and custody matters) and can negatively impact your relationships. If your partner really

is awful, their actions will speak for themselves as things unfold and move forward. The universe has a way of balancing these things out. You do not need to invest your precious time and energy in ensuring your partner receives "justice" for their "crimes."

A final consideration is that it is not possible to truly understand the unique pain of what it is like to come to a decision to go through the process of a divorce unless you have experienced it firsthand. Those who have not gone through that unique form of pain may struggle to comprehend your perspective and feelings. For that matter, even if someone has divorced, no one but you can fully understand your marriage and divorce from your inside experience. Thus, try not to become too concerned or sidetracked by the perspectives and advice of those around you. Keep in mind that while their intentions may be right, their advice might not be the best option for you.

One way to reduce unsolicited questions and comments from those in your life is to make a unified announcement together, requesting your boundaries, whatever they may be, are respected. Technology has made this option a bit more accessible. Sending an email, as a couple, can inform those in your life of the decision you have reached and what type of support you would appreciate, as well as how to respect your clearly outlined boundaries. You can find an example of what this might look like on the following page.

Conclusion

Narcissistic abuse does not only take place in personal and work relationships but also in contact with members of a community and even with public figures.

No matter whether it occurs on a personal or public level, it is vital to be aware of the signs of abuse as awareness of the negative situation is the first step to get out of it.

Narcissists are proud and self-centered individuals who lack empathy for others. They live in a world of their own making, and they believe that they are unique and special. Hence, they always seek to serve their individual needs and won't mind using people as a means to further themselves

Many people have fallen victim to narcissistic abuse in general, and some have dated a narcissist or had an unhealthy relationship with one.

It is not a bad thing to seek love; in fact, one of the basic needs of humans is the need for a sense of belonging and acceptance by other people. There is nothing wrong in seeking love, but in the process of trying to find love, many have fallen victim to unhealthy relationships with abusive people. Essential issues like identifying the behaviors of narcissists in dating, and learning how to deal with the narcissist who seeks control were explained in full details. Why people fall victim to the wiles of the narcissist was not left out as the qualities that make people easy prey for the narcissists were extensively detailed. Psychological effects might linger for a very long time in the psyche of victims, even after they have quit the relationship with the narcissist and as such reading a material like this serves as a precaution not to fall victim to the narcissist's manipulative behavior.

Narcissists don't even think about how their behavior affects others, and this is why they find it so easy to use emotionally abusive and manipulative techniques in their relationships.

Narcissists operate in romantic relationships; it exposes the words they say and the actions they take to abuse victims. Also, empowering strategies as to how to disarm narcissists and how to deal with narcissism in dating have been explained. With the proper management techniques, any victim can get over the emotional abuse and mental manipulation of dating or being involved with a narcissist to go on and lead a productive and fulfilling life. It is usual for victims of abuse to cry after their ordeal and think whatever went wrong with the relationship was their fault, which is what the narcissist wanted; a traumatic experience for the victim

The narcissist is a real-life zombie. Rather than feast on flesh, they feast on you, your compassion, empathy, frustration, stress, and anything adverse they can get you to feel. The narcissist will never change, no matter how long suffering or persevering you are. This is something I keep repeating over and over, because they will promise you, they can change. In fact, they will show signs of improvement! But in the end, it's all a game. They just want to lull you into a false sense of safety and security. They just want to take you even higher up the mountain so that they can dash you and your hopes harder against the rocks in the valley even more devastatingly than they did the last time.

Try to understand that as far as the narcissist is concerned, you exist purely for entertainment purposes. Your thoughts, ideas, and emotions — your whole life — has no meaning to them at all. I'd like to assume that this is not the case for you. I want to believe that you value yourself enough never to let another narcissist treat you the way they have always done.

There is no reason to settle for friendships, relationships, or love that is subpar. If the "love" makes you feel worthless, then it isn't love. Narcissists give love a bad rep. They make it hard for people to trust others, and even worse, they make it hard for you to trust yourself. The narcissist will never stop being the way he is. You can cry, beg, yell, kick, pray, do whatever you want to. The narcissist will remain a narcissist, barring divine intervention. This is a cold, hard truth that everyone needs to swallow. Only until you accept this truth can you begin to look for different, healthier ways of dealing with the narc while protecting your sanity and identity.